Agincourt

My Family, the Battle and the
Fight for France

Sir Ranulph Fiennes was the first man to reach both poles by surface travel and the first to cross the Antarctic Continent unsupported. In the 1960s he was removed from the SAS Regiment for misuse of explosives but, joining the army of the Sultan of Oman, received that country's Bravery Medal on active service in 1971. He is the only person yet to have been awarded two clasps to the Polar medal for both Antarctic and the Arctic regions. Fiennes has led over 30 expeditions including the first polar circumnavigation of the Earth, and in 2003 he ran seven marathons in seven days on seven continents in aid of the British Heart Foundation.

In 1993 Her Majesty the Queen awarded Fiennes the Order of the British Empire (OBE) because, on the way to breaking records, he has raised over £14 million for charity. He was named Best Sportsman in the 2007 ITV Great Briton Awards and in 2009 he became the oldest Briton to reach the summit of Everest.

Agincourt

My family, the battle and the
fight for France

Ranulph Fiennes

First published in Great Britain in 2014 by Hodder & Stoughton
An Hachette UK company

First published in paperback in 2015

1

ISBN 978 1 444 79211 9

Typeset in Sabon MT by Palimpsest Book Production Limited, Falkirk, Stirlingshire

Printed and bound by Clays Ltd, St Ives plc

Hodder & Stoughton policy is to use papers that are natural,
renewable and recyclable products and made from wood grown in
sustainable forests. The logging and manufacturing processes are expected
to conform to the environmental regulations of the country of origin.

Hodder & Stoughton Ltd
Carmelite House
50 Victoria Embankment
London EC4Y 0DZ

www.hodder.co.uk

To Anton and Jill, for the very best of friendships
and for all our work together down the years.

Also by Ranulph Fiennes

A Talent For Trouble
Ice Fall In Norway
The Headless Valley
Where Soldiers Fear To Tread
Hell On Ice
To The Ends Of The Earth
Bothie The Polar Dog (With Virginia Fiennes)
Living Dangerously
The Feather Men
Atlantis Of The Sands
Mind Over Matter
The Sett
Fit For Life
Beyond The Limits
The Secret Hunters
Captain Scott: The Biography
Mad, Bad And Dangerous To Know
Mad Dogs And Englishmen
Killer Elite
My Heroes
Cold

Contents

	Foreword	1
1.	The French Connection	5
2.	The rise and rise of Eustace de Fiennes	15
3.	Geoffrey de Mandeville and other fickle Fienneses	29
4.	Intermarriage, bribery, temerity and indecision	41
5.	Friends and Lovers	59
6.	Wool, wine and war	71
7.	The Buying of Broughton	95
8.	So much Christian blood spilled	105
9.	When men of good breeding think nothing of killing	115
10.	Fair stood the wind for France	137
11.	The actions of the tiger	161
12.	Fiennes to the fore	181
13.	A family at war	199
14.	A Vaste Multitude Yielded Up in Death	217
15.	La Mort de Fiennes	237
16.	Another Fiennes loses his head for losing the War	257
	Postscript	287
	Appendix: The Arming Of An English Man-At-Arms, c.1415	289
	Acknowledgements	299
	Bibliography	301
	Picture Credits	303
	Index	305

THE FAMILIES OF FIENNES & BOULOGNE

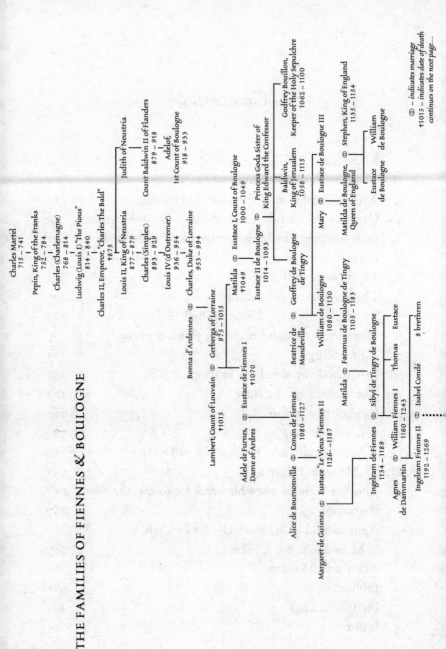

King Edward I ⊗ Eleanor de Braose

Humphry de Bohun, 3rd Earl of Here

Humphrey de Bohun, 4th Earl of Hereford ⊗ Elizabeth

King Henry IV, Bolingbroke, Duke of Lancaster ⊗ Mary de Bohun

2 generations

King Henry V
King Henry VI
King Henry VII (House of Lancaster)

Ingelram Fiennes II ⊗ Isabel Condé
1192 – 1269

Sibyl de Filiol ⊗ Giles de Fiennes †1316

William de Fiennes II (killed Courtrai) ⊗ Blanche de Brienne

Maud Fiennes ⊗ William de Fiennes II

Robert Fiennes   Lord John Wake ⊗ Joanna Fiennes

Margaret Fiennes ⊗ Edmund Mortimer

John Comyn

Roger Mortimer, Earl of March (adultery with Queen Isabel of England)

Edward I

Edmund, Earl of Kent ⊗ Margaret Wake

Joan, "the Fair Maid of Kent" ⊗ The Black Prince

King Richard II

Richard, Duke of York

Richard III

5 generations

Sir John Fiennes, Baron of Fiennes & of Tingry (fought army of Mahaut, was prisoner in Louvre) 1270 – 1340 ⊗ Isabel de Dampiers

Sir Robert Fiennes of Fiennes and of Tingry, Constable of French Army (1356 –1370) 1308 – 1382 — no issue

(Nephew) Robert Fiennes (killed at Agincourt 1415)

Fiennes Cousins also killed at Agincourt (Jean and Louis du Buis de Fiennes)

Through Robert's niece, the French Fiennes line passes to the family of the Dukes of St Pol and to Richard Woodville, father of Elizabeth the wife and Queen of King Edward IV

William de Saye II ⊗ Beatrice Talbot de Mandeville
†1144

Geoffrey De Saye I ⊗ Alice de Cheney
1155 – 1230

William de Saye III ⊗ Sibyl Marshall
1215 – 1272

Mary ⊗ William de Saye IV
1253 – 1295

Idonea Leybourne

Geoffrey de Saye III ⊗ Geoffrey de Saye IV
1281 – 1322   1304 – 1359

John ⊗ 3rd Lord Clinton †1399

Idonea de Saye

William 4th Lord Clinton †1432

Guy de Beauchamp, 10th Earl of Warwick ⊗ Maude de Beauchamp

3 generations

Richard Beauchamp, 13th Earl of Warwick (3rd cousin of James and Roger Fiennes; Fought beside them for Henry V)

Sir John Fiennes 1275 – 1339 ⊗ Joan Jordaine

Sir John Fiennes ⊗ Maude de Monceux

William Fiennes †1359 ⊗ Maude de Monceux

Robert Fiennes   John Fiennes

Beatrice de Brewer ⊗ William de Saye 1340 – 1375

John de Saye 1373 – 1382

Elizabeth Batisford ⊗ William de Saye †1399

Joan de Saye, Countess of Hereford ⊗ William Fiennes, Sheriff of Sussex 1357 – 1405

Robert Fiennes

Sir John Cornwaille (stepfather) ⊗ Elizabeth Holland ⊗ John Holland Earl of Huntingdon

Roger Fiennes (Treasurer) 1384 – 1449 ⊗ Elizabeth Holland

Sir Richard Fiennes (The Lord Dacre in 1458) 1433 – 1483 ⊗ Johanna Dacre

Emeline Cromer ⊗ James Fiennes 1394 – 1450 (executed)

Elizabeth Fiennes ⊗ Alexander Iden

William Cromer (executed with James)

Sir William Fiennes 1428 –1471 ⊗ Margaret Wykeham

Elizabeth Fiennes ⊗ John 6th Lord Clinton †1478

Author's Note

To avoid using phrases like 'my ancestor' tediously often in the text, the names of my ancestors and their close families are displayed in italics, for clarity.

Foreword

While in Brussels in 2013 negotiating with Belgium's great explorer, Alain Hubert, for his help over the removal of heavy snow vehicles and my team of five men from Antarctica, his wife took me to the Central Square and showed me a magnificent statue of my ancestor, *Godfrey de Bouillon*, the first King of Jerusalem, and to this day a hero of the Belgian people.

On the way back to the Huberts' Polar Foundation we passed along Fiennes Street, a reminder of the importance of my family in medieval times in the complex world of war between the 'French' and the 'English'.

Only a week later, back in England and with key Belgian support assured, I received a phone call from the editor of Hodder, part of the global French publishing group Hachette, to ask if I would be interested in writing a book about the Anglo-French Wars to coincide with the six hundredth anniversary of Agincourt, the great battle of 1415 made famous in Shakespeare's *Henry V*.

Why me? was my immediate reaction. Surely a military historian would be a more apt choice for such a story? 'You,' replied my editor, 'have the distinct advantage over most historians because of your direct Anglo-Norman ancestry whose members, during the Hundred Years War, commanded both the French and the English armies and were closely related to the kings and queens at the very nerve centre of all the Anglo-French wars. In fact it is undeniably arguable that your family members both started and later lost the war!' Throughout this book I have put the names of my ancestors and their close families in italics.

So, with no polar expedition on the immediate horizon, I visited *Martin Fiennes* at Broughton Castle, where our family have lived since Norman times. He and his father, *Nat Fiennes*, the twenty-first *Lord Saye and Sele*, had helped me five years previously to delve into the extensive family records held in the castle attics, and at that time, although no professional archivist, I had found the study fascinating.

This opportunity to search further into the medieval Anglo-Norman wars and our family's involvement therein was, to me, a gift from the gods.

Where most historians use the term 'English' to describe the medieval Anglo-Welsh armies, I have sometimes called them British. The various mongrel armies that opposed them across the Channel I have dubbed as either Norman or French.

In describing those bloody times when my 'French' cousins killed their 'British' relatives, I have tried to remain impartial – not always with success.

The enmity between France and England is an ancient one that can nowadays be treated with humour. On arrival at the London 2012 Olympic Games, President François Hollande thanked Britain for 'rolling out the red carpet for French athletes to win medals'. This light touch of sarcasm was doubtless in retaliation for Prime Minister Cameron's earlier comment that he would 'roll out the red carpet for French businessmen fleeing the high rates of tax' that Hollande had proposed for France. The truth is that the two countries have been jealous and suspicious of one another since the Norman Conquest of 1066, which was led by my direct ancestor Count Eustace of Boulogne, the army commander of William the Conqueror.

The series of wars involving Edward I and his successors, called the Hundred Years War by historians, was the direct outcome of the Conqueror's victory at Hastings in 1066, where Eustace proudly carried the flag of the invasion. To be more specific, the Hundred Years War started as an argument between Edward III and Philip VI of France over feudal lordship principles, and this was caused by the fact that, after Hastings, the English (Anglo-Normans) owned huge areas of France through inheritance and/or marriage.

The war took place in two phases. Between 1337 and 1380 there was a series of invasions with the express Viking-type purpose of ravage, plunder and destruction in order to keep the French on the defensive, thereby safeguarding the Anglo-Normans' possessions in France. For many years in Aquitaine and Gascony, the inhabitants preferred English rule and provided large numbers of soldiers for the English armies.

There were no standing armies in Britain until the seventeenth century, so an army had to be raised for a specific campaign, after which the soldiers would head back home with their pay and, hopefully, some worthwhile plunder, or even some ransom money.

During the 350 years between the battles of Hastings and Agincourt, the fighting skills and methods of both the two great armies underwent considerable change, as did the attitudes of their successive monarchs. So to understand Agincourt, you need to understand what leads up to it. The first chapters that follow detail the countdown to the incredible Battle of Agincourt and its aftermath.

Ranulph Fiennes
Exmoor 2014

I

The French Connection

25 October 1415

Before the cold gleam of daylight spread over the sodden trees and tents of Maisoncelles, France, King Henry V sent out orders to prepare for battle. The order for silence still held. The smell of woodsmoke as fires died down vied with the foul body odour of the soldiers scurrying through the gloom to the whispered orders of their sergeants.

Four men, all knights, were sheltered in a barn, unable to sleep. They were keen for action, any action, to break the dread anticipation of waiting for death or worse. They had all seen the horrendous wounds sustained in medieval battles. After donning their full battle armour with considerable help from their pages, they bade each other God's blessing and went to the camps of their men.

These knights were *Roger Fiennes*, his brother *James Fiennes*, *Roger*'s brother-in-law *John Holland* and *Roger*'s stepfather *John Cornwaille*. All four were my direct ancestors.

If ever a single line of kinsmen had, over four centuries, a continuous influence on British history, then I claim that role for my direct ancestors and their immediate clansfolk.

In every age there have been aggressive monarchs and dictators who thrived on and lived for war, or who tried to focus their subjects' minds on foreign conquests when things were bad at home.

Just as the spark that led to the great wars of the twentieth century involved a chance assassination in Sarajevo, so certain acts of favouritism to foreigners in the English court of King Edward the Confessor during the eleventh century caused intense jealousy to rage in the heart of the most influential baron in the land, the Viking descendant Harold Godwin of Wessex.

We, my direct ancestors that is, were the main foreign favourites who caused this rift and were thus directly the cause of the Anglo-Norman war that followed, including, in 1415, the bloody Battle of Agincourt where Fiennes blood flowed on both sides.

To understand the Battle of Agincourt we have to go back 400 years. To explain why Edward the Confessor was linked with the Fiennes clan involves a brief history of northern Gaul, the land of my ancestor *King Pepin*, his son the *Emperor Charlemagne* and the latter's direct descendant *Count Adelof of Boulogne* (born AD 918).

Adelof's fiefdom included the village of Fiennes a few miles south of Boulogne which, during the past millennium had been a local barony subject to successive sovereigns: counts of Boulogne, dukes of Burgundy and kings of England and France. A welter of counties, duchies, principalities, kingdoms and empires, positioned on what would become the international boundary between France and Germany, were involved.

The land of Fiennes is mostly low and level, but rises to a higher plateau and eventually to tableland. A series of plateaux are cut by river valleys. The terrain is traversed from south-east to north-west by low hills and forms the watershed between the basins of the North Sea and the English Channel. Côte d'Opal, which thrusts north-westwards towards England, and extends on its western side from Cap Blanc Nez to Cap Gris Nez, is known as the Boulonnais, the Bononia of ancient Gaul. Caesar fortified its principal city, which eventually became the see of the diocese of Boulogne. Its coastline is broken by many a port from which the Romans set forth in conquest.

This Boulonnais was an ancient county ruled over by sovereigns who held only nominal allegiance to the kings of France. For the most part, this region gives the impression of a charming Flemish landscape. In the midst of the general fertility, however, lies a vast moorland extending northwards, and on the border of this land of mystery there ran the Roman road over which royal entourages to the Field of the Cloth of Gold once travelled. Here nestles the village of Fiennes, and to the east of it the extensive forest of Guînes.

Charles de Gaulle called this part of the world the 'fatal avenue'. Since the Treaty of Verdun in 843, when the Carolingian Empire was divided among the three grandsons of *Charlemagne*, the Boulonnais has suffered the ravages of warfare, from Agincourt to the Somme. Even before the division of the empire, Celtic Belgae had invaded the area. They were followed by Romans and by Germanic Franks, and eventually by the Valois kings of France who fought the English during the Hundred Years War. The wars of the seventeenth century to establish France's international border continued into the Franco-Prussian War and two World Wars. The soil must be rich in blood and bone.

The county of Boulonnais now forms part of the French department of Pas-de-Calais. Its rulers from 879 through to 1160 stemmed from a junior line of the royal house of Flanders, and at that time it was an independent county. My ancestors, the *Counts of Boulogne*, rulers of the Boulonnais, were nominally feudal lords who rendered homage only to the kings of France. About 1059 *Eustace II, Count of Boulogne and Seigneur of Fiennes* built his castle in his parish of Tingry to consolidate his local power. The immediate region was heavily forested, the hiding place of wolves and bands of brigands. Boulonnais policy during this period was a calculated balancing of the spheres of interest exercised by the dukes of Normandy and the counts of Flanders on either side of the Boulonnais.

The earlier *Counts of Boulogne* had by then already acquired large feudal holdings in England. *Eustace II* left three legitimate sons as well as a bastard who acquired the title *Count of Tingry*. When that line ended in the person of heiress *Sybil de Tingry*, her husband *Enguerrand de Fiennes* then became the joint ruler of Fiennes and Tingry, as well as succeeding to an immense patrimony in England because of the influence of *Matilda*, the last heiress of *Boulogne* who was also his cousin and political supporter.

When *Matilda* married into the House of Blois, it was to Stephen, who was to become both sovereign of the Boulonnais and King of England.

Matilda's uncle, *Eustace of Boulogne*, was married to

8

Princess Goda, the sister of King Edward the Confessor, and the two men, King Edward and *Count Eustace*, were the best of friends. Quite why they had become acquainted in the first place, despite the then considerable geographical barrier of the English Channel, deserves explanation.

The Anglo-Saxon settlers of the ninth and tenth centuries fought waves of Viking raiders, their most successful leader being Alfred the Great. One of Alfred's line, Ethelred the Unready, ordered the massacre of all Danes in England, but Viking reinforcements forced his exile to Normandy. While there, his daughter, Goda, married my ancestor *Count Eustace of Boulogne*.

After a brief spell of Danish rule under King Canute, Ethelred's son, Goda's brother, was recalled from exile and became King Edward the Confessor. He brought many Norman friends with him to the English court and placed them in positions of power, much to the annoyance of the English nobles, especially Lord Godwin of Wessex, the most influential baron in the land. Thus began a power struggle between Edward and his friends from his days in exile under Duke William of Normandy, ranged against the Viking English forces of Harold Godwin.

A third party then entered the ring in the person of my cousin *Count Eustace of Boulogne*. He had been threatened by the French emperor and decided that it would be wise to retire for a while to the English court of his brother-in-law, King Edward, where he soon learned to loathe Harold Godwin.

Following a scuffle in Dover, Godwin's soldiers killed twenty of *Eustace*'s retainers, and this gave King Edward good reason to exile Godwin to Flanders (now Belgium).

A year later Godwin returned at the head of a Flemish army and Edward, a weak man, became a mere puppet king. It was later claimed by Duke William of Normandy that, while Godwin was in Flanders, Edward had promised William the throne of England on his death.

When King Edward, the last of twenty-five kings of the Wessex dynasty all based in England, died in 1066 with no sons, Godwin seized the throne. This enraged two would-be claimants, one of whom, King Harald Hardrada of Norway, attacked from the north while Duke William prepared an invasion fleet on the French coast. *Count Eustace of Boulogne* lent William many ships and agreed to be second-in-command of William's army.

Godwin marched his army of Anglo-Danes north and defeated the Norwegians at Stamford Bridge. Only three days after that battle, Duke William and cousin *Eustace* landed at Pevensey. After a forced march south, Godwin's army clashed with the Norman and Boulogne forces on a hilltop near Hastings.

Duke William's chaplain wrote of the battle: 'The Normans furiously carried out their attack on the main body of the English host. There were present in this battle, *Eustace Count of Boulogne*, William Count of Evreux, Rodulf of Tossey . . .'

Duke William, armed only with a broken lance, was more formidable than others who brandished long javelins. With a harsh voice, he called to his main army commander, *Count Eustace of Boulogne*, who, with fifty knights, was about to give the signal to retreat. *Eustace* came up to the duke and said in his ear that he ought to retire 'since he would court death if he went forward' and is depicted offering this advice on the Bayeux Tapestry.

If only Duke William had listened to cousin *Eustace*'s advice to retreat, then the Norman occupation would never have happened and nor would the long years of bloodshed of the subsequent Hundred Years War.

But William won the battle, Godwin collected an arrow in his eye and, sad day for the Anglo-Saxons, we Normans had arrived in Britain. William had himself crowned in London on Christmas Day as Saxon villages all around were torched by his soldiers. He ruled with immense cruelty, trampling the native English underfoot. By the end of his twenty-one-year reign, 5 per cent of the 2 million inhabitants of his British territories were Gallic imports appointed by the king to control a rigid caste system with a Stasi-type spy network and a meticulous census of all citizens and their possessions, known as the Domesday Book. This recorded the wealth of some 13,000 settlements down to the last goat and hen, so that an unavoidable tax burden could be levied, chiefly to pay for his mercenaries.

William stole some 5,000 estates from their Saxon owners along the borders of Scotland and Wales, and in the so-called Pale region of Southern Ireland and gave them to Normans in return for their pledge to fight for him whenever needed. Only the mountain regions of Wales remained as the last redoubt of the native British.

Despite the efficiency of the Norman occupiers, occasional revolts flared, especially when the King was in Normandy fighting the King of France or other neighbours. Late in 1067 the men of Kent decided to get rid of the Normans by the simple expedient of inviting my feisty ancestor *Count Eustace* to spearhead their revolt. By then he was fed up with his erstwhile Norman ally and saw no reason why parts of

England should not become Boulogne, rather than Norman, controlled.

So in 1067 a second invasion force arrived from France and took the countryside around Dover from the Normans. Sadly, the key Norman bastion of Dover Castle held out against the Boulogner siege long enough for a superior Norman relief force to arrive, and *Eustace* sensibly hightailed it back to Boulogne. William was apoplectic and he confiscated land, including a huge chunk of south-east England, which he had nicknamed the Honour of Boulogne and awarded to *Eustace* after Hastings. Several years later with no further bad behaviour and professed loyalty to King William, cousin *Eustace* was given back most of the Honour.

The behaviour of the Normans in Britain mirrored that of whites in South Africa in the apartheid era. No intermarriage was allowed with Saxons, who had become second-class citizens in their own land.

Eustace and many other Boulogne or Norman lords lived mostly on their French, not British, estates, and they continued both to fight and to intermarry with each other. Important towns and major villages gave their names to their lords' families, as was true of my ancestors who came from towns such as Boulogne, Fiennes, Saye, Guînes and Ardres, and all sooner or later married into each other's ruling families.

Did Britain and its people actually benefit in any way from the Norman invasion? Were the new Norman aristocrats, who supplanted their Saxon counterparts, better for the well-being of the general populace? Was their governance from an economic and social viewpoint an improvement on that of the overthrown system of King Edward the Confessor and his English Saxon predecessors?

Economically, William did nothing to promote trade, other than to establish the first Jewish colony in London. In terms of the law, the Normans introduced their 'trial by battle' system, whereby the defendant and his accuser fought one another to establish who was guilty of the original crime. This seems to me to be no improvement on the existing Saxon method of establishing guilt by 'trial by ordeal', where the accused was thrown into a river to see whether they floated or sank. Normans had the considerable privilege of being able to select a third option of purging themselves via 'an unbroken oath'.

Unfortunately these days, despite my Norman DNA, when caught speeding I do not automatically qualify to avoid the heavy fine or, worse still, points on my licence, as awarded to drivers of Saxon heritage.

William's policy of ensuring internal security by building castles involved punitive taxes on local communities, while large numbers of Englishmen were recruited into Norman armies as mercenaries to fight William's French enemies. French became the encouraged and socially acceptable language, even though the Saxons were probably a more civilised race in many ways and at most levels of society than were the Normans. Both groups shared a good mix of Viking blood.

Large numbers of Englishmen were recruited into Norman armies as mercenaries to fight William's French enemies, and the status of English women suffered a considerable decline. Whereas the two sexes had, in Anglo-Saxon times, experienced a general state of equality, the Normans imported their firm belief as to women's inferiority. After all, St Paul had clearly indicated that this was a Christian rule of life. Women should show blind obedience, first to their father and then to their designated husband.

Although Hastings is generally described as a battle between the French and the English, the reality was a struggle between a Norman duke, whose main enemy was the King of France, and Harold, a West Saxon Viking earl with zero English blood in his veins.

Hastings resulted in the union of two lands – England and the Duchy of Normandy. But a century and a half later the last of the Norman kings of England lost the duchy to the French. The result would be the Hundred Years War.

2

The rise and rise of Eustace de Fiennes

William of Normandy was to rule the British with a rod of iron for twenty-one of his sixty years, altering many of their existing laws and customs. Born illegitimate, he was known as William the Bastard, so he would be happy to learn that he is now generally remembered as William the Conqueror.

He treated the British as second-rate citizens, and his only claim to their throne was as great-nephew of Edward the Confessor's mother, which made him that king's second cousin once removed.

Like many of his British subjects, William was descended from Viking forebears, who had invaded northern France 150 years before and then spent their time fighting each other. As Duke of Normandy, William had conducted various campaigns against both the King of France and his immediate neighbours, including Brittany, Maine, Anjou and Boulogne, and had learned that aggression and cruelty paid dividends.

After his initial victory at Hastings, William took Dover

and London with ease, burning several towns and bridges for good measure. To protect Londoners from invaders, he ordered the building of the Tower of London and, satisfied that the British would remain supine, if not grateful, he went back to Normandy only three months after the invasion.

While still under thirty years of age, William had fought off attacks by two of his own uncles who had armies and castles in different parts of Normandy, and in 1054 when attacked by the King of France he had, by laying waste to large swathes of Norman countryside, vanquished the French army and won the peace which a decade later enabled him to attack at Hastings without having to look over his shoulder.

One secret of William's ongoing military success was his habit of confiscating the lands of his vanquished enemies and handing them over to his high-ranking key supporters who were often known as 'the companions of the Conqueror'. These included several of my ancestors to whom he gave great chunks of land previously owned by Anglo-Saxon families.

His second-in-command at Hastings, *Count Eustace of Boulogne*, was granted various English estates including in the south-east the so-called Honour of Boulogne and, in Somerset, the manor of Martock, previously held by Queen Edith, widow of Edward the Confessor.

Another well-rewarded 'companion of the Conqueror' was *Lord Eustace de Fiennes*, who died four years after Hastings and whose progeny would later take over as heirs to the counts of Boulogne.

Yet another ancestor who was granted land in England by the Conqueror was a neighbour of *Count Eustace* called *William de Saye* who came from the local village of Saye (close to Fiennes). The subsequent fortunes and lands of the Sayes would be subsumed by the Fiennes family in the mid-fourteenth century.

Overall we did pretty well out of William's land-grabbing habits and his rewards-for-the-boys schemes.

On the plus side, William's rule included the founding of Norman buildings, both churches and castles, which remain among Britain's finest. He also instituted some new and repressive laws that cut down a good deal of the existing crime throughout his realm in days when murder, rape and anarchy were commonplace.

The Bastard's biographer, William of Poitiers, summarised his rule thus: 'enforcing the Truce of God, he checked all outbursts of violence and he protected the poor, the widows and the orphans. The countryside, the castles and the towns found in him a guarantor of stability and safety for their possessions.' This glowing report probably owes much to the biographer's desire to please, and it should also be stressed that England was a larger, more fertile land than Normandy, and its Christian laws had been established in the seventh century, 300 years before the Christian conversion of the Normans. For twenty years prior to Hastings, Edward the Confessor had ruled over relatively prosperous, peaceful and cultured conditions compared with the ongoing internecine strife common to most of northern France.

In 1067 William left England to the tender mercies of two trusted aides, of whom an Anglo-Saxon journalist wrote: 'They built castles far and wide throughout the land, oppressing the unhappy people, and things went ever from bad to worse.'

There were, during William's personal absence, recurring local revolts. Uprisings in the south-west were easily subdued by the Norman armies (by then heavily bolstered by English mercenaries and press-ganged recruits). The northern English, the Welsh, the Scots and the Danes all tried their luck against the Normans during the six years that followed Hastings, but William's network of eighty castles manned by loyal retainers and his army's lightning-quick responses to each new threat invariably saw off all his enemies. For instance, two years after Hastings, a Danish army liberated the city of York from its Norman garrison. William's vengeance was extreme. Even though the Danes fled at the approach of his army, he slaughtered the townsfolk. Local chronicles described the aftermath: 'It was horrible to behold human corpses decaying in their houses, the street and on the roads, swarming with worms whilst they were consumed by corruption with an abominable stench . . . There was no village inhabited between Derby and York; they became lurking places for wild beasts and robbers and were a great dread to travellers.'

The year 1069 was William's most dangerous due to uprisings on many sides, but his responses, according to one modern military historian 'must rank as one of the most outstanding military achievements of the age'. The end result was the overall conquest of Britain within six years, at the end of which his rule of repressive terror saw a period of paralysis and peace with a backdrop of famine and devastation described by historian Sir Frank Stenton as 'distinguished from ordinary warfare by a deliberate attempt to ruin the population of the affected districts . . . Within the country ravaged at this time, vast areas were still derelict after seventeen years.'

The Norman writer Ordericus Vitalis wrote: 'William, in the fullness of his wrath . . . destroyed at once all that could serve for the support of life in the whole countryside lying beyond the Humber.'

None the less, William dedicated a great deal of time to establishing Christianity throughout his Norman empire on both sides of the Channel. He did his utmost to encourage total celibacy among all newly appointed priests, which was an extremely tall order since most priests at the time had one or more wives and, quite often, a number of mistresses. Prostitution was also rife and equally hard to suppress.

As his enemies in France increased their aggression in the 1070s, so William's army included more British soldiers. Britain was a richer and more populous country than Normandy, with over a million people to tax and to use for armed manpower, and William did both with vigour.

Two of William's uncles, his own son and heir Robert, rebellious dukes of Anjou and Brittany and at times King Philip I of France all led armies against William in Normandy at various points of his twenty-one-year stint as King of England. He needed eyes in the back of his head, as well as the instant armed forces that his feudal system reliably provided in both England and Normandy.

As to the specific tactics William's armies used to overpower his opponents, massed cavalry charges with the lance, sword and crossbow backed up by mercenary bands of infantry were highly effective although, especially towards the end of his reign and in France, not invincible.

When, in 1085, Norman England was threatened by a Danish invasion coinciding with a number of internal rebellions, William needed to pay for mercenary forces from France to help out, but was faced with a lack of funds and so decided to investigate thoroughly the available wealth of his British subjects.

He sent out tax inspectors to complete meticulous records village by village and to list all property down to the scraw-

niest piglet. The result was the Domesday Book, the fore-
runner of today's HM Revenue and Customs.

William, over two memorably awful decades from the
viewpoint of the Anglo-Saxons, replaced their aristocracy,
most of their social and economic systems, and even their
official language, with those of the Normans.

The chronicles of Ordericus Vitalis summarised the effects
of William's reign on the Anglo-Saxons: 'The native inhabitants were crushed, imprisoned, disinherited, banished and
scattered beyond the limits of their own country while his
own vassals and adherents were exalted to wealth and honours
and raised to all offices of state.'

The Domesday records show that half the value of all
England was then owned by a mere 200 men, including my
ancestor *Eustace of Boulogne*. Most of these 'honour' liege-
lords were absentee Normans with huge estates on the other
side of the Channel.

By the end of William's reign there was no question of
any rift between the Anglo-Normans and the Normans of
Normandy, for both sections of the Anglo-Norman Kingdom
shared the same autocratic ruler, aptly named the Conqueror.

On campaign in France in 1087, William's army ranged
against his French enemies consisted of both Norman and
British soldiers. William died that year after an accident when
riding and, on his deathbed, told his priest: 'I persecuted the
native inhabitants of England beyond all reason. Whether nobles
or commons, I cruelly oppressed them; many I unjustly disinherited; innumerable multitudes, especially in the county of
York, perished through me by famine and sword . . . I am
stained by the rivers of blood that I have shed.'

At the time of William's death, his oldest son Robert was

actively campaigning against him on the side of the French king, so William naturally bequeathed the kingdom of England to his second son, also William.

He would almost certainly have wanted to hand over Normandy to his son William as well, in order to ensure continued peace between the two parts of his prized kingdom. But Robert had, at an early age, been solemnly and irrevocably invested as the hereditary Duke of Normandy, and so, despite their many differences, William confirmed that Normandy was Robert's.

To his third son, Henry, William left the sum of £5,000.

It would take a goodly slice of luck for William junior and, after his death, his brother Henry to keep the peace between the two halves of the Anglo-Norman union.

William Rufus, so called because of his florid face, never married and his English court 'squirmed,' it was said, 'with fornicators and sodomites'. His rule in England was even harsher than his father's had been and he was constantly at war with his elder brother Robert.

Out hunting in the New Forest one day in 1100 Rufus was killed by an arrow from an unknown source. His younger brother Henry was participating in the same hunt that day, and many people suspected him of the murder.

The obvious successor to Rufus was his brother Robert, but he was away crusading in the Middle East so Henry usurped the throne of England under the principle that possession is nine-tenths of the law. Nobody stood in his way, and certainly nobody mourned the passing of the obnoxious Rufus.

It would take many weeks, Henry knew, for the news of his brother's death to reach Palestine and for Robert to hear that he had been elbowed aside yet again, but Henry lived in fear of the revenge that Robert was likely to exact once he returned to Europe.

The fact that a fierce civil war between Henry I, King of England and Robert, Duke of Normandy was avoided can be attributed to the remarkable success of Duke Robert's army commanders, two of the sons of cousin *Eustace of Boulogne* of Hastings fame, against the crusaders' Muslim enemies. The elder of the two crusading brothers was *Godfrey of Bouillon* (whose statue in Brussels I have mentioned in the Foreword of this book).

Duke Robert, rightful heir to the English throne, was the titular head of the Norman crusading army commanded by my kinsman *Godfrey*, who had sold most of his French estates to payroll the 40,000 knights and infantry in his army, including bands of British, Flemish and German mercenaries.

Godfrey's army was the first of various Christian armies to reach Constantinople, and from there, via Beirut, Jaffa and Bethlehem, their target city of Jerusalem where he and Robert of Normandy were at the forefront of the fighting, as was *Lord Eustace Fiennes* of Castle Fiennes near Boulogne.

The Fatimid Shias defended the Holy City with stubborn skill until *Godfrey*'s men finally broke through the defences in July 1099 and, in the ensuing two days of carnage, massacred 40,000 inhabitants, including women and children.

Eyewitness records of the occasion stated:

Wonderful sights were to be seen. Some of our men cut off the heads of our enemies, others shot them with arrows so that they fell from the towers, others tortured them longer by casting them into the flames. Piles of heads, hands and feet were to be seen in the streets of the city. It was necessary to pick one's way over the bodies of men and horses . . . Our men discovered that the Saracens had swallowed gold coins. So they burnt great heaps of bodies so that the stomachs and intestines of the dead released the precious metal into the human ashes.

All Jewish survivors were collected in a synagogue and burned to death. As the main architect of this victory, cousin *Godfrey* was voted by the crusaders to be the First Keeper of the Holy Sepulchre, an honour that had been turned down by Duke Robert. The crusaders then moved on to take further Saracen strongholds with *Godfrey* and Robert ever at the front of the battle.

Soon after King Rufus was slain by an arrow in the New Forest, cousin *Godfrey* was killed in the same way, and his brother *Baldwin* took over with the title of First King of Jerusalem, which kept the Holy City in our family for a little longer. But Duke Robert headed back home, arriving just a few weeks after his brother Henry was crowned. Robert's crusading successes were soon known throughout the land, and many of Britain's most powerful Anglo-Normans supported his claim against that of the usurper, Henry.

But the latter was cunning and knew his brother well. He assured Robert that he could keep all Normandy and would be paid the huge annual sum of £2,000 in return for Henry being able to keep the English crown. This cosy deal suited Robert, since it gave him the money to continue his beloved crusading.

Once Robert, placated by the brotherly deal, was back in his Norman duchy, Henry began to plot his downfall, for he would never be safe with the rightful keeper of the English crown lurking just across the Channel.

The late William Rufus had, during his fairly short rule, alienated various powerful Anglo-Norman barons, and Henry handed out goodies to gain their support. He married the daughter of a Scottish noble, by whom he had a son, but as a sideline he sired more than twenty bastards, including half a dozen daughters who he married off to potential enemies, a royal policy described by historians as sex 'for politics not pleasure'.

As soon as Henry was certain of enough baronial support in Britain, he invaded Normandy, captured Robert at the Battle of Tinchebray in 1106 and locked him up for the next twenty-eight years in Cardiff Castle. There is no proof, but contemporary journals suggest that Robert was murdered by unknown parties. This left England and Normandy once again sharing the same ruler.

With all likely claimants to his English throne out of the way, Henry, although the first Norman king to speak fluent English as his first language, spent very little time in England, as he focused on leading his armies against incessant attacks from his mainland neighbours, especially the King of France. For these wars, Henry raised troops and taxes in Britain where, in his absence, his carefully selected governing magnates and their bevies of Domesday civil servants maintained a reasonable level of peace and prosperity, at least in comparison with Henry's predecessors.

Keen to avoid the family infighting of the previous three rulers, Henry cultivated his one son (another William) to be brought up in the image of his father, but, sailing back to England in 1120 after a campaign abroad, this young William's ship struck a rock and all but one of the passengers were drowned. Henry, clearly a practical man and a pragmatist, then groomed his only other legitimate child, his daughter Matilda, to be his heiress, and he married her off to one of his chief rivals, the Count of Anjou, Geoffrey Plantagenet.

At this point, Henry could, he would have thought to himself, die at any point, safe in the knowledge that his daughter and her Plantagenet husband would rule England and Normandy with no nasty brothers lined up to usurp them.

But he then made a fatal error by giving great wealth and important estates to his favourite nephew and Matilda's first cousin (the grandson of William the Conqueror). This lucky noble was Count Stephen of Blois who, in 1125, married none other than the granddaughter of my ancestor, *Count Eustace of Boulogne*. Her name was also Matilda, but she was often called Maud, so I will call her *Maud* for the sake of clarity. This Stephen of Blois was a sharp cookie who had a lot to live down, for his father of the same name was notorious throughout Europe as a deserter from the First Crusade.

Stephen junior happened to be in Boulogne with his wife *Maud* when, in the spring of 1135, his uncle King Henry died of food poisoning while on campaign in Normandy. Fortunately for Stephen, Henry's nominated heiress, his daughter Matilda, and her husband Geoffrey Plantagenet were at the time in faraway Anjou. So, taking a usurper's leaf out of the late Henry's copybook, Stephen together with cousin *Maud* took the next ferry from Boulogne to Dover and thence to London where he knew that he had the support of key Anglo-Norman magnates, who preferred him as king rather than the female Matilda.

Stephen claimed that Henry had on his deathbed changed his mind about the succession and named him, Stephen, as his heir. Enough people in high places chose to believe him, and Stephen was crowned King of England. A few months later our *Maud*, heavily pregnant with yet another *Eustace of Boulogne*, was crowned queen, the first of my ancestors to sit on an English throne.

In contrast to William the Bastard and Rufus, King Stephen relied on compromise and diplomacy. To keep the rightful heiress to the crown, Henry's daughter Matilda, quiet, he accepted highly unfavourable and temporary treaties with her and her powerful husband, Geoffrey of Anjou. This worked for a while but, only four years after Henry's death, Matilda attacked Stephen's army and at the Battle of Lincoln captured and imprisoned him. Queen *Maud* fought on and rescued Stephen, who continued to rule with an easy-going style.

For the next nine years a low-intensity civil war flickered on and off in England between the forces loyal to Stephen and *Maud* and those of the queen they had dispossessed, Matilda. The loyalty of my relatives was split between the two sides.

Meanwhile, in the Holy Land a new crusade was being fought which involved the King of France and his wife, a lady of legendary beauty and fierce temperament, Queen Eleanor of Aquitaine. During this crusade she conducted an adulterous affair with her own uncle, and her husband later divorced her. Only eight weeks later Eleanor married again, this time to Henry, the son of Matilda, the claimant to the English throne.

With the ex-Queen of France as his wife, this Henry Plantagenet was now in control of the vast Angevin empire of Anjou, Aquitaine and Normandy, an area almost half the size of modern France. In 1153 he and Eleanor forced King Stephen, by then sick and weary, into a treaty whereby on his death the crown of England would pass to Henry. This key agreement was the work of various court favourites, including *Queen Maud*'s nephew, my kinsman, *Faramus of Boulogne*.

Stephen duly died a year later and Henry became King Henry II of England and Duke of Normandy. His Plantagenet dynasty would rule through fourteen kings over the next 300 years.

So, in simple terms, the late Henry I's nephew, Stephen, was peacefully succeeded by Henry I's grandson, Henry II. This new King Henry kept in his royal court many of my ancestors and their kin who had emigrated from Normandy and Boulogne, being the family of *Queen Maud*.

When Henry II took the throne he was well aware that our family had fought and died for his mother as well as for Stephen, but he generously let bygones be bygones so that all retained the royal favour at the change of regime.

King Stephen had showered favours on those Fienneses who had stood by *Queen Maud* during his time in prison, awarding the queen's nephew, *Faramus of Boulogne*, the key job of Warden of the Cinque Ports and Constable of Dover Castle, where for the next five centuries one of the main towers was named the Fiennes Tower. Stephen had also given to *Faramus* the lordship of Clapham and Carshalton in Surrey, and to his daughter *Sybil* the estates of Ash, Martock and Widdicombe in Somerset. On Stephen's death, all the lands of the counts of Boulogne passed to *Sybil* and thence to her husband, *Ingelram Fiennes*.

By the time Henry II took over the crown of England and the dukedom of Normandy, the Fiennes family and their

Boulogne predecessors had been in powerful positions of influence over the actions of all four Norman kings from the Battle of Hastings to the ending of the civil war.

Thanks to his marriage to Eleanor of Aquitaine, and his various other European connections, Henry was by far the most powerful monarch in Europe, ruling more land in what is today's France than did the French king himself. On top of which he proved to be a wise and sensible ruler, quickly ridding Britain of the anarchy and on-off civil war conditions of the past two decades.

Although the King of France had declared Eleanor to be barren, she produced eight healthy children for Henry. Sadly, their four sons proved to be a treacherous, disloyal bunch who, throughout much of Henry's successful thirty-four-year reign, caused him non-stop headaches with their plots against him, the final one even involving his queen, Eleanor.

Henry died a successful king but an unhappy man.

By the time of the 1086 Domesday records, the Fiennes family already owned major estates in eleven different counties, all appropriated from the Saxons. One, *John Fiennes*, who had 'fought with valour' at Hastings, also retained extensive properties in Normandy, as did most of his fellow Norman invaders.

3

Geoffrey de Mandeville and other fickle Fiennesses

Prior to the arrival of Henry Plantagenet, many Anglo-Norman barons had taken advantage of the semi-collapse of royal authority under weak King Stephen for two decades, and had become petty dictators against a background of chaos and fear. Henry II's father, Geoffrey of Anjou, from the point of view of Norman class hierarchy, was a mere count who had the good fortune to marry King Henry I's daughter, Matilda. So when his son became their new king, many of the Anglo barons saw him as a comparatively low-born immigrant and, initially, a target of much snobbish hostility.

But, luckily for the Anglo-Saxons, their luck was about to change, for Henry II proved to be an exceptionally enlightened and successful monarch. Thanks to his parentage he succeeded, aged twenty-one, to the greatest empire in Europe, including all of the British isles and more of France than was ruled by the French king.

To correct the gross injustices that King Stephen had allowed through his laissez-faire attitude of compromise between powerful barons and bishops, Henry ruled that all grants of land, wealth and privilege made by his predecessor (to whom he always referred as 'the usurper') were null and void. He proved an extremely effective governor, strategist, administrator and minister of justice, and he gradually earned the respect, if grudgingly, of the barons. Many historians of today regard him as the founder of English common law.

Unfortunately, Henry's life was to be blighted, as seems the norm with medieval ruling families, by his own children. His four sons were truly a nest of vipers who spent much of their lives fighting against their father and each other, especially John, the youngest and most treacherous. John started life as the least favoured royal son in terms of land, despite being Henry's favourite of the brood, because Queen Eleanor was forty-five years old when she gave birth to him and, by then, all the couple's vast territories from Normandy to Spain had already been designated to John's elder brothers.

Naturally jealous that this huge chunk of French territory should be ruled by the kings of England, the French kings plotted to put matters right.

France had its origins in the division of my ancestor *Charlemagne*'s great Gallic empire back in 814, when the kingdom of the West Franks was created. *Charlemagne*'s successors were feeble and anarchy prevailed for the next century until in 987 the Count of Paris, Hugh Capet, announced himself as the 'first King of France'. His dynasty, the Capetians (including their branch lines, the Valois and the Bourbons) ruled France until the abolition of the monarchy in 1793, enforced by the guillotine, not the English.

In King Henry's day the current French king, Louis VII (whose ex-wife he had married), ruled Paris and the regions to the city's immediate north and south. But powerful leaders, whose allegiance to the Capetians was often purely nominal, ruled huge fiefs much larger than those of the king. The greatest of these feudal vassals was King Henry II of England, so the French kings, Louis VII and especially his successor Philip II, did all they could to stoke up the rivalries between Henry's four treacherous sons. This they did with considerable success, and key to King Philip's diplomatic trickery were the ongoing strains between Henry and his son Richard Lionheart.

Following John's birth in 1167, Eleanor left Henry altogether and set up her own headquarters in Poitiers, capital of her native Aquitaine, where she brought up Richard on a diet of tournaments between knights. When he was fourteen, Eleanor installed him as Duke of Aquitaine.

Meanwhile, back in England, King Henry announced that the majority of his empire would go to his eldest son, Henry. None of his sons were content with their promised inheritances, each worried that their father would live for decades before they could actually 'rule' anywhere and, worse still, that he would change his mind and give everything to his favourite and youngest son, John.

Goaded by the Capetian King Philip of France, conspiracies, rebellions, diplomatic marriages and major battles between the sons and father, with one or more son being on the father's side from time to time, ensued right up to King Henry's death. Queen Eleanor, over in Poitiers, normally took the side of her sons against her husband, which resulted in Henry declaring her a prisoner under house arrest and keeping her in a castle for sixteen years. Matters were a touch simplified when two of the brothers died, leaving only Richard and young John to contend their inheritance.

King Henry's last days involved an undignified flight from an army led by the King of France allied to his son Richard and, deeply hurtful, joined also by his favourite son, John.

When Richard took the crown of England in 1189, it was the first time in over a century that a royal accession was achieved without bloodshed or controversy.

By all accounts, King Richard was given to violent rages and his lifelong dream was to defeat the infidel in the Holy Land. To that end he taxed his British subjects heavily, although during the ten years of his reign he spent only six months at home. In his absence abroad, his rule in England was maintained by loyal retainers, including many of his father's and my kinsfolk in the royal court. After a few weeks in England he would soon be off again to France, which is why, in that wonderful little book *1066 and All That*, he is nicknamed Richard Gare de Lyon.

The great Turkish Muslim leader known as Saladin had, two years prior to Richard's coronation, taken Jerusalem back into the hands of Islam and, by way of tit-for-tat revenge on cousin *Godfrey Bouillon*, First King of Jerusalem, had ordered the killing of all the city's defenders. Other Christian-held cities in the Holy Land also soon fell to the Saracens, and the Pope sent pleas for another crusade to all Christian lands, especially to France and to England.

Since King Richard rightly feared that his enemy Philip of France would encourage his brother John to usurp the throne of England if he left on a crusade, he delayed his departure for almost two years before responding to the Pope's call to arms. But in 1190 he finally set out with a great and costly army, after leaving Ireland, much of Normandy and rich estates in England to brother John. He did not, however, have an heir of his own as he was probably homosexual, nor did he appoint John, or anyone else, to be his successor should he die in the Holy Land.

While Richard carried out largely successful battles and sieges with his crusaders, brother John acted, for a while, as his surprisingly faithful regent in England.

Richard's most successful single crusade achievement was the siege of the coastal port of Acre, one of the longest sieges ever recorded and during which three of my ancestors were killed fighting for Richard: *Sir Ingelram Fiennes* and his cousins *John* and *Tougebrand Fiennes*. Subsequently *John*'s family gave the plot where they buried his heart to the citizens of London: a place known today as Finsbury Square.

Philip of France returned early from the crusade and offered John all the French lands held by Richard. Tempted by this rich prize, John put together an army and was about to set out when the seventy-year-old Queen Eleanor, on learning of his plans, sailed to England and forced her wayward son to desist from this new treachery.

One reason for John's competitive behaviour with Richard and his other brothers has been attributed by historians to an inferiority complex caused by his short, stocky build. At 5 foot 5 inches tall, he was considerably shorter than his unusually tall (and reputedly more handsome) brothers.

When he learned of John's betrayal, King Richard decided to head home, but on the way back he was kidnapped and imprisoned for eighteen months by an enemy, Duke Leopold of Austria, who offered him for ransom to the highest bidder.

While John strove to ferment a civil war against Richard, loyal supporters of the latter worked to raise funds for the

huge ransom payment. Three of these loyalists were my kinsfolk – *William de Saye*, his son *Geoffrey* and his father-in-
law *Geoffrey de Mandeville*. They eventually collected many
tons of silver, the equivalent of three years of England's
entire tax yields at the time. This they took to Germany in
chests in February 1194 and proudly brought the crusade-
famous King Richard back to England.

Unbelievably, Richard pardoned his brother John, and
together they spent the next four years, as did my two *Geoffrey*
relatives, fighting King Philip.

To retake his Angevin lands seized by Philip during his
German imprisonment, Richard used a highly professional
force to besiege castles, defend against constant counter-
raids by Philip's local attack groups and, when the rare
opportunity arose, to attack major French armies at full
strength.

This army of Richard's did not consist of men who, traditionally, served a set number of weeks by contract and would
then head home whatever the military situation at the time.
Instead Richard paid mercenary forces with specialist skills
who would work for him for as long as they were paid. Some
of his men specialised in the tunnel-digging mine warfare
and siege-engine technology required to destroy castle walls.
Others were Genoese crossbow infantry, Welsh longbow and
dagger commandos and various mercenary groups who fought
for anyone who paid them and who took pride in their ruthless reputations.

Was Richard himself by nature cruel and vindictive?
Following the long siege of Acre he sanctioned and watched
the public beheading of over 2,000 of his Turkish enemies
when their leader Saladin failed to pay their ransom on time.

Such barbarous acts were, however, nothing unusual at the time, nor were they 100 years later when Muslims recaptured Acre and killed all the Christian inhabitants.

In the spring of 1199, while besieging a French castle, Richard was wounded in the shoulder by a crossbow bolt and died of gangrene poisoning. He passed his kingdom in its entirety to his erstwhile scheming brother John. There is, as they say, nowt so queer as folk.

As John well knew, Philip's burning ambition was to rule all of France and he and various rebellious barons attacked Norman lands. Resistance crumbled, key castles yielded, and it was increasingly clear that many Norman barons were ready to declare allegiance to France and no longer to England. By early June 1204 John had lost all Normandy and he knew that Philip would soon go for Anglo-Norman territories in the rest of France.

Back in England John needed to raise big money and a well-provisioned, professional army if he was to regain Normandy, never mind prevent the loss of his southern French territories.

He also contrived an important alliance with those Flemish and northern French coastal fiefdoms, especially Boulogne, whose heiress *Sybil's* son, *William Fiennes*, married *Agnes de Dammartin*, the sister of *Count Renaud of Boulogne* and John's key ally on the French coast.

Philip of France also recognised *Renaud* as a vital chess piece in the war against England and did his best to woo him. When this failed, the French attacked Boulogne and Flanders, but John backed up *Renaud* and saw off the French.

When I first learned medieval history in the 1960s I was taught a simplistic version of the evil King John who was forced by the will of common people to give up his despotic ways and agree to freedom for all under a law of equals called Magna Carta.

The reality was, of course, far more complex and certainly did not involve an uprising of the populace against the monarchy. Rather it was the revolt by a mere handful of great magnates from various counties led by my kinsman *Geoffrey de Mandeville* in London and a couple of dozen other barons, mostly from wealthy land blocks in the north and the Midlands. Early on in 1214 John had begun to discover exactly which of the English-based Norman barons he could rely on. But some wavered like today's floating voters. One such was the contemporary *Fiennes* family boss, *William*, lord of the great Martock estate in Somerset, which he had been granted by the son and heir of King Stephen, *William of Boulogne*. However, when John levied heavy taxes on *William*, the latter complained vocally, refused to pay, was put on John's blacklist and for a while had his estates confiscated.

William's cousin and friend was the hugely wealthy *Geoffrey de Mandeville*, one-time bearer of King Richard's ransom money to Germany, and he, like *William*, became incensed by John's taxes. Together with *Henry de Bohun*, Bishop of Hereford, whose son *Humphrey* married *William Fiennes*'s daughter *Maud*, *de Mandeville* nudged the disgruntled barons around England into open revolt.

Two factors brought discontent into the open under John. The first was his 1214 defeat in France by the armies of King Philip and his son Prince Louis in both Aquitaine and Flanders. This bitter defeat ended with the signing of a five-year truce, although nobody expected it to last.

Back in England John felt vengeful towards the various barons who had turned down his recent requests from the battlefront for vital reinforcements and cash. So he demanded new taxes.

Matters came to a head in the spring of 1215 when kinsman *Geoffrey de Mandeville*'s group of dissident magnates arranged to meet the king. However no agreement could be reached so John ordered their estates to be seized. Cousin *Geoffrey* therefore attacked London, arriving there with his armed force shortly before John's own men. He had the City plundered, burned down Jewish properties and besieged the king's guard in the Tower of London.

Somehow mediators persuaded both sides to meet on 15 June 1215 at a Thames-side field called Runnymede, near Windsor, where a draft document of an agreement was to be signed by the king and by a nominated group of twenty-five barons.

There were sixty-three clauses in this 'Magna Carta' (as it was subsequently described) and although the barons had intended that it would apply to *their* main grievances, it was clearly written to apply 'to all freemen throughout the realm'.

Although John did show every sign of intending to comply with the Agreement and sent copies of it far and wide throughout the Kingdom, the more extreme barons, including three of my kinsfolk, clearly did not trust the King.

William Fiennes, a long-time supporter of the King, was one of those barons who withdrew his aid at that crucial point of the revolt, as a result of which his estates in Somerset were confiscated by the Crown.

Trust soon broke down and when the king raised a mainly mercenary army that soon successfully besieged several of the barons' strongholds, *Geoffrey de Mandeville* appealed to Philip of France to invade, join the rebels and take over as King of England. In response John split his army in two, and his most famous general, the Earl of Salisbury, attacked *de Mandeville*'s forces in London, but failed to dislodge them. Meanwhile, the king took his own army north, besieging rebel castles and burning rebel-supported towns on his way to Dunbar on the coast east of Edinburgh.

In May 1215 Prince Louis landed unopposed on the south coast and marched to London where his French troops re-inforced *de Mandeville*'s. At this stage, I am sorry to say, he was joined by my fickle kinsman, *Baron William Fiennes*, who also laid siege to John's strongholds in Dover and Winchester, but both held out through the summer.

Early that September, John's army moved against rebels in the east of England, aiming to cut off his enemies in the north from those in London and the south. But, as his advance party crossed the River Ouse near its confluence with the Wash, they were caught in quicksand and then by the returning tide. John, sick with dysentery and gout, died a few days later, naming his eldest son Henry, then aged nine, as his successor, and as regent the seventy-year-old William Marshal, legendary tournament ace and survivor of many battles fought beside Henry II and Richard I.

On his accession things definitely looked grim for young Henry, King Henry III as he now was. Over half of England was occupied by Prince Louis of France and his allies, the revolting barons. Apart from Dover Castle, of which *Ingelram Fiennes* was constable, the entire south-east was in enemy hands.

A major battle ensued when the barons attacked the main

royal army at Lincoln. The result was a convincing victory for the king's men, and when Prince Louis sent for reinforcements from France, his great fleet was destroyed in the Channel by the highly efficient fledgling navy that John had put together over the previous decade. His galleys could be propelled by sail or oars or both, and an early version of Royal Marines armed with crossbows crouched ready on deck to shoot steel bolts or flaming arrows of Greek fire which, like napalm, was difficult to extinguish with water. They also used chemical warfare by manoeuvring until, upwind of the French, John's sailors released clouds of pulverised lime from pots. This acidic dust blinded the French sailors, who were easy to kill once their ships were boarded. The last major foreign invasion force, prior to the Spanish Armada, was thus beaten off.

Soon afterwards, Prince Louis of France sued for peace and, on an island in the Thames, a treaty was signed that allowed him and his men to head back to France with their tails between their legs.

So John's Angevin son, Henry, and not Louis of France, became England's eighth monarch since the Conqueror.

Following the reign of King John and his bitter fighting with the French, the last remnants of 'class' discrimination between Saxon and Norman Englishmen disappeared, and those Anglo-Normans who still owned estates on both sides of the Channel had to make up their minds whether to become English or French because Normandy had become as assuredly French as today's Texas is American and not Mexican.

King John and his successors were truly kings of England, unlike William the Conqueror and his sons who had called themselves kings of the Anglo-Normans.

Likewise, King Philip ensured that his Capetian dynasty began the process of taking over most of today's geographical France, with Normandy as just another province. He forced Anglo-Normans to decide where their true loyalty lay. My family split both ways. Those who reverted to their French roots left England for good, while others prospered on their English estates and lost their French property.

My family were at the very heart of the revolt against John and of the Charter or Magna Carta that evolved from it. Of the twenty-five barons who signed the Charter, three were Fiennes kinsfolk: *Henry de Bohun*, the Bishop of Hereford; *Geoffrey de Mandeville*; and *Baron Geoffrey de Saye*.

The Charter is today acknowledged worldwide as being the earliest influence on the historical process that led to the rule of today's constitutional law. In 1987, some 700 years after Runnymede, *Oliver Fiennes*, the Dean of Lincoln, brother of the twenty-first Lord Saye and direct descendant of signatory *Geoffrey de Saye*, exhibited his cathedral's priceless copy of the Magna Carta all over the United States. It forms, after all, the basis of the American Bill of Rights.

4

Intermarriage, bribery, temerity and indecision

I n 1216, less than a year after Runnymede, the main
security clause, giving the twenty-five barons the power
to enforce the Charter's rules, was withdrawn by the royal
circle of the regent, leaving the barons toothless. Their
response, as always, was to refuse the king's next request for
cash. Since, from an early age, Henry had nurtured a strong
desire to recapture territory in France lost by his father, he
was always in need of money and was therefore always having
to cede power to those with the purse strings.

In search of allies to enable him to reclaim Normandy,
Henry used the normal tactics of intermarriage and bribery.
In 1227 he assumed full power as king, and in 1230, aged
twenty-three, he led his first major attack on the forces of
the French king Louis IX, the son of Prince Louis who had
invaded England when Henry was nine.

Having secured sufficient funds and allies, Henry then
squandered an excellent opportunity to regain valuable land,
including Bordeaux, by temerity and indecision.

Then in 1236 the king married the comely Eleanor of Provence, who brought over from the south of France a host of her fellow countrymen unable to speak English but who were nonetheless given top jobs in the Church and in government. This soon permitted them to trap wealthy English heiresses, which further upset the 'native' English, who included Anglo-Normans of several generations' standing with no remaining territory over the Channel.

The most powerful of these recent immigrants were the new queen's own uncles, William of Valence, Peter of Savoy and Boniface of Savoy, the last being appointed as Archbishop of Canterbury. England, as in the days of William the Bastard, was now ruled, or rather misruled, by a gang of imported mandarins with zero knowledge of English laws, customs or administration – a true recipe for anarchic disaster.

On top of all this, Henry, by 1242, had somehow raised sufficient tax to allow another of his half-hearted efforts to retake lost lands in France. Two major defeats resulted at the battles of Saintes and Taillebourg. He gained no land but lost the last English port of Poitou.

Henry was helped, unlike so many previous kings, by having an actively loyal brother, Earl Richard of Cornwall, who had married Henry's wife Eleanor's sister, one of many marriages Henry organised between his English nobles and foreign royals.

His queen naturally supported her own foreign relations, the Savoyards, when favours were available to grant, whereas Henry had long favoured the powerful Lusignan clan. The resulting royal quibbles served to destabilise the throne and to hinder Henry's ongoing attempts at improving his affairs in Gascony, which by the early 1240s was his only remaining

French territory, long retained by England due to the wine trade centred in its capital city of Bordeaux.

In 1253 Henry sailed south for Gascony, leaving Queen Eleanor and his brother Richard as regents. This trip proved to be his most successful military foray and he achieved his aim of sorting out threats from neighbouring Aragon and Castile, besieging rebellious locals and generally ensuring that all Gascony remained tied to the English crown. He left three Fienneses in charge of his army in Gascony: *Ingelram*, his son *William* and his brother *Baldwin*.

The next diplomatic move that Henry planned was to place his brother Richard in line for the papacy, and to that end he made peace with the King of France. After all, he sensibly recognised all French territories were, but for Gascony, already lost. Unfortunately for Henry, although the resulting Treaty of Paris did lead to peace with the French for the next twenty-five years, it also had the unfortunate consequence of converting Gascony from an English sovereignty into a mere fiefdom held in liege status to the King of France. This was a monumental diplomatic error and was made worse by the fact that it failed to achieve Henry's aim of securing the papacy for his brother. His reputation back home was severely damaged by the whole sorry episode, and by 1258 trouble loomed once again.

At that time Henry's elder son and heir, Prince Edward, was nineteen and itching to exercise his personal prowess. He fell out with his equally ambitious mother, Queen Eleanor, and the two of them ended up supporting two different power factions.

Led by Henry's own brother-in-law, Baron Simon de Montfort, a group of armed barons closed in on the king at a Westminster meeting of Parliament. They did not actually arrest him, but de Montfort became, for the next seven years, the de facto ruler of England with Henry, to all intents, a mere puppet ruler. Although the detailed troubles between the king and his magnates were different, the basic struggle was simply a continuation of the evolution process of the Charter and of democracy itself.

King John had been forced into the Runnymede confrontation and Henry's comeuppance was the takeover by de Montfort's clique as a result of general dissatisfaction with his rule on four counts. There was his expensive and fruitless attempt to obtain the papacy for his brother Richard, his equally costly failures to retake or at least retain French territories, his expensive gifts to foreign favourites and, worst of all, his placement of these hated immigrants into key positions of power over the people of England.

De Montfort forced both Henry and his son Edward to sign a new version of the Runnymede Charter, titled the Provisions of Oxford, which enforced the holding of three annual Parliaments, the existence of a committee to approve all financial affairs of the realm, another committee to 'advise' the monarch long-term on all matters of governance, and the appointment of twenty-five barons (à la Runnymede) to conduct immediate reform of the government.

Over the next few years, de Montfort gradually lost the support of many of his barons, who grew suspicious of his own autocratic ambitions. So, a cunning diplomat, he engineered a new power base by increasing the parliamentary pool with lower classes of knights and representatives of different counties and towns. And, although he was himself clearly a foreigner with paper-thin Englishness, he transformed himself in the eyes of the general public into 'the shield and defender of the English' against the imminent (illusory) threat of French invasion and foreign rule. His hypocrisy was phenomenal, his own notorious father of the same name had led French armies against the mountain fortresses of the Albigensian 'heretics' in southern France and had suppressed them with torture, terror and massacre. While he retained his personal dictatorship of England, de Montfort's consummate PR skills succeeded in uniting the country in a deep resentment of foreigners in general and with a new pride in English nationhood. This tide of antipathy towards immigrants was then, in 1263, steered by de Montfort against all those of his fellow foreigners who stood in his way, including the queen herself.

With King Henry isolated in the Tower of London, the queen escaped by boat down the Thames, but she was forced to retreat when crowds on London Bridge pelted her with rocks and garbage.

An abbey chronicle of the time recorded: 'Whoever did not know the English tongue was despised by the masses and held in contempt.' One new statute Henry was forced to sign included a passage that confined any position of governmental office 'to native-born men' and expelled foreigners from such jobs for ever.

Despite all his successes and restrictions on the autocratic potential of future monarchs, de Montfort was himself increasingly deserted by many of his early supporters, retaining a shrunken power base confined mostly to London and the Midlands. Then, late in October 1263, the Pope, hoping to avoid an armed clash in one of 'his' main Christian kingdoms, sent in a mediator, but to no avail and civil war followed.

Early in 1264 Henry and his son Edward gained an initial

victory at Northampton, but a month later, at Lewes, de Montfort retaliated by crushing the royal army and capturing Henry, Prince Edward and Richard of Cornwall. My forebears who fought for the king at Lewes that day included *Sir Giles Fiennes* and the famous knight *William de Saye, Lord of Sele* (a village in Kent).

De Montfort was now the ruler of England, basing his regime's support not on the magnates, most of whom hated him, but by calling upon low-level country knights and town burghers to form what amounted to an embryonic House of Commons. However de Montfort's absolute power turned many against him, and when in 1265 Prince Edward escaped his imprisonment he was quickly able to raise a substantial army, largely due to the defection from de Montfort's side of the powerful Earl of Gloucester.

And on a hot summer's day in the scenic Vale of Evesham, Prince Edward, with his lifelong companion *Ingelram Fiennes* fighting valiantly at his side, cornered the far smaller de Montfort force and massacred them and their leader without mercy.

For much of his life Prince Edward had been an ardent admirer of his aunt's husband, Simon de Montfort, who was also his godfather, and at one point had even plotted with de Montfort against his father, King Henry. Then, at Evesham, Edward had commanded the army that destroyed de Montfort and literally tore him to pieces. Winston Churchill wrote of Edward: 'in Edward I the great Earl [de Montfort] had found his true heir.' According to another historian: 'The victor of Evesham was the true pupil of the vanquished.'

For the last seven years of his rule King Henry lapsed

into mild senility, and Prince Edward's regency included a bunch of Fienneses from Henry's court, such as *Michael Fiennes*, who for many years was Edward's chancellor and who encouraged the regime to adopt most of de Montfort's social reforms.

By 1268 England was sufficiently at peace for Edward to join the Eighth and last Crusade, even though Henry was increasingly senile, indecisive and focused on the completion of his great building works at Westminster Abbey.

When in 1272 King Henry died after a reign of fifty-seven years, his heir Edward, by then in his early thirties and married to Eleanor of Castile, was well into crusading and so confident that he had no threats to fear back home that he returned only in 1274 to be crowned at Westminster.

A number of my kinsfolk had achieved top jobs with influence and estates in England via intermarriage with previous royals. Now, through Edward's marriage to Eleanor, another batch of Fienneses arrived on the scene.

Queen Eleanor's great-aunt, *Agnes de Dammartin*, was the mother of *Ingelram Fiennes*, which ensured his already strong position in the royal court. He and his sons were to marry into the royal family and their descendants would include future kings of England. Early in Edward's reign, *Ingelram*'s son and heir *William Fiennes* married the daughter of the King of Jerusalem, *Blanche de Brienne*, the first cousin and best friend of Queen Eleanor. *Ingelram*'s younger son *Giles* had been brought up in the royal court alongside Prince Edward and he, in his turn, married off his relations to the upper echelons of influence and wealth.

Giles's sister, *Maud Fiennes*, married *Humphrey de Bohun, Earl of Hereford and Essex*, and Constable of England. In royal records this *Maud Fiennes* is referred to as, 'the noble damsel *Maud*, cousin of Queen Eleanor'.

Prince Edward and the likes of his close friend and contemporary, *Giles Fiennes*, were infamous for their unruly behaviour in their teenage years. They had been brought up together, taken lessons from the same teachers, hunted and jousted together and later fought side by side in the wars in Wales, Gascony and Scotland. *Giles* also joined Edward and Eleanor in the Holy Land on Crusade.

When still a young prince, Edward, a martial arts enthusiast, was proud of his reputation as 'the best lance in the world', and at Lewes he had fought beside my kinsman *William de Saye*, who was himself a famous warrior, having captured six knights single-handed at the Battle of Saintes.

Another cousin, *Ingelram*'s brother *Michael*, was no great soldier but he was trusted by King Edward who promoted him to be his chancellor, a key position in terms of the king's tax-raising abilities and so vital in carrying out any successful military campaign.

From cradle to grave and from battlefield to treasury, King Edward could always fall back on his clique of loyal Fienneses.

Edward was a popular prince, tall and handsome, well known for his jousting prowess and, being friendly with the Pope's representatives in England, he took advantage of their diplomatic skills and ecclesiastic influences to heal many of the deep wounds resulting from the civil war. How to turn past enemies into friends was a forte of his, for he could be very charming when he wished.

In 1270, with father Henry growing ever more senile but safely enthroned in a peaceful and prosperous nation, Prince Edward, his beloved Eleanor and a band of his favourite knights went to join King Louis of France on the Eighth Crusade.

The great Muslim leader Saladin was long gone, but a worthy successor as scourge of the Holy Land Christians appeared in the form of Baibars, a Russian Mongolian slave who had joined the personal bodyguard of the Sultan of Egypt and, out hunting one day, he stabbed his boss in the back and declared himself Sultan. Thereafter, he devoted his life to crushing all forms of Christianity in the Holy Land, besieging the castle redoubts of the Knights Templar and reducing the Christian territory to a tiny part of the region won by previous crusaders.

Louis gathered a mighty host of 60,000 men and over 1,000 boats, whereas Edward could only manage 1,000 knights, and even that in terms of taxes raised was three times more than the entire cost to his father Henry for the reconstruction of Westminster Abbey.

Louis and many of his army died of dysentery at Tunis, after which his second-in-command, his brother Charles of Anjou, agreed a truce with the local ruler and meekly took his entire army back to France.

Prince Edward's tiny host, joined by his younger brother Edmund and his wife, did their best to confront the devilish Baibars. While they never succeeded, Edward did manage to gain long-lasting pan-European fame and hero worship by making a few daring raids, capturing Acre and sacking Nazareth, killing everyone who lived there.

After sixteen months on crusade, Edward decided that he could do no more with his motley band because the various groups of Christians still holding out in isolated pockets of the Holy Land constantly bickered among themselves, and even traded with their great enemy Baibars to buy off his aggression. So Edward fixed a ten-year truce with the jumped-up Mongol, which at least allowed Christian pilgrims access to key parts of the Holy Land. He was recovering in Sicily from an assassin's attack with a poisoned dagger when news reached him of the deaths of his son John, his uncle Richard of Cornwall and his senile father, King Henry III.

Since England had been well ruled by the likes of *Chancellor Michael Fiennes* for the previous few years of Henry's dotage, Edward, although now officially monarch of Britain, felt no great inclination to rush home before some relation usurped the throne in the customary Angevin manner of so many of his predecessors. Instead, he was confident that the man he had appointed as his regent, *Roger Mortimer*, the son of *Margaret Fiennes*, would keep his throne safe while he enjoyed life for a while before taking on the full stresses of kingship.

The king loved to joust at tournaments, for he was exceptionally talented with a lance and sword, and he took his Eleanor and his gang of favourite knights (aka the royal court) from one European cousin's realm to another, jousting all the way for two long years before heading back to his British subjects. These jousts very often consisted of mock battles where, even though the combatants wore full armour and grasped war lances with wood-blocked tips, there were still a great many severe injuries and deaths. At one over-serious tournament in which Edward had previously taken part in Nottinghamshire, several knights were wounded and subsequently died.

In Gascony Edward spent a year sorting out local trouble-making dukes and arranging marriages for his many children to the most troublesome of them. In Paris he pledged his loyalty to King Philip III, the King of France, as overall liege-lord of his Gascon lands and, stopping off in Burgundy, he accepted the personal jousting challenge of the Count of Chalons for a battle royal, the most ambitious tournament in living memory where 1,000 knights on either side clashed in a giant arena. The count did his best to drag the king off his horse, which annoyed the latter's knights, and the fight very nearly turned nasty. Edward was subsequently admonished in a friendly manner by the Pope that he must forsake dangerous teenage sports now that he was a heroic Christian king.

Back at last in Britain after four years abroad and two years after his father's death, Edward settled to the onerous task of making all parts of the British Isles into a single nation under his rule. He would go down in history as the Hammer of the Scots, but he started his reign by concentrating on Wales.

Just as William the Conqueror had given great areas of England to Norman barons, so in Wales Norman baronial dynasties had taken over huge chunks of the land, especially in the border counties. These Welsh Norman magnates had become so powerful by Edward I's day that they could even build castles and attack the Welsh without first checking with the king. The two most influential (and often confrontational) barons of these so-called Marcher lands were *Humphrey de Bohun,* the husband of *Maud Fiennes*, and *Roger Mortimer,* the son of *Margaret Fiennes.*

Although Edward's three predecessors had done their best to subdue the more rebellious of successive Welsh kings and princes, their attention had often been diverted by troubles in France or from homeland rebel barons. Edward had no such worries at the start of his reign, and his crusading experiences had given him the know-how as to the best methods to counter the guerrilla tactics of the northern Welsh in their mountain redoubts. He attacked along their coastline as well as through thickly forested land and he used experienced mercenary forces, including southern Welshmen. It was these Welsh mercenaries who specialised in the use of the longbow who were soon to teach English generals that the correct application of longbow archers could defeat any enemy, even heavily armoured cavalry squadrons.

At the time of Edward's succession, Llewelyn, the Prince of Wales, who married the late Simon de Montfort's daughter, was causing trouble alongside his brother David. Poor Llewelyn's severed head soon spent time on a stake at the Tower of London, and David, considered to be more guilty than his elder brother, was dragged over cobbled streets, hanged until almost dead, then had his entrails removed and burned and all four limbs cut off and sent for display in four English cities. His head was kept on show in London in an iron grilled container to retain any bits that might try to escape once putrefied.

The next year, 1284, Queen Eleanor gave birth to her sixteenth child with Edward, a son born in Wales and also named Edward. All his brothers were to die of natural causes, but he was proclaimed at birth to be the first English Prince of Wales. This was intended to placate the naturally rebellious Welsh and did seem to work quite well for a while, allowing King Edward to concentrate on trouble elsewhere.

Edward's many Welsh campaigns as prince, and later as king, taught him a new battle-winning form of warfare by ensuring that his armies always blended squads of expert archers, usually mercenaries from Wales and Cheshire, with his heavy cavalry. So his enemies were killed either at long distance with arrows or at close range with spears. In his last Welsh campaign against the Llewelyns, his army of 15,000 included 9,000 Welsh archers.

An arrow shot could be expected to be accurate at a maximum distance of around 200 yards. However the range of maximum effect was under 100 yards, shooting level. The British began to develop the medieval war-bow in the late fourteenth century in order to counter heavy cavalry charges. They favoured wood from the yew tree because of its particular ability to 'return to shape', meaning its elasticity. Yew logs were mostly imported from Italy, Ireland and Spain. Then professional bowyers split the logs into staves some seven feet long and three inches thick, which they waxed to prevent splits developing during a standard twelve-month period of seasoning.

Different bowyers had special ways of shaping their bows, and their apprentices were sworn to secrecy never to reveal these skills. The average bow of this type was able to draw a weight of about 120 pounds when a 28-inch arrow was at full tension just before release. Only an abnormally powerful person was strong enough to achieve such a draw action and professional archers' bodies were lopsided as a result of years of practice. The power of their fist-grip was vice-like, and they used three, not two, fingers on the bowstring.

The only feather considered serviceable for use with arrows to be shot from medieval war-bows was that from the wing of the grey goose, glued and/or sewn on to the arrow shaft.

Arrowheads were fashioned from locally mined iron and

were bodkin-tipped with simple iron points without leaf-shaped barbs. The effect was ideal for point-loaded impact in an attempt to penetrate armour or cause injury through the armour.

Edward I learned the hard way, from Welsh guerrilla troops, about the extreme effectiveness of the longbow and bodkin-tipped arrows against even the latest Italian armour when used by expert archers. So he hired archers from Wales and from the semi-Welsh natives of neighbouring Cheshire for his own armies in order to fight against all his enemies (including the Welsh).

Although, like professional bowyers and fletchers, there were dedicated arrowsmiths, the majority of arrow manufacture came from local blacksmiths.

Future British armies, whether fighting at home or abroad, evolved Edward's new focus on longbow troops and how best to use them into a fine and murderous art.

Anticipating imminent new wars with the French, Edward replaced his old friend *Michael Fiennes* as chancellor with one Robert Burnell, who proved adept at raising the considerable tax revenues needed to maintain a standing army.

Edward, like his father Henry before him, reacted only mildly to ever more provocative moves by his French counterparts. But in 1293 Philip IV, known as Philip the Fair, seriously alarmed Edward by occupying the 'English' wine capital of Bordeaux on the pretext that English pirates had destroyed a French fleet in the Channel.

So in 1294 Edward assembled a major force in Portsmouth, with the intention of regaining the Gascon lands that he had learned to love during the three-year period he had spent there during the previous decade.

Philip's seizure of Bordeaux was followed by his announced aim to confiscate all of Gascony from English rule, and Edward found both his magnates and his bishops sufficiently indignant – they probably enjoyed their Gascon wines – that they granted ample funds for his war chest without the normal quibbles.

A few weeks before Edward was due to lead his fleet south, a fresh Welsh revolt occurred, and so he divided his force in half and set out to crush the Welsh. The other half of the army sailed to Gascony under the command of various leaders, including Edward's loyal but uninspiring brother, *Edmund*, the son-in-law of *Joanna Fiennes* and his close comrade, my kinsman, *William de Saye*. This operation did not go well, for only half of Gascony was recovered, and the key city of Bordeaux was held by the French.

Once Edward's army had subdued the Welsh, he took a smaller force to Flanders to help the Flemings against the French, but the resulting new tax requirement proved the final straw to magnates back home who threatened serious trouble if Edward continued his expensive war games. This inspired him, in 1302, to take advantage of a major setback to the French army in Flanders at the Battle of Courtrai, which forced Philip the Fair to agree a truce and to restore all of Gascony to King Edward. Marsh and bogs at the battle site helped a motley army of Flemish soldiers armed with long spears to defeat the cream of Philip the Fair's heavy cavalry and some 40 per cent of the French aristocracy. Ten thousand Frenchmen died that day, no prisoners were taken by the Flemings and Flanders never became French territory. The Fleming victors stripped the enemy of all their valuable armour, as a result of which the battle became known as the Battle of the Golden Spurs.

The Battle of Courtrai was, to the Flemish and to Belgian Flemings to this day, their version of Agincourt, which they still celebrate as a national holiday.

William Fiennes who had for many years stood by Edward and had been his close companion on his great crusade, fought at Courtrai for the French and was killed.

Having, after a fashion, reached relatively satisfactory conclusions to his warfare and diplomacy in Wales and Gascony, Edward was able to focus on his fervent ambition to unite all Scotland as part of his kingdom.

In 1296 John de Balliol, then King of Scotland, renounced all agreements that he had previously arranged with Edward, so the latter marched north with a powerful army largely consisting of Irish and Welsh mercenaries. At Berwick on the border, the de Balliol stronghold, Edward, accompanied as always by his old comrade *Giles Fiennes*, stormed the town and, over the next three days, executed 7,000 of the inhabitants – Britain's most notable mass murder. De Balliol was briefly shut up in the Tower but was then allowed to emigrate to France. A year later a little known Scottish knight, William Wallace, managed by sheer force of personality to unite the clans and conquer all of Scotland within a few months.

Fiennes relatives were involved in Edward's Scottish troubles in various ways. The husband of *Joanna Fiennes*, Lord John Wake, who had fought at the storming of Berwick, joined the 25,000-strong army that Edward raised to stamp out the Wallace revolt. Wake had a small squad of his own and the rank of captain under the command of the Bishop of Durham. The army met up with Wallace's hordes near the town of

Falkirk, where the English won a resounding victory. Captain Wake was killed there. His wife's sister *Margaret Fiennes* married the nephew of the exiled John de Balliol, whose name was John 'Red' Comyn. This Comyn was a close claimant to the Scottish throne and was murdered in a church by Robert the Bruce just before Bruce became King of Scotland.

The Battle of Falkirk marked the end of Wallace's rebellion. He escaped alive, but was later captured by a pro-English Scot and was taken to London to be hanged, drawn, beheaded and cut open prior to his limbs being sent to various Scottish cities.

So, by the spring of 1303, Edward was the undisputed ruler of all the British Isles and of all Gascony. However, during the war years that produced such a positive outcome, the British people had suffered huge tax rises and the country was, for a while, on the knife-edge of a further civil uprising. Anarchy ruled in much of the country as a result of Edward's frequent absences, so that whereas his early years were famous for their peace and prosperity and the many excellent legal practices he had introduced, his later years were notorious for the lawlessness of his lands. Bands of armed men known as trailbastons, so called after the heavy cudgels with which they were often armed, roamed town and country, robbing and raping with impunity. Contract killers offered their services openly at local markets, the crown jewels were stolen from the treasury, and juries were routinely intimidated.

It was in the spring of 1306, with King Edward, then aged sixty-six, celebrating the pregnancy of his second wife Margaret, a sister of Philip the Fair no less, that he heard the news, referred to above, that Robert the Bruce, scion of a long line of Scottish Norman barons, had murdered his rival John Comyn, husband of *Margaret Fiennes*, and had then, after being quickly crowned King of Scotland, raised the flag of independence.

Edward's rage at the Bruce knew no bounds and, while planning retribution, he fell seriously ill. Realising that he was not up to leading another campaign, he charged his eldest son, Prince Edward, to take over. But the prince was no warrior, and he failed to respond to this first test of leadership. Aged sixty-eight and close to death, the old king sailed west from Carlisle to join his army and died a few days later.

5

Friends and Lovers

Edward was brought up with five of his sisters, since all his brothers, by his father's first marriage, died while he was a child. He was close to his sister Elizabeth, who was married off to one of Britain's top magnates, the Marcher *Lord Humphrey de Bohun, Earl of Hereford* and son of *Maud Fiennes*. Edward's mother died when he was six and the following year his doting grandmother, Eleanor of Provence, also died.

Edward once described my kinsman *John Fiennes*, later a traitor to him, as 'my cousin and tutor'. He and a dozen fellow courtiers' children were brought up and taught together by *John Fiennes* and other court nobles with no particular teaching credentials other than apparent loyalty to the crown.

Had the prince studied the genetic tendencies of the *Fiennes ancestors of his teacher John and his brother Robert*, who were later to aid his murderer, he would have done better to banish them both at an early stage. At some point, while still a teenage member of Prince Edward's rowdy court circle,

John was given to bad behaviour. Records still exist of King Edward I writing to the Bishop of Exeter asking him to be 'gracious' to *John* for 'breaking up the Bishop's property'. And, a few years later, *John* was accused in court, with a gang of fellow courtiers, of breaking John de Foscle's dyke at Ashrugge in Wiltshire and of felling his trees.

I only learned of *John*'s misdemeanours in Wiltshire when, in 1965, I was myself detained briefly in Chippenham Prison and heavily fined for blowing up a concrete dam in Castle Combe, not far from Ashrugge.

One of Edward's fellow child students, the son of a loyal Edward I administrator from Gascony, was Piers Gaveston who, over their teenage years, became the prince's bosom friend, adviser and lover.

For the usual diplomatic reasons, young Edward was betrothed to Isabella, a daughter of the Count of Flanders who, at the time was having a romantic affair with the above *John Fiennes*. They had met when *John* led negotiations on behalf of Philip of France with the Count of Flanders, her father, to end the French/Flemish wars.

On one occasion French troops under *John*'s command cornered and destroyed a large group of raiders and, following subsequent negotiations to end the fighting, *John* acted for the French and became friendly with the Count of Flanders and even more friendly with his beautiful young daughter, Isabella.

Thanks to his successful arbitration with the Count of Flanders, *John* was used by King Philip of France to negotiate with Edward I over various French/English disputes. My family still possess a record of a letter in French written 600 years ago by *John* to the King of England on behalf of King Philip. Whether or not King Philip knew that his envoy *John* was making love to the daughter of his Flemish enemy who was betrothed to another potential enemy, Prince Edward of England, is not known. All turned out well because *John* married Isabella and Prince Edward's Flemish betrothal was, in fact, switched to a more illustrious bride, King Philip's own daughter, another Isabella.

John was prone to switch, as his father *William* had done, from working with the French to helping the English, since his family had extensive lands on both sides of the Channel. Prince Edward, on becoming king, would use *John*, as Philip had, as his intermediary with the Count of Flanders.

Quoting from various sources, including Ranulf Higden, the 'Monk of Chester', the teenage Prince Edward was described both before and after his succession to the throne of England as 'lazy and incapable', 'totally unfit to rule', 'handsome and physically strong, but weak in character' and 'a big, dull, unmannerly oaf'. It was also said that he preferred the company of prostitutes, musicians, ribald actors, craftsmen and even country labourers to his own kind. And that he was over-generous to friends while cruel to servants. Above all, he was disastrously in thrall to his friend and lover, Piers Gaveston. Chronicles of the times refer to the prince's indulgence in 'wicked and forbidden sex'. The Meaux Abbey chronicle states that he 'took too much delight in sodomy'.

Back in the early twelfth century homosexuality was no great deal, and Anselm of Canterbury wrote that, 'Up to now this sin was so common that hardly anyone was ashamed of it.' But by Edward I's reign attitudes had hardened against it and offenders were often punished by castration, or even immolation. So the prince and Gaveston were, at the very least, openly risking the disdain of the public at all levels.

Rapidly ailing, the old king prepared for a new attack on the Scots. He died on his way north and the prince was crowned without apparent objection from any quarter.

After his father's death, Edward's first act as king was to halt further aggressive acts against Scotland, which was a popular move since all campaigns involved tax demands. But then he appointed Gaveston as Earl of Cornwall, thereby positioning this already detested Gascon upstart as senior in the royal hierarchy to many of the great earls and dukes. This great title should, by tradition, have gone to Edward's younger brother Edmund. This was an ill-judged move by Edward, and his premature downfall was from then on a likely outcome.

He further insulted the noblesse of England by marrying Gaveston to his niece, the Countess of Gloucester, and, worst of all, by appointing Gaveston as his regent when, in January 1308, he went to France to marry his fiancée Isabella, the daughter of the King of France.

The general jubilation at the peace likely to follow this coming together of French and English royal bloodlines was short-lived due to yet another Gaveston-related blunder. At the coronation of Isabella as Queen of England, Gaveston carried the crown and, after the service, Edward gave him the very best of Isabella's royal jewels. Her French uncles, who were at the wedding, reported to her father that Edward clearly loved Gaveston more than he loved Isabella.

A few months after the coronation, a powerful group of barons, armed to the teeth, forced the king at a Westminster Parliament to exile the hated Gaveston. He did so under duress, but he vowed that he would exact revenge on those responsible and would retrieve Gaveston at the earliest opportunity, which he did in 1309. But after a renewed exile the king defied the barons by appearing in public at Windsor in the autumn of 1311 with Gaveston at his side. So the magnates under the Earl of Lancaster prepared for civil war.

Gaveston was captured without difficulty and summarily beheaded. The king was grief-stricken and swore revenge on the perpetrators. But civil war was averted since the main cause for strife had been Gaveston. In the winter of 1312 Isabella gave birth to the future King Edward III.

Early in 1313, after a visit to France by the king and queen together, a couple of conciliatory banquets were shared by Edward and his hated cousin Lancaster. If from then on the king had behaved with a degree of common sense, his reign might today have been remembered for its positive features rather than for its follies and Edward's selfishness.

But a new version of Gaveston was soon identified, or rather two of them, a father and son both named Hugh Despenser. Both had served Edward I on his various military campaigns and in government. Edward II now alienated many magnates by giving land, wealth and great influence to these two Despensers, exactly as he had with Gaveston. His relationship, especially with the younger Despenser, was rumoured to be homosexual.

My kinsman *Humphrey de Bohun* felt threatened by Despenser moves on his Marcher lands and he appealed for help from the ever anti-Edward Earl of Lancaster. The Marcher lords then banded together and their forces attacked Despenser properties all over England, and the king was eventually forced to exile both men and replace them with Marcher appointees. But, soon afterwards, he launched a successful attack on the allied forces of the Marcher lords and the Earl of Lancaster at the battles of Shrewsbury and Boroughbridge. Lancaster was beheaded and two members of the leading Marcher family, the Mortimers, were sent to the Tower for trial. The elder of the two soon died in prison of starvation, but the younger, *Roger Mortimer*, survived, and for some reason his death sentence was commuted to life imprisonment in the Tower, an act of mercy that the king would live to regret.

The two Despensers were immediately recalled and restored to their previous positions of influence. One of those few individuals who had stayed constantly loyal to Edward since he was a prince in his teens and who had fought for him against Lancaster and against the Scots was my kinsman *Geoffrey de Saye*, the son of *William de Saye*. An early mention of this *Geoffrey* was in criminal proceedings records of 1318 when he was briefly gaoled for 'consorting with the outlaw Robert Coleman'. But Edward had soon released him and restored him to royal favour.

Another lifelong friend who was a successful fighter in most of Edward's campaigns, but who died before Borough-bridge was *Giles Fiennes*, the first of that name to establish himself as an English, rather than an Anglo-Norman, resident. His descendants were well established, with at least six large estates in England.

After *Giles* there were English Fienneses and French ones. You had to make up your mind, or have it made up for you by regal decree. For instance, the Wendover Estate records note: 'Moreover *John Fiennes* had the living of the manor of Wendover but, being afterwards attainted for adhering to the French, he lost all.'

In 1322 the two sons of *William Fiennes* (killed at Courtrai) still wavered as to which side of the Channel they preferred. The elder son Jean (often called *John* in English chronicles), the baron of the Fiennes and Tingry estates in France, was voted leader of the barons of Artois in their local fight against the territorially aggressive Countess Mahaud. He was briefly imprisoned in the Louvre but was later released when he served the King of France against the Flemings. For a while Edward II had granted this *John* the tenancy of previous Fiennes land in Martock in Somerset, but his sister *Mary* (aka *Margaret Fiennes*) had married the Marcher lord *Edmund Mortimer*, and their son *Roger* had been, as noted above, locked up in the Tower with a life sentence.

Edward spent much of 1323 travelling the regions previously held by his enemies and suppressing any dissent, but while he was away the arrogant and dictatorial Despensers were creating new enemies.

The King of France at this time of confusion requested that Edward attend court in Paris to pay due homage for Gascony and to sort out recent troubles there. The Pope suggested that the person most suitable to reach a peaceable solution between Edward her husband and the French king her brother was Queen Isabella. By way of avoiding the homage ceremony, Edward (on the advice of the Despensers who were fearful of their fate if the king, their protector, left England) pleaded sick and sent his thirteen-year-old son Prince Edward in his place.

With his wife and son in France, Edward enjoyed a tour of friendly castles and manors unaware that *Roger Mortimer*, his long-time Marcher enemy, was engineering a cunning revenge. Locked up in the Tower, he seemed powerless.

Although no proof exists in any record, it is highly likely that, from 1322 when the younger Despenser appears to have become King Edward's lover, à la Gaveston, the queen began to turn against her husband. She must have been a consummate diplomat, for she gave the king no hint of her feelings, but she followed a careful plan for revenge on the Despensers. Her great ally, the Bishop of Hereford, paid two Londoners to help *Roger Mortimer*, the son of *Margaret Fiennes*, to escape from the Tower by making his guards drunk and then providing him with a rope ladder with which to head for freedom. *Mortimer* fled at once to France where he was given sanctuary by his uncles *John* and *Robert Fiennes*, both of whom, at that time, had had their English estates confiscated by Edward for 'adhering to the French'.

Edward wrote to the brothers addressing each as 'my kinsman', but using threats if they did not give up *Mortimer*. I can find no response to the king's threats from either brother, but royal records state that *Robert*'s 'warhorse was confiscated' (presumably from Wendover).

Another Fiennes relative who actively plotted with Queen Isabella was *Lord Thomas Wake* (the son of *Joanna Fiennes*), who she was later to install as Constable of the Tower of London.

Back in England, hostility towards the king increased day by day. In March 1324 Parliament, including the majority of those barons who had backed the king at Boroughbridge, now demanded that all the rotting corpses that had been hanged there and left on gibbets over the past two years be taken down and buried.

In September 1325 the king heard that his queen and *Roger Mortimer* were lovers and plotting together, and had gathered together a powerful army, including a group under *John* and *Robert Fiennes*. In September 1326 Isabella's army landed unopposed in England with her son the prince, and she found massive support wherever she went, including in London.

The king fled to Bristol with the Despensers and a few loyal supporters. They were finally betrayed and arrested in Wales. The elder Despenser was put to death and the younger was brought before the queen and many barons, who passed the following sentence on him:

> that he should be drawn on a hurdle, attended by trumpets
> and clarions, through all the streets in the city of Hereford,
> and then conducted to the market-place, where all the people
> were assembled; at that place he was to be bound on a high
> scaffold, in order that he might be more easily seen by the
> people.

First, his privates were cut off, because he was deemed a heretic, and guilty of unnatural practices, even with the king, whose affections he had alienated from the Queen by his wicked suggestions. His private parts were cast into a large fire kindled close to him; afterwards, his heart was thrown into the same fire, because it had been false and traitorous, since he had by his treasonable counsels so advised the king, as to bring shame and mischief on the land, and had caused some of the greatest lords to be beheaded, by whom the kingdom ought to have been supported and defended; and had so seduced the king, that he could not or would not see the Queen, or his eldest son, who was to be their future sovereign, both of whom had, to preserve their lives, been forced to quit the kingdom. The other parts of Sir Hugh thus disposed of, his head was cut off and sent to London to the Queen.

The reader may wonder at this Froissart description of a medieval execution. I have found a number of versions that differ. Indeed, there is still much controversy among historians about hanging, drawing and quartering and what it meant and how long it took victims finally to die. However, it is generally agreed that the *drawing* aspect referred to the victim being tied to a hurdle which was attached to the tail of a horse and then drawn to the place of execution (generally Tyburn in England). Some historians will argue that the drawing referred to the drawing of the organs from the body.

Hanging, drawing and quartering was the official punishment for treason but only for men; for modesty reasons women were burned (very rare in England before the sixteenth century). There are various accounts across the centuries that describe victims dying at various points during their ordeal. If a victim was popular or won the sympathy of the crowd then they may have been dead before they were cut down from the gallows; a kindly executioner would wait for them to breathe their last or the crowd would pull down on their legs to ensure a swift end. Failing this, the victim may only have been hanged for a few seconds before they were cut down to ensure they were fully conscious for the coming torment. If they had passed out they would be revived with vinegar. In these instances victims tended to remain alive until their chests were torn open and their hearts pulled out. A seventeenth-century account records that one of the Gunpowder plotters cried out after his heart had been plucked out.

Edward II was forced to sign his own abdication in favour of his son and was imprisoned in Berkeley Castle. The queen installed *Mortimer* as her regent while Prince Edward was still a junior. She thanked those Londoners who had murdered various key Despenser stalwarts in the city and she promoted the two locals who had helped *Mortimer* to escape from the Tower, one of whom she made Mayor of London.

Two feeble attempts to rescue Edward failed dismally and merely encouraged the queen and *Mortimer* to face the fact that he would remain a potent threat to their regency so long as he remained alive.

In September 1327 Edward's death in prison was officially announced and his body was laid out for a public medical inspection to show that he had not been murdered. However, the truth came out slowly but surely and is summarised in the chronicle of Geoffrey le Baker.

> His wife Isabella was angered that his life which had become most hateful to her should be so prolonged. She asked advice of the Bishop of Hereford, pretending that she had had a dreadful dream . . . that her husband would at some time be restored to his former dignity and would condemn her, as a traitress, to be burned or to perpetual slavery. The Bishop of Hereford was feared . . . And so letters were written to Edward's keepers. [These men] believed that the favour of Isabella and the Bishop made them secure [and they] took control of the castle . . .

Then began the most extreme part of Edward's persecution:

> He was shut up in a secure chamber, where he was for many days and almost suffocated by the stench of corpses buried in a cellar hollowed out beneath him. Carpenters who worked

beneath the window of his chamber heard his laments. When his warders perceived that the stench alone was not sufficient to kill him, they seized him on the night of 22 September . . . and held him down. They thrust a plumber's soldering iron, heated and red hot, guided by a tube inserted into his bowels and thus they burnt his innards and his vital organs . . . He shouted aloud so that many heard his cry both within and without the castle and knew it for the cry of a man who suffered violent death. Many in both the town and the castle of Berkeley were moved to pity for him.

Thomas Gray's poem written three centuries later describes Edward's last moments:

> Mark the year, and mark the night,
> When Severn shall re-echo with affright
> The shrieks of death, thro' Berkeley's roofs that ring,
> Shrieks of an agonizing King!

Queen Isabella, in widow's weeds, attended her late husband's funeral. And she ruled all England with her lover *Mortimer*.

6

Wool, *wine and war*

On the death of his father, King Edward III, then aged sixteen, was firmly under the control of *Roger Mortimer*, who was wont to walk in front of him in public and whose control over the ever-popular queen was complete. At least for the first two years of his regency.

Henry, the Earl of Lancaster, the son of Edward II's nemesis, was appointed as guardian of the young king, but he soon found that even he could access his young ward only via *Mortimer*. This naturally alarmed him and, with many other nobles, he began to plot against the regent.

Mortimer, for his part, rewarded all those who had helped him rise to power, including personal friends and relatives like *John and Robert Fiennes*, who had housed him in France after his escape from the Tower, and who were given back all their estates in Surrey and Somerset.

The chronicles of the mayors and sheriffs of London for 1188–1274 summarise the Mortimer regency: 'The Queen and *Sir Roger Mortimer* assumed unto themselves royal power

71

over many of the great men of England and Wales, retained the treasures of the land in their own hands and kept the young King wholly in subjection to themselves.'

Once Edward III rid himself of *Mortimer*'s domination, he was to see himself as the true King of France.

England at that time controlled the wine-lands of Gascony in the south of France, and, in the north, had a warm alliance with the Flemings of Flanders due to their mutually profitable wool trade. So, when Edward married into the Flemish Hainault royal family, tensions with France increased and this alone could have sparked off the wars that followed, which became known as the Hundred Years War.

Additionally, previous royal French/Anglo-Norman intermarriages had led to Edward's mother having a senior claim on the French throne when King Charles IV died. The French, however, reckoned that any male French relative of the dead king was more acceptable than Edward the Englishman, whatever the legal niceties.

In 1330 *Mortimer*, still young Edward's regent, made a basic error of judgement when he had the king's uncle, his own cousin the Earl of Kent, arrested. He was, in *Mortimer*'s mind, the most likely claimant to the throne, should the king die. Since he, *Mortimer*, had by then clearly planned to become king, the Earl of Kent must go.

An agent provocateur planted by *Mortimer* managed to persuade Kent that his half-brother, the late King Edward II, had not after all 'died' in Berkeley Castle, but was alive and, with his, Kent's, help, could be restored to the throne. Kent took the bait, was duly arrested for planning treason and speedily beheaded.

Edward's guardian, Lancaster, realised that *Mortimer*'s

next target must be the young king himself, so he advised Edward to strike first.

At night with two others, Edward entered *Mortimer*'s headquarters, Nottingham Castle, by way of a secret passage, killed *Mortimer*'s two guards and arrested *Mortimer* in front of the queen. *Mortimer* was sent to the Tower and was condemned to death by a committee of peers for various offences, including the murder of Edward II and his half-brother, the Earl of Kent. He was drawn and then hanged at Tyburn on a robbers' gallows.

The queen was treated gently by her son and she spent the rest of her life in retirement in Norfolk.

With *Mortimer* out of the way, the young king showed himself adroit at handling the magnates and parliaments of Britain and managed, until the last years of his fifty-five-year reign, to avoid arguments with his nobility, who served him faithfully at home and abroad.

During his reign, my family moved into a number of key positions in England and in France; indeed they commanded the army and navy of *both* warring countries at the peak of the Hundred Years War.

On the English side, the Fienneses intermarried with the Sayes and became a powerful family entity. *Geoffrey, the first Lord Saye* and *William of Wykeham* and *William Fiennes* all became entwined during Edward's reign, which is why my great-grandfather bore the complex title in 1907 of *John Twisleton-Wykeham-Fiennes, seventeenth Lord Saye and Sele*.

Geoffrey de Saye, son of the *Geoffrey* who was always loyal to Edward II, had two daughters, one of whom, *Idonea*, married *John, Lord Clinton*, who was one of Edward III's greatest warriors. And *Geoffrey* himself became Edward's Admiral of the Fleet, as well as a great land general at such battles as Crécy. His other daughter, *Joan*, became the sole heiress of the *Saye* fortunes, and she married *William Fiennes*. During Edward III's reign the Fiennes family absorbed the name and fortunes of the Sayes through this marriage. The *Wykehams* would come next.

One family problem was caused in 1337 when Edward declared war on France and laid claim to the French throne. The last links whereby Fiennes members could happily feel both Norman and English were irrevocably split, at which point *Ingelram's* son *Giles* elected to be English, while his brother *William's* family became wholly French. *Ingelram's* daughter *Maud* had married *Humphrey de Bohun*, the Constable of England, and their great-great-granddaughter *Mary Bohun* married King Henry IV. *Mary's* sister *Eleanor* married Thomas of Woodstock, the youngest son of Edward III.

Not long after *Ingelram's* two sons went their separate ways, and during Edward III's reign, one descendant, *Geoffrey de Saye*, was Admiral of the English fleet and the other, *Constable Robert Fiennes*, commanded the French army. On 5 March 1327 *John Fiennes*, having 'declared for the French', had his estates at Martock and elsewhere promptly removed by Edward III, and these and his manors were granted to other more faithful subjects of the House of Plantagenet.

At the time of his accession, Edward's French lands were Aquitaine, Poitou and the Channel Islands. The French naturally coveted these regions, and through the early to mid-1330s built up both their army and their navy.

Early in 1340 Edward's spies sighted a great armada of French, Genoese and Spanish warships massing in the Channel harbour of Sluys in readiness for the invasion of England. The Hundred Years War had begun.

Edward ordered his admiral, *Geoffrey de Saye* (my great to the power of twenty grandfather) to prepare his fleet for war and set out to confront the would-be invaders. The king and queen were both on board.

On reaching Sluys port, the English could not penetrate the mass of French vessels since they were all chained together, so they turned about as though in retreat which provoked the French into untying their ships and giving chase with the midday sun in their eyes. The English square-rigged chunky boats turned about again and their massed archers rained down arrows on the French and Genoese cross-bowmen. The fighting raged all night, and in the morning those French vessels that still had live crewmen fled the battle. Some 20,000 Frenchmen died as against 4,000 English and Welsh. For many years thereafter the English held sway in the Channel, which was to prove vital for subsequent invasions of France.

Following his heady victory at Sluys Edward desperately wished to follow up with a major invasion and decisive victory over the French, but the necessary funds were not forthcoming from London.

Edward's army's hierarchical structure reflected the accepted class system of the day. Career officers with experience commanded the smaller fighting units where control of individuals counted most, whereas large formations were usually led by major nobles or officers who, after distinguishing themselves in battle, obtained wealth, status and estates.

Edward had learned at an early age the best way to mix his key weapons, the longbowmen of Wales and their cousins from Cheshire with his foot soldiers and heavy cavalry, and to select the best site for a given battle from which to milk every available advantage of elevation and protective features.

He also learned the advantages of various Channel crossings when attacking different French ports in order to invade different provinces, which often depended upon which provincial boss had a friendship treaty with him at the time, rather than with the French. In this respect a royal daughter marrying a local duke was worth a great many soldiers. Queen Philippa did her best by producing this supply line.

Edward's most oft used ports needed favourable winds to reach in days when no dependable Met Office existed and when even a brief storm could be disastrous. But given good conditions, Edward could reckon on reaching Calais within twenty-four hours, the Norman ports in three days and Bordeaux in ten days.

Edward had to content himself with a smaller invasion of Normandy in 1346. My kinsman, the *Earl of Warwick*, following the marriage of *Maud Beauchamp* to *Geoffrey de Saye*, was in command of this invasion force. During their attack on the city of Caen, *Warwick*'s army killed 3,000 citizens and gained rich booty, but failed to tempt the ill-trained French army into a decisive battle. Edward's men – 4,000 mounted knights, 5,000 Welsh and Irish spearmen and 7,000 Welsh and Cheshire archers – pushed on south from Caen, laying waste to the countryside, burning houses and defecating in waterholes.

When they laid siege to various castles, even with limited siege materials, they were often successful, but my French kinsman *Robert Fiennes*, the elder son of the *John Fiennes* who had sheltered *Roger Mortimer* on his French estate, was the French army captain most successful at relieving English sieges, including those of Amiens, Rheims, Tonerre, Auxerre and Regennis. Because *Robert* financed his own armed unit, he eventually went bankrupt, although by the time the two armies eventually met, King Philip had promoted him to command the French army as Constable of France.

Since the English army's commanders included the young Prince Edward, known as the Black Prince, whose wife's great-grandfather was *William Fiennes*, and fighting alongside the English king were my kinsfolk the *Earl of Warwick* and *Geoffrey de Saye* of Sluys fame, we were, as a family, pretty much in charge of both sides at the ensuing Battle of Crécy.

Once the French Constable had mustered all his troops, they totalled a massive host of 40,000 men. Of those, 15,000 were Genoese crossbowmen protecting the cream of the French cavalry, with foot soldiers from many of Philip's allies, including Germany, Savoy, Luxembourg and Bohemia.

When Edward's spies told him the size of the French force, he realised that direct confrontation was maybe not such a good idea after all, unless he could locate an ideally defensive location. He needed to cross the Somme, but could find no bridge, and the French were closing rapidly from behind. Promising a great reward to locals, he found one farmer, named Gobin Aqueche, who agreed to guide the English to the hidden causeway of Blanchetaque. The man's name is now a French word for traitor, as is Quisling in Scandinavia.

Arriving at the tidal crossing in the early morning, Edward's bowmen waded across the estuary with water up to chest-level in places.

A French river guard of 4,000 men defended the far bank, but their crossbow range of 100 metres was less than the 200-metre killing range of the longbow, and the Welsh archers, half-submerged though they were, were able to decimate the enemy and force a crossing for the rest of the army in the nick of time.

Next day, ten miles from Blanchetaque and on the edge of the great forest of Crécy, Edward drew up his battle lines with care. With some 16,000 men to face 40,000 he knew that he could only win by using the ground well, and this he undeniably did. The edge of the forest, the town of Crécy, and a marshy stream all provided good flanking obstacles, and where the ridge line, along which he assembled his battalion, was less steep, Edward's archers dug pitholes just ahead of their foremost rank.

The royal standard was proudly planted, the same dragon banner that King Harold had flown at Hastings, in the epicentre of the 2,000-metre-long defensive front. And there they awaited the arrival of the enemy. Apprehension at such a time is unavoidable. In the 1960s in Arabia, fighting the Soviet-trained People's Front, I well remember the mounting fear, the bowel-loosening thought of bullet-damage and my small Omani force being overrun in enemy territory. The worst times were those when waiting, sweating hour after hour in oppressive heat by day and with the whine of mosquito clouds by night, knowing that the enemy was close by.

Edward's men waited and watched. Their enemy's lines stretched across a wide front, the approaching sound of their drums and battle cries deadened by a rainstorm. Great flocks of crows flapped overhead as the first move was made by Philip's men. His Genoese crossbowmen, several thousand of them marching ahead of massed cavalry lines, aimed to shoot their deadly steel bolts from a maximum range of 100 yards.

As at Blanchetaque, the superior range of the Welsh longbow proved the death knell of the Genoese. Steel-tipped arrows bombarded the crossbowmen long before they could use their own weapons to any effect. Those not killed or maimed would have retreated, but the French cavalry, their horses snorting and rearing with fear and their proud knights ablaze with testosterone, advanced screaming their war cries as they trampled and crushed their own retreating crossbowmen. Longbowmen now concentrated on horsemen, or in most cases their mounts, for their arrows had the potential to penetrate even the plate armour fixed to the heads and chests of many of the chargers.

As darkness fell, successive waves of charging cavalry piled in chaos into the heaps of their dead and dying predecessors. Some French foot soldier battalions reached the ridge line in strength and engaged the British in the dark. The teenage Black Prince fought hard and impressed all about him. Not bad for a sixteen-year-old.

Fifteen separate charges by the French during that long summer night failed to break the English lines, and after four final attacks with fresh divisions in the morning, the French gave up, King Philip nursing an arrow wound in his face.

Local Crécy churchmen moved through the mounds of the dead and tallied the number of French knights by their heraldic coats of arms. They counted 4,000, a number that Edward was keen to proclaim back in Britain by way of justification for war taxes. One of the French commanders was the legendary, almost blind King of Bohemia, whose family crest was appropriated by the young Prince of Wales for his own. Its three white feathers are still the device of today's Prince of Wales, as well as that of the Welsh Rugby Union.

Acknowledging the key part in the victory at Crécy by the Welsh, the prince made all of them freemen and allotted each man an acre of land.

Records indicate that the total losses sustained by Edward's army at Blanchetaque and Crécy were fewer than 200. Elated at their unexpectedly easy victory, they moved on immediately to besiege the key deep-water port of Calais early in September. Edward's long-term plans to rule France required an easily attainable harbour as a bridgehead for invasion, and nowhere was geographically more suitable than Calais.

My family had, down the centuries since their ancestors *Charlemagne* and the *Count of Boulogne* had ruled the region, treated Calais and Boulogne as their own. 'Our' village of Fiennes (pronounced Fee-en) is ten miles south of Calais in the region known as the Pas-de-Calais. Twelve miles from the suburbs of Boulogne and three miles from the village of Guînes, the population of Fiennes is today about 900 and the Château de Fiennes in Tingry village is now just a ruin (destroyed by Henry VIII). The nearby woods, still impressively extensive, are known as the Forest of Fiennes, and their highpoint, Fiennes Mountain, is 163 metres above sea level. From the summit on a clear day you can look over and above Calais and see the coast of England.

Because a double wall and wide tidal moat protected the castle and the town, Edward spent over a year camped around his target, knowing that he could starve out the garrison sooner or later with little risk of a relief attack by the French after their Crécy setback.

The famous French *Chronicles* by Jean Froissart (an Anglo-Norman), written in 1370, describe the siege and its aftermath.

'In 1346 the King of England, Edward III, had laid siege to the French town of Calais, desiring to claim the town and its castle as his own. The siege dragged on into 1347 as the citizens of Calais were slowly deprived of provisions and food. Their last hope was dashed when King Philip of France withdrew his army, after determining that a battle with the English would result in severe losses for his own troops.

The citizens of Calais had fought bravely in resisting the long siege and had inflicted heavy losses on the English invaders. However, they now realized that their only hope was to throw themselves on the mercy of the King of England. Weakened by hunger and constant deprivation, they decided to pursue negotiations with the King.

From the battlements of Calais, Sir Jean de Vienne, the military commander of Calais, called out to King Edward's spokesman, Sir Walter Manny, 'All of us here will die, or else go mad with hunger unless the noble king whom you serve takes pity on us. Please beg him humbly to have mercy on us. Allow us to leave just as we are, and he can have the town and citadel and everything in them.' But Sir Walter replied, 'We must warn you that it is not the King's purpose to let you go free as you suggest. The inhabitants of Calais have caused him much trouble and have cost him dearly in lives and money. He is greatly angered against them.'

On hearing of the citizens' pleas from Sir Walter, Edward decided that six of the foremost citizens should surrender to him: 'I will do with these six as I please,' said the king, 'but the rest I will spare.'

'When this news was reported to the people of Calais there was much weeping and sorrow. Even Sir Jean was moved to tears. Finally the town's wealthiest citizen, Master Eustace de Saint Pierre, came forward saying, 'It would be a terrible thing indeed to allow so many to die, when there appears a means to avoid such misfortune. An act of such merit would surely find favour in our saviour's eyes. Let me be the one delivered into the King of England's hands.' Other greatly respected citizens volunteered to accompany Saint Pierre including Jean d'Aire, brothers Jacques and Pierre de Wissant, *Jean de Fiennes* and Andrieu d'Andres.

Sir Jean delivered these men to Sir Walter, asking him to intercede with King Edward in order to prevent the death of the six. Sir Walter replied, 'I do not know what the king will decide, but I promise you I will do all that I can.'

When the captives were led into King Edward's presence, he looked at them with fierce anger in his eyes. The king hated the people of Calais because of the losses they had inflicted upon his army in the past. Though the six burghers of Calais knelt before him and pleaded for mercy, the king's anger would not subside. He ordered that they be put to death immediately.

The nobles and knights present also begged the king to show mercy, including the brave Sir Walter, yet still the king refused. 'The people of Calais have killed so many of my men that it is only proper that these six should die in their turn.'

At this point, the Queen of England, Philippa, who was present during these events, was moved to intercede. Though she was pregnant at the time, she fell to her knees before the king and weeping said, 'My lord, since I crossed the sea to join you, at great danger to myself, I have never asked of you a single favour, but now I ask you in all humility, in the name of the Son of the Blessed Mary and by the love you have for me, to have mercy on these six men.'

The king remained silent for a time and finally spoke, saying, 'My lady, I might wish you were anywhere but here. Nevertheless I cannot refuse your request, though it be against my will. These men are yours to do with what you like.' And with that the Queen thanked her husband the king and had the halters taken from the necks of the prisoners. They were presented with new clothes and fed an ample dinner. Whereupon they were given safe passage through the English army and released to freedom.

The captain of the six lucky burghers and the youngest, a professional baker, was the cousin of *Constable Robert, the Lord of Fiennes*, who throughout the year-long siege had made constant attacks on Edward's siege force from his base of St Omer, one of which, in April 1347, in the surrounding country near Arques, succeeded in killing 700 men.

Had Edward spotted the relationship of his arch-enemy *Robert Fiennes* to the young burgher of Calais, he might well have been less merciful. As it was, *Jean* became more famous in French history than *Robert*, as the 'bravery' of the burghers became legendary, and in 1884 they were immortalised in bronze with life-size statues sculpted by Auguste Rodin.

From 1347 to 1558 Calais and its hinterland, including the

village of Fiennes, would remain in English hands, and it was known to the French as Le Pays Conquis (the conquered country). The local French population were evicted following the town's surrender and their places and jobs were taken by English settlers. Thereafter, the citizens were considered as English as the denizens of Jersey or the Isle of Wight. After its eventual reunification with France, they called it Le Pays Reconquis. The history of Calais is a microcosm of the Hundred Years War as the English Plantagenet monarchs and their French Valois rivals struggled for control of France.

Robert Fiennes, like his father *John*, had not always fought for the French king but had been involved in local activities against him when only thirteen years old. His nickname is first mentioned at that time as Moreau, meaning 'dusky shiny black', presumably due to his swarthy complexion. He and his father joined Philip's army in 1337 to repel the English invasion and he was promoted to Commander of St Omer during a period of siege, from where he made many successful sorties.

In 1340 his father died and *Robert* became Lord of Fiennes and of other Calais regions. He fought for the crown in Brittany and in Gascony in the mid-1340s, and, again based in St Omer, constantly harassed the English garrison of Calais after its fall to Edward.

Late in December 1349 *Robert* plotted with the governor of St Omer, during a period of local truce with the English, to conduct a sneak attack on the by then fairly sleepy garrison of the town. Sadly, a spy reported the plot to King Edward and Sir Walter Manny, the governor of Calais, who laid an ambush with 300 foot soldiers and 600 archers commanded by the king himself. On realising that he had been betrayed,

Robert rallied his small force at the bridge of Nieulay and fought through the night, killing many English before he retreated.

Not long after the victory of Calais, the Scottish King David invaded England, but he was easily defeated by an army of various northern English barons. These two successes allowed Edward to raise enough money and men to defend Calais against counter-attack. With at least 30,000 men, it was larger than any English army previously raised.

It would be many decades before such a strong army could be recruited again because, in 1348, the Black Death began its rampage, killing over a third of the entire population of Europe and Britain. One of the early deaths was that of King Edward's daughter, Joan, who was in Bordeaux at the time.

The plague originated in 1338 in central Asia, a region where bubonic plague was and still is endemic. Reaching the Crimea via China and India by 1347, it spread rapidly thence to Sicily, Italy and Spain. By early 1349 Edward was advised to stay away from a London Parliament as the city was full of the disease.

The bacteria-carrying flea was hosted by rodents, especially the large black rat, and the symptoms included swollen glands which seeped blood and pus from the armpits, neck and groin, accompanied by heavy subcutaneous bleeding, hence the black appearance of victims. At the same time great purple bubbles or 'buboes' grew overnight to the size of crab apples. Excruciating pain and sudden fits of vomiting blood followed, and then, more often than not, death. A slightly different bacillus added septicaemia to the symptoms and a third concentrated in the lungs so that victims coughed away their lives.

From the date in 1348 when a French sailor arrived in Weymouth and brought the disease to England, it took only three years to kill off nearly 30 per cent of the nobility, 40 per cent of the clergy and half the population as a whole: about 2 million people.

In Europe nearly 25 million victims died in pain and fear and many died of economic hardship and starvation. Records tell of a single estate where 5,000 sheep died when their owner and all his farmhands died. Women left without family to protect them suffered for, as Thomas Brinton, the preacher, recorded, 'On every side there is so much lechery and adultery that each man lusts after the wife of his neighbour or keeps a stinking concubine.'

With far fewer workers to till the barons' estates, the survivors demanded and gained higher wages. This is well summarised by a first-hand account written at the Cathedral of Rochester and now in the British Library:

A great mortality . . . destroyed more than a third of the men, women and children. As a result, there was such a shortage of servants, craftsmen and workmen, and of agricultural workers and labourers, that a great many lords and people, although well-endowed with goods and possessions, were yet without service and attendance. Alas, this mortality devoured such a multitude of both sexes that no one could be found to carry the bodies of the dead to burial, but men and women carried the bodies of their own little ones to church on their shoulders and threw them into mass graves, from which arose such a stink that it was barely possible for anyone to go past a churchyard.

My ancestor *Eustace de Boulogne*, right, with William the Conqueror. Eustace's advice to William to retreat, as depicted here in the Bayeux Tapestry, went unheeded.

The statue in Brussels of *Godfrey de Bouillon*, son of *Eustace de Boulogne*, and legendary leader of the First Crusade.

Effigy of Eleanor of Aquitaine and Henry II. Through his marriage to Eleanor, and his various other European connections, Henry was by far the most powerful monarch in Europe, ruling more land in France than the French king himself.

Following the long siege of Acre, during which three of my crusader ancestors were killed, King Richard I sanctioned and watched the public beheading of his Turkish enemies when their leader Saladin failed to pay their ransom on time.

Crusaders use a catapult to bombard a city with the severed heads of their enemies.

Successful battles and sieges required men with specialist skills in tunnel-digging. Here soldiers are mining a tunnel under cover of a movable shelter.

The execution of Hugh Despenser, 1326. Condemned to death by Isabella and *Mortimer*, 'he was to be bound on a high scaffold, in order that he might be more easily seen by the people.' Illustration from Froissart's Chronicle.

A mid-thirteenth century illustration of an English pirate being dragged to his execution.

French cavalry fall into a ditch, which had been camouflaged by twigs, at the Battle of Courtrai in 1302, during which *William Fiennes* was killed fighting for the French.

The battle of Sluys, 1340, marked the beginnings of the Hundred Years War. Edward III's Admiral was *Geoffrey de Saye,* my great to the power of twenty grandfather.

Edward III crossing the Somme – as the French hold the far bank of the ford at Blanchetaque – before the Battle of Crécy, 1346.

At Crécy, the superior range of the British longbowmen, most of whom were Welsh, sounded the death knell of King Philip's Genoese crossbowmen. The Commander (or Constable) of the entire French army was my kinsman *Robert Fiennes*.

Jean de Fiennes – study in bronze for the *Burghers of Calais* by Auguste Rodin.

The six Burghers of Calais, among them *Jean de Fiennes*, kneel before King Edward to plead for mercy for the citizens of the town.

The Black Prince copied his father Edward III's tactics of plunder and pillage of the French countryside and its towns.

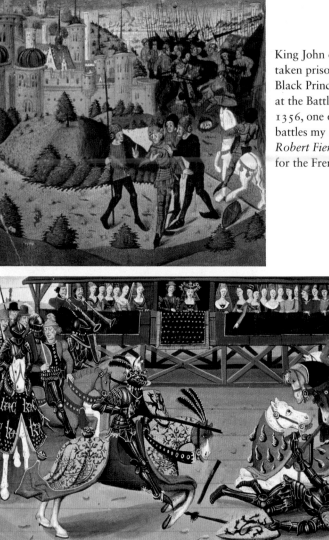

King John of France is taken prisoner after the Black Prince's victory at the Battle of Poitiers, 1356, one of the many battles my ancestor *Robert Fiennes* fought for the French.

A reputation for skill in the tournament was the best way of achieving recognition and even fame, and certainly increased your chances of survival in battle.

One side effect of the Black Death appearing during the ongoing war against the French was a surge of English patriotism and popular pressure to get rid of French as the official administrative tongue. By the end of the century French had almost disappeared, even among nobles and the clergy. So a new generation emerged who wrote prose and poetry in the English vernacular – Chaucer being a fine example.

In France this same wages issue led to peasant rebellions or *jacqueries*, and great swathes of countryside were ruled by armed bands. The man charged by the king to deal ruthlessly with this problem was *Robert Fiennes*.

Following the accession of King John of France, the Black Prince, based in an extravagant court in Bordeaux, plundered Gascony and south to the lush Mediterranean provinces, gaining rich booty in the process until, focusing on his ambitions to win another glorious Crécy, he took his army into north-west and central France. He copied his father's tactics of so damaging the countryside by plunder and pillage, a form of warfare known in France as *chevauchée*, that the king would have no option but to meet him face to face in battle in order to avoid the destruction of his country's economy, the misery and starvation of his people and, of course, a huge loss of tax revenues.

Chevauchées were well summed up by the French herald, Honoré Bonet: 'In these days all wars are directed against poor labouring people.' Anybody suspected of knowing the whereabouts of hidden grain, wine, animals or poultry was cruelly tortured until they produced the goods. Everything not edible or valuable was destroyed and burned. Peasants were beaten up, hanged or roasted alive at the whim of passing armies, whether regular or mercenary. Throughout much of France, alongside a growing hatred of the English, there blossomed a feeling of togetherness caused by fear, and this helped King John and his successors turn the provinces into a single nation under a powerful central monarchy for the first time. The Black Prince's *chevauchées* accelerated this process.

The major confrontation that the Black Prince was seeking took place near the town of Poitiers in September 1356. Some 50,000 men on the French side clashed with 9,000 English and Welshmen. King John had clearly not digested any of the lessons learned by King Philip at Crécy, for he sent wave after wave of foot soldiers against English cavalry and pressed suicidal attacks with futile and fatal persistence against the superb defensive ridge-top position of the Black Prince.

Apart from gaining yet another victory over a numerically superior French force to enhance his brilliant reputation, the Black Prince came away with a number of prisoners of prime importance, including, as a stroke of luck, King John himself, who was taken to extremely comfortable lodgings in Windsor Castle. King Edward, meanwhile, spent the next two years sending diplomats back and forth to the de facto ruler in Paris, the discredited Duke of Normandy who had fled in panic from the action at Poitiers but was acting as regent for King John's nineteen-year-old son Charles.

Edward's bargaining position was extremely strong since, not only did he hold King John, but Paris, in turmoil, was virtually ruled by a mob, and armed gangs of brigands roamed many of the provinces. To press home his initiative, in 1359 Edward himself led a *chevauchée* into the French heartlands. The fact that this foray was not wholly successful was largely due to the efforts of *Constable Robert Fiennes* who, after Poitiers, had taken full command of the French army. In 1359 *Robert* also fought various rebel factions and reinstated the king's law with successive sieges of rebel cities, including Auxerre and St Valery.

In April 1360 the dauphin (the French equivalent to the Prince of Wales in Britain) sent *Robert* to England to parlay with King Edward. These talks led to the Treaty of Brétigny, which in return for Edward renouncing his long-held claim to the French throne, Normandy, Anjou and Maine, gave him full sovereignty of Aquitaine, Poitou, Guînes and Calais. This amounted to one-third of all France, to which bounty was added, as a ransom for King John, the sum of 3 million gold crowns.

One or two English barons in France soon broke the terms of the treaty, and both kings used *Robert Fiennes*, with his Anglo-French family connections, as a key diplomat to arrange punishment for the relevant English malefactors. In July that year Edward gave *Robert* safe conduct to move freely in England and in English parts of France in order to act as his troubleshooter to keep the peace.

Robert used this trusted position with Edward to request that some or all of his father *John*'s estates in Surrey and Somerset be returned to him. However, by 1362 Edward had alienated *Robert* by ceding Fiennes lands near Calais to the English. *Robert* was furious and refused to let English troops enter his castle, which was then besieged by an army of several thousand, but they were called away before *Robert* had to surrender. Castle Fiennes remained undamaged until 1543 when English troops of King Henry VIII laid waste to the region and razed the castle to the ground.

The Brétigny truce allowed the French monarchy time to regroup and to form a standing army. Nationalism was gathering strength in both England and France, which meant less potential for setting Frenchmen of one province against another, whereas the French could, and increasingly did, set the Scottish against the English. Also, as a nation, France was far bigger and more powerful than Britain. In 1363 King John of France died while still a prisoner in England, having failed to raise his sky-high ransom, and his son Charles V took over with the sole ambition of reversing all the concessions made to the English at Brétigny.

Charles V was growing in monarchical power at the same time as King Edward was beginning to show his age. After Poitiers, and despite ongoing small-scale victories by the Black Prince, Edward's personal energy dimmed. For the last decade of his fifty-five-year reign, the king descended slowly into senility and, as no regent officially took up the reins of power, all the great gains of Crécy, Poitiers and Brétigny were gradually lost during the 1360s and 1370s.

One of the key ingredients to military success became increasingly difficult to obtain, as trained longbow archers died in their thousands, as did every other professional, in successive waves of the Black Death. Edward ordered the Sheriff of London to 'cause public proclamation to be made that everyone strong in body, at leisure times on holiday, use in their recreations bow and arrows . . . and learn and exercise the art of shooting; forbidding all and singular on our behalf that they do not after any manner apply themselves to the throwing of stones, wood, iron, handball, football, handyball, cambuck, or cock fighting, nor other such like vain plays, which have no profit in them . . . under pain of imprisonment. Witness the King at Westminster, the 12th day of June.'

During the winter of 1369 Kind Edward fell for the charms of a woman called Alice Perrers, whose origins have been guessed at by many historians but never proved. Whatever they were, she managed to dominate the king during his dotage and had influence over his policies. He gave her royal jewels and great estates, including the Fiennes lands of Wendover. These had been confiscated from *Robert Fiennes* when he was Constable of France and had been given to another of my kinsmen, *William of Wykeham*, a friend and adviser of King Edward. He, in turn, was made to hand it over to Alice Perrers.

During the late 1360s the Black Prince's health began to deteriorate, and from then on his energies were sapped. Charles V seized his chance and set his armies the task of confiscating all English-claimed land. One major city soon lost to the French was Limoges, which was much favoured by the Black Prince, and he reacted by besieging it, although by then he had to be carried, sick and weary, in a litter. When his men at length breached the walls and took the city, the Black Prince ruthlessly ordered the execution of 3,000 citizens. He then retired until his death in 1376, and one of his younger brothers, John of Gaunt, Duke of Lancaster, became the king's main army commander and, in all but name, his regent.

In 1369 Queen Philippa, much loved by Edward despite his open affair with the, by then, notorious Alice Perrers, died. Edward mourned Philippa deeply and allowed his involvement in the affairs of the realm to lapse both at home and abroad.

The Fienneses on both sides of the Channel did well in these times.

Constable Robert, after a period of friendship with King Edward, was imprisoned in England after objecting to having Fiennes Castle and other properties near Calais nominated as 'English lands'. Released fairly quickly, he returned to King Charles in Paris and was ordered by the king to command the siege of Ardres, which was held by a strong English garrison. Despite repeated attacks by *Robert*'s 1,000-strong force, the siege failed, and soon afterwards he had to retreat to his nearby Castle Fiennes, which the English attacked. They failed to take the castle but they laid waste to all *Robert*'s surrounding lands.

During his years of army command, *Robert* completed a remarkable tour of military successes against various powerful French rebels. In 1361 he took the key town of St Esprit and evicted the mercenaries on behalf of the crown. He was made governor of Languedoc and Lieutenant of the King in Artois, Champagne, Boulogne and Flanders. He defeated bands of mercenaries along the castle lands of the Loire and was named Captain of the King in the countries of the Somme. In 1380 he resigned as Constable of France and commander of the French army and handed over to Bertrand du Guesclin.

By then the French army and navy had not only reduced English-held land in France to Calais and a thin strip of the Bordeaux–Bayonne coastal area, but had begun to raid and destroy southern coastal towns in England, including Hastings and Rye.

While *Robert* held sway in France, the Fiennes family in England furthered their positions of influence, largely by intermarriage with the heiress of *William of Wykeham* and with the heiress of the great lines of the *Counts of Boulogne* and the *Sayes*.

It began with *John Fiennes* (grandson of *Giles*), who married Maud de Monceux, the heiress of Herstmonceux Castle near Hastings. Their son *William* married *Joan de Saye*, heiress of the Saye and Boulogne fortunes, who was the daughter of Admiral Geoffrey Saye, victor of the Battle of Sluys. The couple had one son, *William*, who married *Elizabeth Batisford*. *William* and *Elizabeth* had two sons: *Roger*, who married *Elizabeth Holland*; and *James*, whose grandson William married Margaret Wykeham, the heiress to *William of Wykeham* and his seat, Broughton Castle near Banbury.

My kinsman *William of Wykeham* came from humble farming stock in Hampshire, became clerk of works for royal properties and, working at Windsor Castle, impressed Edward III who promoted him to be Bishop of Winchester and later chancellor of England. When Edward III was ageing and John of Gaunt was effectively regent, the latter quarrelled with the chancellor, who resigned. He would later become one of the richest men in England. All his properties gained during Edward's reign would eventually accrue to the Fiennes family and his surname would be added to ours.

As King Edward's personal rule faded to impotence, he depended on *Chancellor Wykeham* as his chief adviser. A contemporary Chronicler wrote of *William*: 'All things were done by him and without him nothing was done.' This naturally upset the King's most senior brother, John of Gaunt.

Edward died of a stroke in 1377, but his eldest son and heir, the Black Prince, had died the previous year, which left a question mark that would later lead inevitably to civil war. John of Gaunt had *William of Wykeham* exiled, but powerful bishops restored him to power.

Edward had appointed his grandson *Richard*, eldest son of the Black Prince and his wife, *Joan Fiennes*, as his successor, and John of Gaunt, *Richard*'s uncle, did not dispute this.

All the early victories of Edward III's long reign had, in the end, proved temporary, as had his attempts to establish a lasting peace with France.

7

The Buying of Broughton

When King Edward died in 1377 he had three surviving sons: John of Gaunt, the Duke of Lancaster; Thomas of Woodstock, the Duke of Gloucester; and Edmund of Langley, the Duke of York. None of them would inherit the throne because it fell to Richard, son of their eldest brother, the Black Prince, who died in 1376, whose right to be the next King of England was undisputed.

The inheritance factor, which was later to cause immense problems, was that of yet another brother, second in line after the Black Prince, who had also died but had left a daughter. That daughter was, by English law, the heir to the throne after Richard. She was to marry into the troublesome family of my kinsmen, the *Mortimers, the Earls of March*, thereby giving them a direct claim to the throne should Richard have no heir.

However, Richard would grow up to wish that he had no uncles. They were to cause him nothing but trouble and, after his death, competition between their progeny would result in eighty years of bloody civil war.

The eldest brother, John of Gaunt, acted as regent, and his son, Henry Bolingbroke, was brought up and educated beside *Richard*. John of Gaunt was for a while rivalled in power-play by the Earl of March, but the latter died young. In years to come the descendants of these two men would form the bitterly opposed houses of Lancaster and York.

When *Richard*, the great-grandson of *Joanna Fiennes*, was ten years old, he was crowned King of England. Unlike his father and grandfather, he was a lover of peace, not war, so he did his best throughout his two-decade rule to avoid trouble on all fronts. The Black Prince's wife, *Joan Fiennes*, remained close to her son *King Richard* through his teenage years, but had no say in the politics of the day.

Richard's family crest was that of the Count of Anjou, who had married the mother of Henry II who had fought King Stephen and his wife *Maud Fiennes*. The *genêt* flower was in Latin *planta genista*, which, corrupted to Plantagenet, became the dynastic name of the seven successive English kings after Henry II, kings who had ruled much of France and then, by young *Richard*'s reign, lost it again.

Gaunt's regency involved continued war in France which went from bad to worse and drained England of cash reserves. The only answer, as always, was to tax everyone, but since the Black Death had drastically lessened the number of the taxable, the populace grew ever more resentful. Gaunt and his Parliament showed little sympathy and became the target of the people's hatred.

By 1381 people all over England were refusing to pay the basic poll tax, and local mobs would attack tax collectors. This was understandable when you read records of certain poll tax collectors who behaved in a ruthless manner, especially in the south-east of England where among others my kinsman *James Fiennes* was a county tax collector.

These royal representatives moved from village to village, heavily armed, and demanded the minimum tax from every adult. One such collector in Kent, John Legge, gained notoriety by parading every inmate of a village and checking those girls whose parents claimed they were too young to pay tax. He lifted their skirts and checked with his fingers which ones he graded as 'under poll age'. It is not difficult to imagine the hatred such behaviour engendered towards the likes of Legge and their royal masters. The Peasants' Revolt that followed was directed not at the fourteen-year-old Prince Richard but at his government.

By all accounts young Richard was tall with long fair hair and delicate features. He hated war unless no viable alternative existed and, although possessing a quick Plantagenet temper, was normally given to conciliation and well-thought-out diplomacy. He hated the world of tournaments so dear to his father, but he encouraged all forms of art, music and culture. He promoted the author and poet Geoffrey Chaucer, and my kinsman the architect *William of Wykeham*. Keen on all aspects of fashion and up-to-date devices, Richard is credited with the invention of the handkerchief, the codpiece and the private lavatory.

The year after the Peasants' Revolt, Richard married Anne, the daughter of a traditional enemy of England, the King of Luxembourg and Bohemia. This marriage was a considerable advantage in all Richard's efforts to end the ongoing Hundred Years War. Additionally, his new wife (like him, only fifteen years old when they married) turned out to be a perfect companion and lover.

Although homosexuality was never Richard's penchant, he did shower lavish gifts on his favourites, especially Simon Burley, the tutor of his youth, Robert de Vere, who became the under-chamberlain and Michael de la Pole, the chamberlain. These favourites became a royal clique whose influence was thought by many, including Richard's two key uncles, Gaunt of Lancaster and Thomas of Gloucester, to be a threat to their own power.

Another great favourite of the king's youth was Thomas Mowbray, the Earl of Nottingham, but his jealousy of de Vere soon turned him fatally against Richard.

In 1387 trouble between Richard's clique and his two uncles, Gaunt and Gloucester, came to a head. Gloucester put together a powerful group, known as the Lords Appellant, who demanded the exile of de la Pole. Chief among them were the Earl of Arundel, Mowbray, the previous royal favourite, and *Thomas Beauchamp, the Earl of Warwick*, the second cousin of my kinsman *Sir William Fiennes*, whose mother was *Maud Beauchamp*. The Warwicks were to become heavily involved in the ups and downs of Richard's later years. Also involved as a key Appellant was Richard's cousin Henry Bolingbroke, the son of John of Gaunt.

Fearing execution, Robert de Vere raised a small army which fought the forces of the Appellants at Radcot Bridge, near Oxford. The battle ended with the flight and permanent exile of de Vere. The Appellants then captured the king and called a meeting of Parliament so that they could legally depose him. He, in turn, accused them of treason.

The resultant Merciless Parliament, as it came to be known, did not reach a decision which would allow the legal execution of the Appellants' targets, let alone the deposition of the king. So they abandoned attempts to fulfil their aims legally and had Simon Burley executed. De Vere fled into exile and having established power over Richard, the five Appellants held sway for a while.

Richard manoeuvred carefully against the Appellants, setting his uncle Gloucester against Henry Bolingbroke, the son of Gaunt, who both had their eye on the throne. He allowed the unpopularity of the Appellants' rule to sink in over the following years until, in 1389, he announced that at twenty-two years old he was ready to rule without any form of regency.

The ruling council, tired by then of the Appellants, supported Richard's bold declaration, and for the next ten years he ruled as a monarch in tandem with a two-house Parliament, often playing the Lords off against the Commons. He also instituted a rule of terror against individuals who opposed him.

In 1394 his beloved wife Anne died and, two years later, in pursuit of his lifelong desire for a lasting peace with France, he married Isabella, the seven-year-old daughter of King Charles VI of France, which resulted in a twenty-eight-year peace treaty.

This raised the king's general popularity several degrees, since peace meant less onerous taxes, although the Gloucester faction nonetheless accused the king of wrongful use of taxes for his exorbitant royal lifestyle. The king managed to persuade the Lords to categorise this accusation as treason, and Richard pounced on his long-term Appellant enemies that spring. His three main opponents, Gloucester, Arundel and Warwick, were arrested. Arundel was executed, Warwick was imprisoned, and uncle Gloucester was exiled to Calais where he was later murdered, probably at the instigation of the king.

The two younger members of the Appellants, Henry Bolingbroke and Thomas Mowbray, both erstwhile childhood and teenage comrades of the king, remained unpunished and, indeed, were given new titles. Bolingbroke's ageing father, John of Gaunt, remained loyal to Richard to the last and died in 1399.

Richard's revenge on his Appellant enemies now appeared to be complete, and at home he continued to conduct life in his royal court with extravagance.

Richard promoted my kinsman *William of Wykeham* to be Chancellor of England, by which point this one-time clerk of the works had become the richest man in Britain. He purchased Broughton Castle in Oxfordshire which, when his subsequent descendant and heiress *Margaret Wykeham* married my great to the power of fifteen grandfather, *William Fiennes*, in the mid-1440s, became our family castle, as it remains today.

William of Wykeham also founded Winchester College and New College, Oxford, to consolidate a firm link between public schools and universities, making both colleges available, through scholarships, to the 'poor and indigent'.

He also invented a process called Founder's Kin, by which his descendants could gain favourable rates for their education at both colleges. Sadly, this family perk ended in 1868 after 500 years in existence, so I just missed out (by eighty-eight years).

Others of my ancestors involved with Richard's reign included *Lord John Clinton*, one of Richard's loyal army generals, and, in the arduous job of collector of taxes for Sussex, *Robert Fiennes*.

Robert's father, *William*, inherited a fine red-brick castle at Herstmonceux, near Hastings, from his heiress mother, *Maud Monceux*, as well as a fortune through his heiress wife, *Joan de Saye*. Joan's sister, *Idonea*, married the above *Lord John Clinton*.

Robert's eldest brother, another *William*, served as a loyal county bureaucrat to the king as Sheriff of Sussex and Surrey and as Constable of Pevensey Castle.

In 1397 the two youngest of the five original members of the Appellants, Henry Bolingbroke and Thomas Mowbray, had been magnanimously treated by Richard, unlike their elder colleagues. But with the benefit of hindsight that apparent generosity was merely due to the king biding his time for a more diplomatic occasion to take his revenge.

That moment came when Bolingbroke and Mowbray fell out with one another. It is conceivable that both men suspected that the king had not really forgiven them, so each thought to gain brownie points with Richard by stressing their personal loyalty to him. What better way than by denouncing the other man?

This is exactly what Bolingbroke did, telling Richard that Mowbray had approached him the previous month and, warning him that they were both in danger of regal wrath, suggested that they strike first at the king. Bolingbroke said he was deeply shocked at this proposal and was now warning the king of Mowbray's intentions. He then added his further suspicions that Mowbray had been involved in the murder of the exiled Gloucester.

A committee sat to decide on Mowbray's guilt, but could not reach a decision so the matter was to be resolved by a traditional trial by combat.

However, at the last minute Richard announced that he would make an immediate decision on the guilt, not only of Mowbray but also of Bolingbroke, since the latter could not have been an innocent party or Mowbray would not have put the plot to him in the first place. The king sentenced Bolingbroke to ten years' exile and Mowbray was exiled for life.

Mowbray died a year later, and so in early 1399 did John of Gaunt. This left Richard with a chance to confiscate Gaunt's entire wealth and estates because Bolingbroke, his heir, could not inherit while in exile as a traitor. Stupidly, Richard underestimated the reaction of the now disinherited Bolingbroke.

So Richard, having checked that his appropriation of the Gaunt (Lancastrian) empire was legal, went ahead and, having peremptorily extended Bolingbroke's exile to a lifelong sentence, officially confiscated his inheritance, the greatest estate in all Britain.

The King then made the most stupid error of his life by underestimating the natural reaction of the exiled and now disinherited Bolingbroke.

Assuming that all was now well at home, Richard set out for a long campaign to deal with troubles in Ireland accompanied by his four most trusted magnates and their forces and leaving his ineffective uncle, the Duke of York, in charge of England in his absence.

Bolingbroke seized his golden opportunity and arrived with a small group of followers and some foreign mercenaries in the north of England where his family's support was strongest. He found to his delight that popular feeling was generally hostile to Richard and even in the south-east where the Duke of York might have expected to gather a meaningful force in the name of King Richard, the barons were loath to take up arms for a king who had illegally seized his cousin Bolingbroke's estates on a charge of treason that was commonly thought to be contrived.

When at length Richard returned from Ireland, he learned that the Duke of York, having failed to raise a royal army, had switched sides and joined Bolingbroke.

Richard then found virtually no support whichever way he turned, and was forced to abdicate. Locked up in the Tower, Richard was accused of numerous crimes, including the murder of his uncle Gloucester. Bolingbroke was quickly crowned as King Henry IV.

Richard was moved north to the new king's castle in Pontefract where, a year later, in February 1400, he, aged only thirty-three, was pronounced dead; no witness ever surfaced with proof of murder or, indeed, any specific reason for his death. The suspicion lingered, however, that Bolingbroke had ordered his agents to starve his cousin to death.

Richard's chief legacy was his long peace with France, which was now at risk, for Isabella, the French king's daughter, was now no longer Queen of England.

From a purely domestic English viewpoint, Bolingbroke's coup meant that one extremely popular grandson of Edward III had usurped the throne from an increasingly unpopular grandson of the same king.

8

So much Christian blood spilled

Henry IV, unlike all his predecessors since William the Conqueror, was born in England to an English father and an English mother.

He married an English woman, *Mary de Bohun*, whose ancestor was *Maud Fiennes*, the daughter of *Ingelram Fiennes*. He made his coronation speech in English, the first post-Conquest king to do so. This was an indication that the fashion for upper-class folk to speak French was fading away in the face of an ever stronger sense of English identity, naturally emphasised by the centuries of wars with France as public enemy number one.

Unlike the peace-loving Richard II, Henry approved of warlike policies and saw himself in the shoes of his grandfather, Edward III, winning great victories in France. Unfortunately his dreams were to be ever thwarted by annoying obstacles, such as a shortage of money and recurring rebellions at home in Britain.

The French were ruled at the time of Henry's coronation by Charles VI, who was periodically given to fits of insanity, at which times other members of his family took over the reins of power, however briefly. Unsurprisingly, Charles refused to acknowledge Henry as King of England, since the latter had deposed the daughter of a French king from her position as Queen of England.

Nonetheless, in the summer of 1400 Henry obtained confirmation from the French that they would abide by the twenty-eight-year peace treaty, which enabled Henry to plan to subdue the ever threatening Scots without fear of a French invasion. So he put together an army of 14,000, including two of his teenage sons, the elder being generally known as Prince Hal.

The canny Scots talked peace terms but failed to come to the table. Instead of the major battle that Henry sought, Robert of Scotland kept his forces on the move employing guerrilla tactics until the English were forced, through lack of money, to withdraw. This expensive failure harmed Henry's initial popularity back home. People who continued to support King Richard announced that he was still alive and could be brought back to his rightful place as king. There were several plots to murder Henry, and within a year of his heroic and highly popular coronation he was suffering attacks on several fronts. One meaningful result of the Scottish campaign's failure was Parliament's ever growing ability to prevent monarchs from conducting unpopular campaigns. No English king or queen ever again invaded Scotland.

In France, despite the treaty, the frequently insane King Charles VI was threatening to invade Gascony, and even Calais was under threat. Welsh rebellion was again likely, and Glendower, their leader, was inviting the Scots to join forces against the English. Henry would have loved to lead campaigns in all directions, but Parliament refused further funds.

Harvests were unusually bad that year, so corn, the staple of the poor, was prohibitively costly, and hunger makes for dissatisfaction with governments.

One good thing which did happen to Henry that year was his marriage to Joan of Navarre, whose grandfather was the late King John II of France. For once a royal marriage was the result of mutual attraction between two individuals and not for political expediency.

In 1402 the Welsh attacked the Mortimer army and captured their leader, *Sir Edmund Mortimer*. Word spread that the Welsh had failed to bury the dead of the battle, despite this being a normally well-respected Christian rule of war. Even worse, local Welsh women had descended on the dead and wounded English after the battle, cut off their genitals and forced them into their mouths. Noses were also cut off and inserted into bottoms. So Henry led a Welsh campaign, but the Welsh army merely melted into mist and non-stop rain to avoid confrontation, knowing that the English, always short of funds, would soon have to withdraw.

In 1403 Henry faced a serious revolt from the Percy dynasty of Northumberland, including the famous jouster and Percy heir Harry Hotspur, who had joined forces with the Welsh.

The Percys of Northumberland had helped Henry defeat King Richard, yet now, only four years later, they were raring to get rid of Henry himself. By intermarriage between the families of Hotspur and *Edmund Mortimer*, they shared a direct descendant, the twelve-year-old *Earl of March*, who had a direct claim (as yet another grandchild of Edward III) to Henry's throne. To help their cause, the Percy contingent spread the rumour that King Richard was still alive.

Gathering what forces he could, Henry set out to manoeuvre

between the Percys marching south and the Welsh Glendower Mortimer force from the west. He decided on Shrewsbury as the best point to aim for. His army, one wing commanded by his sixteen-year-old son Prince Hal, moved with great speed, and his forward troops reached the town to secure the key bridges over the Severn, arriving there just before the opposition force.

This meant that Hotspur's men were cut off from joining up with their Welsh allies and his options for manoeuvre were severely limited by the town of Shrewsbury, which was held by Prince Hal's men, the river itself and Henry's main army.

Both sides had large numbers of Welsh and English long-bowmen, as well as cavalry and foot soldier units. Altogether, as historians now judge, each side had some 5,000 men, and, unlike the unwritten chivalric codes of war normally followed in French–English battles, no such rules were in place that day at Shrewsbury. No quarter would be given, no ransoms taken. As with most civil wars, many families were split and joined opposing sides. What followed became the bloodiest battle yet fought between Englishmen on English soil.

Henry, realising that should he fall in battle his army would in all likelihood give up the fight, dressed two of his best knights in his personal livery with his own royal standard flying above them. This offered the enemy a choice of three different areas of Henry's front line to concentrate on.

Henry's vanguard attacked up a slight incline and hundreds were knocked down by the onslaught of deadly longbow arrows. Prince Hal, fighting hand to hand with his visor raised or removed for better vision, took an arrow deep into his sinuses. But he continued to fight.

Seeing that Henry's forward troops were badly weakened

by the arrows of his archers, Hotspur launched a direct charge against the king's position and very nearly managed to kill him. But royal knights, including the wounded Prince Hal, sent in a counter-charge during which Hotspur was slain. Chronicler Waurin recorded:

> It was horrible to hear the groans of the wounded, who ended their lives miserably beneath the hooves of the horses. There was such slaughter of men whose bodies lay soulless that the like had not been seen in England for a long time . . . for as I have heard tell by word of mouth and by writing it is not found in any book of this chronicle that there was ever in the kingdom of England since the conquest of Duke William so horrible a battle or so much Christian blood spilled as in this one . . . King Henry who was concerned in this matter more than any man, disturbed by the defeat of his vanguard, which was destroyed, with a loud voice began to exhort his men to do well, and throwing himself into the battle did many a fine feat of arms so that on both sides he was held to be the most valiant knight, and it was said for certain that on that day with his own hand he slew thirty of his enemies.

With Hotspur dead and the king's forces attacking with new vigour, the rebel army soon began a disorderly retreat, knowing that they had to make a speedy departure or else be cut down as they ran.

It is reckoned that some 1,500 of the two armies lay dead, and over 2,000 lay too badly wounded to escape the throat-slashing that followed at dusk.

One interesting tactic of the battle was the rebels' use, in place of digging pits or placing stakes ahead of their front line to impede attackers, of plaiting together the long stems of the pea plants in the pea field where they awaited their enemy's assault. Whether or not this ploy helped in the fray that followed, Waurin unfortunately fails to record.

Another point of note was the skill of the pioneering war surgeon, John Bradmore, who undoubtedly saved the life of Prince Hal. At the end of the battle Bradmore found that the prince 'had been struck by an arrow next to his nose, on the left side, which had entered at an angle and, after the shaft was extracted, the head remained in the furthermost part of the base of the skull for the depth of several inches . . . I put the tongs in at an angle, in the same way as the arrow had first entered, then placed the screw in the centre and finally the tongs entered the socket of the arrowhead. Then, by moving it to and fro, little by little (with the help of God), I extracted the arrowhead.'

No anaesthetics are mentioned, so the pain of the operation must have been unimaginable. The prince was, of course, scarred for life, but Shrewsbury and the four years he then spent fighting the Welsh in North Wales were to stand him in good stead in his great battles against the French in years to come.

During the previous summer my kinsman *Roger Fiennes, Constable of Pevensey Castle*, had to flee in the face of a French force burning and pillaging his coastal villages. That August the town of Plymouth was sacked, and soon after the Isle of Wight was invaded by Bretons. A French army landed in Milford Haven and linked up with the Welsh to attack Kidwelly Castle and the nearby English-held strongholds.

Desperate for cash, Henry had to resort to means other than tax, and he obtained expensive loans from wealthy individuals like the cloth merchant turned Mayor of London, Dick Whittington.

By the end of 1404 an ominously large French fleet was building up in the port of Harfleur and the Welsh were massing an army in South Wales, but Parliament still refused to give Henry the necessary resources to mount a strong defensive force. By caving in to most of Parliament's demands, even those that clearly limited the powers of the king, Henry persuaded Parliament to allocate enough funds to enable him to defend the realm against a second Conquest.

All around the coast in 1405 defences were made ready, especially along that part of the south coast where French raids normally took place and where my ancestor, *Roger Fiennes*, was responsible for security. *Roger* had taken over the manor of Herstmonceux from his father, *William*, who died that same summer. *Roger* and his younger brother, *James*, would, in time, have a considerable effect on the course of the Hundred Years War.

The king must have thought that 1405 was bound to be a good year with the wherewithal to allow him to lead glorious campaigns in France and in Wales. But it was not to be, for another serious conspiracy to oust him surfaced that spring.

He managed to deal with this and other troubles by ruthlessly executing the main offenders, including the Archbishop of York. This, in turn, horrified senior clerics when, on the very day of the execution of the archbishop, the king awoke screaming that he was on fire and all declared 'Divine retribution'. Medical reports of the time were unclear about any specific royal illness, although some records mention red pustules on the king's face. Leprosy was rumoured, but when his corpse was examined in the late nineteenth century, no known reason for his affliction was ascertained. What is known is that from his first attack in 1405 until his death in 1413, he suffered ever more painful and debilitating attacks of skin disease. But unlike his French counterpart Charles VI, his sanity was unimpaired.

By the end of 1406 Henry had passed his authority to a committee of his close friends and advisers. This annoyed the stalwarts of Parliament since they had begun to learn how to deal with their king. So they forced him to agree to a set of rules that limited his personal powers to those of a teenage monarch, with Parliament as his dictatorial regent.

The king's illness did not prevent him from empowering a second group of his friends and relations to fight his corner against Parliament. These men consisted of his best friend Archbishop Arundel of Canterbury, his eldest son Prince Hal, and his two Beaufort half-brothers. Arundel became chancellor and, in all but name, the Prime Minister. Within a year of Arundel's promotion, he had, with great diplomacy and the on-off support of Prince Hal and the Beauforts, managed to restore the actuality of the monarch's powers versus those of Parliament.

A major event in France that winter was to alter Anglo-French politics for the rest of Henry's reign and beyond.

For many years the intermittent insanity of French King Charles VI had allowed bitter feuding between two royal cousins, the Duke of Burgundy, known as John the Fearless, and the Duke of Orléans, whose family were known as the Armagnacs. Orléans had long been an enemy of King Henry, who was delighted to hear of the duke's murder one dark night in a Paris suburb. The Duke of Burgundy admitted responsibility for the murder of his cousin, and both the Burgundians and the Armagnacs sent envoys to Henry asking for an alliance against their rival faction. Envoys of King Charles arrived in London and a new truce was signed for peace.

The Welsh could therefore no longer hope for help from the French, and Henry need fear no imminent invasion or further attacks on Gascony or Calais. Meanwhile, his son Prince Hal was clocking up impressive successes against the Welsh, and another royal group had, by sheer good luck, captured the Scottish king James Stuart and imprisoned him in the Tower. Henry's long-time enemy Duke Percy of Northumberland, father of Hotspur, tried one last time to oust Henry, but he was easily defeated and killed by a small royalist force. So all seemed to be going well for Henry.

However, that summer Henry's illness worsened. He fell into a coma, his internal organs began to rot, his eyesight faded and the sensitivity of his ever-itching skin increased.

Strains between his main representatives began to show, leading Chancellor Arundel to resign and making Prince Hal plus the Beauforts keen to cut the ailing king out of the entire process of decision-making. A major source of this royal discord was that Prince Hal favoured an alliance with the Burgundians, while Henry preferred the Armagnacs as he felt they were more reliable allies.

In 1411 the king, despite his ill health, rallied with Arundel's support and that of his younger son, Thomas, Duke of Clarence, and forcefully cut Prince Hal out of his threatening position of imminent takeover. The king did, however, support a military mission by the Burgundians to attack the key city of St Cloud near Paris. A thousand British archers won a major battle for John the Fearless of Burgundy, which made both French parties realise the alarming ascendancy of the longbow.

Playing one side off against the other, Henry then agreed a new treaty, signed at Bourges, which allied the British with the Armagnacs. John the Fearless quickly countered this move and had both King Charles and the Armagnacs tear up the Bourges Treaty, thereby uniting both French parties for a while against the English.

By the end of 1411 Henry had managed to regain personal control over Prince Hal and his allies. Reappointing his old friend Archbishop Arundel as chancellor, he planned a campaign to reassert English control of Gascony. He appointed his second son Thomas to lead this army, much to Prince Hal's fury. A public showdown followed, but knowing that his father would soon die and that his succession was fairly secure, the prince sent him a message of unswerving loyalty, and the two men met at Westminster. The king, according to the *Chronicle of England*, said to Prince Hal: 'My right dear and heartily beloved son, it is true that I partly suspected you, and as I now perceive, undeservedly on your part. But seeing your humility and faithfulness, I shall neither slay you nor henceforth any more have you in distrust for any report that shall be made to me. And therefore I raise you upon my honour.'

The king died aged forty-six in March 1413 after an eleven-year reign, with his four loyal sons at his funeral and a united house of Lancaster at the helm of England.

Despite a never-ending series of setbacks and eternal bickering with Parliament, Henry's reign could be deemed a success. The Welsh revolt was over, the Scottish king was under control and the French were fighting each other, while a British army marched towards Gascony. Henry IV deserved to die with a smile on his face.

9

When men of good breeding think nothing of killing

Prince Hal took over a Britain that was relatively prosperous and peaceful. The plagues had, for a while, died away, harvests were reasonable and no civil war was in progress.

Looking back at his predecessors over the previous four decades, against whom his older subjects might have judged his performance, his great-grandfather Edward III was remembered for the long period of ineffective dotage following his early successes, his cousin Richard II for his rule of terror, and his father Henry IV for his speedy descent from general adulation to the realisation that he was no national saviour, nor military hero, after all.

Like many medieval rulers, Prince Hal would be blessed or cursed as a king by the character of his nearest relations, especially his brothers, uncles and sons. Throughout his highly successful reign, he would benefit from the loyalty and skills of his close Lancastrian kin. His uncles, the sons of John of Gaunt, were John, Henry and Thomas Beaufort, all of whom were valuable advisers and supporters, as they had been of his father.

Henry V's legacy, thanks largely to his portrayal by Shakespeare as the ultimate warrior, is that of the victor of great battles. In real life he was no mere macho male, for his court education had instilled in him a love of music and a knowledge of the classics. He learned to write in Latin, English and French and he developed sincere orthodox Christian beliefs. He also collected a considerable library of religious and historical works. Born in Wales, while young he learned to play the harp and to sing.

His father, always a zealous hunter and jouster of repute, made certain that the young Prince Hal was brought up to hunt, whether with falcons or dogs, and to ride large, often unruly horses with one hand always free to hold a weapon for hunting, which was a fine preparation for warfare. Hunting deer in the extensive English royal forests taught each hunter, including kings, skills with the crossbow and the longbow, although this was not the case on the Continent.

Young men today have a great many ways of achieving self-confidence without showing excellence at martial arts, but in Henry's day a reputation for skill in the tournament was by far the best means of achieving recognition and even fame. Since the advent of war could mean a call-up for unlimited national service at any time, tournament fighting experience was also a huge plus in terms of increasing your chances of survival in battle.

Henry IV's tournament fanaticism encouraged many of his nobles to travel from tournament to tournament on an annual basis, like Formula One Grand Prix today. These mock battles took place in most major European countries and caused a great many deaths and injuries, although, as time went on, new rules made things safer, just as they have with modern car races. Lances had multi-pointed spearheads, which meant that the rider's force of impact was spread across the three (or four) points, rather than focused into the single point of a war spear. The shape of the spearhead also meant it was unable to fit through the sights (vision slots) of a jouster's helmet. Nonetheless, the effect of two lances impacting on the upper bodies of their respective combatants, as their galloping horses charged forward, could cause serious injury.

Many tournaments, especially those between grudge-bearing opponents, involved mass combat between charging cavalry squadrons with lances and swords. Strict rules were in place in Henry's day, but when tournaments were first held in France around the time of William the Conqueror, there were very few enforced regulations, and 'arenas' were often wide-open fields of several acres with hundreds of combatants fighting over many hours. One tournament observer of those early days, Bertrand de Born, wrote: 'I love . . . the knights and horses in the meadows in battle array . . . Trumpets and drums and horses . . . when men of good breeding think only of killing . . . nothing thrills me like the . . . sight of the . . . dead with the pennoned stumps of lances in their sides.'

Henry did not become famous, however, as his father had, for his jousting skills because from the age of fourteen he was involved in real warfare in England, Wales and Scotland, where he became adept in the arts of combat, whether the guerrilla tactics of Glendower's Welshmen or the full-frontal bloodshed of civil war battles like Shrewsbury. The deep and near fatal facial wound he suffered at this battle gave him both a deep respect for the critical power of the longbow and a ravaged countenance, which marked him as a true warrior to the men of his subsequent armies.

Prior to his accession, Prince Hal had gained a slightly unsavoury reputation as a teenage rabble-rouser, tavern drunkard, brothel visitor and, with his gang of young nobles, an aggressor of tax officers. His image, in terms of today's Britain, would be more that of a rough-and-tumble Prince Harry than of the couth and gentle Prince William. This was later to serve him in good stead when, as the royal leader of campaigns, he talked in the tavern language of his men. It was noteworthy that, at the time of his coronation and marriage, his dissolute days of binges came to an abrupt halt.

Looking at various drawings of King Henry there is no easy way of describing him at the time of his coronation, but I quote the contemporary and over-the-top diarist, Titus Livius: 'He was marvellously fleet of foot, faster than any dog or arrow. He would often run with two companions in pursuit of the swiftest of does and would always be first to catch the creature.' And a monk described him as 'not fleshy nor burdened with corpulence but a handsome man, never weary whether on horseback or on foot'.

His left cheek carried a wide and livid arrow scar up to the bottom of his eye socket, his lips were thin, his nose long and narrow and his jaw heavy. His hair was shaved into a high head-cap, like a Jewish skull cap. Overall, he looked like an athletic monk rather than a chunky soldier.

When, over the last forty years, I have been selecting individuals for long polar expeditions, one of my main search-points has been to look for people who are not excitable and, when things are looking bad, do not react with pessimism. Nor, when all is briefly going well, do they dance with joy. Likewise, in all the horrific or glorious experiences of Henry's life, he remained on an even keel, never yielding to panic, however dread the emergency of the moment.

He was stern and ruthless when he deemed it best, but he could show an earthy sense of humour and merciful treatment of his enemies when circumstances allowed. He was never cruel for the sake of it, even when ordering an expedient massacre. He could show extreme anger that would make men tremble, but then regain his temper in minutes. He could be patient or apparently rash when reacting instinctively without rational thought or when awaiting the advice of his trusted comrades-in-arms. He was a successful paradox.

And what of Henry's England? After the various plague pandemics, there were some 2 million people and a great many more sheep whose wool provided the country's economic base.

Around the middle of Henry's reign, with his absence on campaign allowing a loosening in law control, crime became rampant as in the early days of his father's rule. Neighbour would prey on neighbour in pursuit of various disputes with magnates protecting their own criminally active staff from the law. Shropshire crime records from 1414 include, 'large scale larceny, homicides and assaults, highway extortion and the protection of known hunted criminals'. To get local law processes to enforce justice was difficult as many magnates close to the crown were themselves guilty of criminal behaviour.

At sea, pirates were hyperactive in the Channel and North Sea, plundering ships, murdering their crews and hurting the country's economy through the theft of wool and cloth carriers. Henry did his best, as did his uncle, Thomas Beaufort, his regent when the king was on campaigns, to stamp out this piracy, but with poor results. Again, senior government officials were often behind the pirates' activities, men such as Lord Thomas Carew who was later to help Henry mastermind his naval activities against the French.

Key to Henry's government were the men who ran his affairs, especially during his long absences, and were responsible for liaising with Parliament and, above all, ensuring that Henry's war chest was always adequately filled to enable him to continue to fight.

Besides his close relatives, there was a group one could describe as governing courtiers. Lancastrian supporters were, throughout Henry's reign, at the heart of power and influence, and for the most part they backed and ably financed his wars.

A number of these key officials were my kinsmen, whose influence on Henry both in England and abroad considerably affected the outcome of the war with France. Four of them have been picked out by most historians who have covered Henry's reign.

Richard Beauchamp, the Earl of Warwick, had served Henry in his teenage years and had been at his side at the Battle of Shrewsbury and on campaigns in Wales. He joined the Royal Council in 1410. He was a close cousin, friend and business associate of *James Fiennes*. (*James*'s paternal grandmother was *Joan*, the youngest daughter of *Geoffrey de Saye* and *Maud*, the daughter of *Guy de Beauchamp, the tenth Earl of Warwick*.)

The grandson of this *James Fiennes, Sir William Fiennes*, married *Margaret Wykeham*, the heiress of Henry IV's chancellor, *William of Wykeham*, a close adviser to Prince Hal in his teenage years.

James Fiennes's elder brother *Roger* married *Elizabeth Holland*, the sister of *Sir John Holland*, a hero-to-be of Agincourt and other battles, who fought beside King Henry and was brought up by his stepfather, *Sir John Cornwaille*, also a hero of Agincourt.

This *John Holland* was also my kinsman by way of his grandmother being *Joan Fiennes of Kent* (who later married the Black Prince).

Both *Roger* and *James Fiennes* were themselves loyal knights who fought at Agincourt in the company of their cousin, the *Earl of Warwick*.

On the other side of the Channel, the King of France, Charles VI, was beset with all manner of problems, and without the benefit of the loyal circle of relations supporting King Henry. King Charles suffered from a form of intermittent insanity which no physician had been able to diagnose, much less cure, so whenever mad periods possessed him, his queen and his heir, the dauphin, ruled with the unreliable support of various royal dukes and great regional magnates.

At times King Charles would grow violent so that his close ministers and servants were wont to grease their arms so that he could not seize them. His main belief when suffering from insanity was that he was a great mirror of glass that might shatter at any moment.

In 1413, a few weeks after Henry's coronation, a Paris mob led by a butcher named Caboche attacked the royal palace. They subjected the royal family to various indignities and removed from the court all advisers and ministers with known Armagnac connections. They murdered many and replaced them with Burgundians, so John the Fearless, Duke of Burgundy was naturally suspected of involvement.

Later the king recovered his full faculties for a while and showed enough regal influence to execute many Burgundians and to threaten John the Fearless himself, who fled from Paris, only to return in February 1414 with an army. He failed to enter the city and was later chased by an Armagnac force led by the dauphin.

This force managed to take one Burgundian castle at Compiègne, but had trouble besieging the great castle of Soissons, where my French kinsman *Ingelram de Bournonville*, the son of *Jean de Bournonville* and *Mahaut de Fiennes*, held out against the Armagnacs. *Ingelram*'s garrison consisted of a few dozen foot soldiers from Picardy and Artois and a group of English mercenaries sent by Prince Hal, who at that stage favoured the Burgundians despite his father having allied himself with the Armagnacs.

The dauphin's force, in due course, took the castle and executed *Ingelram*. His army then behaved like animals. Many of the English mercenaries, mostly archers, were blinded and hanged, despite a chivalric law of the day that protected foreign auxiliaries from execution. What the Armagnacs then did to their fellow Frenchmen was to be talked about for generations as being far worse than the ravages of any English, or even Saracen, army. They conducted wholesale murder of the citizens in and around Soissons, raping women of all ages, including nuns, and pillaging churches for treasure.

Not long after this nadir of the French civil war, the Burgundians struck an uneasy truce with King Charles and the Armagnacs. Through 1414, both groups were in constant touch with English envoys, including my kinsman, *the Duke of Exeter*.

King Henry had one long-term aim, which was to become King of France which he believed was his legal and dynastic right, in the same way, back in 1066, that Duke William of Normandy believed that he should, by rights, be King of England. As a great admirer of his great-grandfather Edward III, Henry shared that ancestor's belief that the pursuit of inherited rights to a throne, be it that of England or France, was to follow the dictates of a divine will.

In fact, the oft-made claims of both Henry IV and Henry V to the French throne were specious and stood up to no genealogical set of rules. However, both kings managed to persuade themselves, their various armies and some of their tax-producing parliaments that they should have inherited the French crown through the bloodlines of their ancestor Edward III, whose French mother Queen Isabella was the last surviving child of King Philip the Fair of France.

If ever such a hereditary argument had been thoroughly followed, then the English heir to the French throne would have been another senior descendant of Edward III, *Edmund Mortimer of the Marches*.

This comes about since Edward III's inheritance should have passed to his second son Lionel, and not to his grandson Richard II. From Lionel's only child Philippa, the inheritance would then have passed to her *Mortimer* children. This was not the understanding of the two Henrys following the removal of Richard II. The throne of France, as far as they were concerned, was theirs by divine right. Henry IV had failed to claim it, but his son Prince Hal, from a very early age, was determined to do so. Whether by diplomacy or intermarriage or warfare, he would claim the French throne from mad King Charles. At some point in 1414, the year after his coronation, he set the wheels of invasion in motion.

There were three prevalent factors that made it a good time for Henry to pursue his dream. A majority of the English magnates had experienced an unusually long period of comparative peace and they were itching for the romance and possible riches of renewed combat. Second, the factional infighting in France divided that kingdom and greatly weakened its capacity for self-defence. And lastly, the powerful English clerical faction were fearful of Parliament's menacing and increasing tendencies to confiscate Church riches, so a new war would nicely divert their focus elsewhere.

As with Henry IV, who several times found his campaign preparations interrupted by troubles at home, so Henry V could never turn a blind eye to domestic problems in the hope that they would await the end of the campaign at hand.

One such problem came about as a result of the religious opinions of an Oxford theologian named John Wycliffe, whose teachings had been approved, in their initial format, by John of Gaunt and by Henry IV. In January 1414 spies told Henry of a conspiracy to murder him and his brother John by disciples of Wycliffe's philosophy, which was known as Lollardy. Wycliffe had died, but a new champion of the Lollards had sprung up in the unlikely shape of Sir John Oldcastle, who, for many years, had loyally served the crown and fought beside Henry in Wales.

The Church had, during Henry IV's reign, decided that Lollardy was a heresy, since it stressed that true Christians should strictly follow the ways of the Bible rather than the dictated rules of the Church. It challenged the orthodoxy of the clerics and was a precursor of Protestantism.

When Oldcastle openly championed Wycliffe's teachings, he was imprisoned but escaped from the Tower and, when King Henry received word of his plot, he was rearrested at a meeting in London. Alarmed at the wide popularity of the movement, Henry decided to stamp heavily on all heretics. He had thirty Lollards hanged and seven burned to death, thereby gaining the grateful approval, not only of the Church in Britain, but also of Sigismund, the Holy Roman Emperor, the man in charge of selecting popes.

Henry was not personally against the Lollards' doctrines, although his own beliefs were along orthodox lines, nor was he by nature intolerant. Only four years previously he had come upon a single Lollard being put to the flames and had intervened by dragging away the flaming pyre and offering the man a pension for life if only he recanted. But, following the 1414 uprising by Oldcastle and his countrywide followers, Henry saw that heresy and treason had become two sides of the same coin and he would thereafter crush both without remorse.

The details of the Oldcastle plot, when they were revealed, involved pathetic preparations and no more than a few dozen conspirators. Nonetheless, there were known to be many sympathisers of all classes, and a number of public burnings drove practising Lollards underground.

In addition to the Lollard plot, Henry had the usual problems with the Welsh and Scots for, despite his many campaigns over the past five years, both countries had agreements with the French and were thus ever-present threats. If he took a powerful army to France, Henry could never assume that his homeland would not be invaded in the same way that his father had removed Richard II when the latter's army was in Ireland.

The diplomatic game was one of deception, counter-deception, duplicity and sudden changes of direction, which could occur overnight, given a marriage between previously hostile countries or the ever powerful papal influence of Sigismund the Holy Roman Emperor switching from favouring one Christian country over another.

Henry would have to ascertain that his diplomacy achieved minimal support for France from the likes of the Emperor, Spain, Flanders and Brittany, and maximum chaos between French factions, especially between the Burgundians of John the Fearless and the Armagnacs of the dauphin.

Henry's best hope of becoming King of France lay with Duke John the Fearless, whose fight was not with mad King Charles but with the various Armagnac dukes who were his rivals for power and wealth. If John could be persuaded that his power base would best be served if Henry took over the throne in Paris as nominal ruler, but delegated power and policy to John, then all could be achieved with minimal military effort and expense.

As an additional and potentially key chess move, Henry offered his hand in marriage to the French king's daughter, Katherine.

Henry never trusted diplomacy alone to accomplish his French ambitions, so while his envoys talked peace with all parties, he quietly planned for war. And his plans were made with meticulous care and attention to detail. His years of campaigning in Wales were to prove key to making minimal administrative errors.

When planning major polar expeditions, I have to raise sponsorship, which takes years. On one occasion my wife and I spent seven years obtaining 1,900 sponsors, including ones for an aircraft, an icebreaker and crews of specialist volunteers. And all along, we had to plan to start our expedition at a certain season of the year due to weather conditions.

Henry and his team had, likewise, to have everything ready to cross the Channel at the optimum period of good weather, but, as for the Allied D-Day invasion in 1944, the crossing date and the route had to be kept secret from the enemy. No easy task.

Having aimed to set out from England in the summer of 1415, Southampton was identified as the best port of embarkation. If his key target city was to be Paris, the seat of the king, then a number of French ports could serve as possible landings, but the port of Harfleur, at the mouth of the River Seine, had long appealed to Henry as it had served generations of French pirates, being in a perfect position from which to attack English shipping, to make raids on English coastal towns and also to send troops to help Welsh and Scottish revolts.

To be sure that his invasion of France was seen by all at home and abroad, especially by Sigismund, as a worthy 'legal' quest to claim legitimate rule of France, Henry needed to demonstrate right up to the last minute that above all he sought peace with King Charles and that he would agree to a very reasonable treaty of compromises. This was the practice of hypocrisy as a fine art.

Within a month of his planned attack on France, he was still sending peace-seeking messages to King Charles, a typical one of which read:

> May there be peace during our reign . . . We bring glory upon ourselves through knowing that, ever since the day we took possession of our throne . . . we have been quickened by a living love of peace, out of respect for Him that is the author of all peace, and we have worked hard with all our forces to establish a union between us and our people, and to put an end to these deplorable divisions that have occasioned such disasters and caused the shipwreck of so many souls in the sea of war. This is why we have repeatedly and most recently again sent our ambassadors to your serenity for, and touching, this important concern of peace.

On the same day that Henry sent this to King Charles, he commanded all his relevant subjects to come post-haste to London in order to tell them that their 'national service' call-up was imminent.

The French response was along the lines that the king 'would do all he could to arrive at the peace so desirable for all mortals' and that he had sent a new embassy to England to achieve peace. This was annoying, since it gave no excuse for Henry to start the invasion.

Less than a fortnight before the late summer date beyond which the weather window for invasion was likely to expire, Henry sent off a final message that must have made the French realise that the invasion could no longer be avoided by mere diplomacy.

Most serene prince, our cousin and adversary, the two great and noble kingdoms of England and France, formerly joined as one but now divided, have been accustomed to stand proud through all the world by their glorious triumphs. The sole purpose of their unification was to embellish the house of God, that holiness might reign and peace be established throughout the Church, and to join their arms by a happy accord against her adversaries, to subdue the public enemies. But, alas! The discord that plagues families has troubled this harmony. Lot, blinded by an inhuman feeling, pursued Abraham: the honour of his brotherly union is buried in the tomb, and hatred – the sickness inherent in human nature and the mother of fury – comes to life once more. Nevertheless, the judge of all, who is susceptible neither to prayers nor to corruption, is the witness of our sincere desire for peace; we have done in conscience everything within our power to achieve it, even to the extent of an imprudent sacrifice of legitimate rights that we have inherited from our ancestors, to the prejudice of our posterity. We are not so blinded by fear that we are not ready to fight to the death for the justice of our cause. But the law of Deuteronomy commands that whoever prepares to attack a town begins by offering it peace; thus, since violence, the enemy of justice, has ravished for several centuries the prerogatives of our crown and our hereditary rights, we have done out of charity everything within our power to re-enter possession of our rights and prerogatives, so that now we are able by reason of the denial of justice to have recourse to the force of arms. Nevertheless as we wish to be confident of a clear conscience, we now address you with a final request, at the moment of setting out to demand from you the reason for this denial of justice, and we repeat to you in the name of the entrails of Jesus Christ, following the example shown us by the perfection of evangelical doctrine: friend, give us what we are owed and by the will of the Almighty avoid a deluge of human blood, which has been created according to God; restore to us our inheritance and our rights that have been unjustly stolen, or at least those things that we have demanded earnestly and repeatedly by our various ambassadors and deputies, and with which we would be contented in respect of God and in the interests of peace. And you will find us disposed on our part to forego 50,000 crowns of gold of the sum that we have been offered as dowry, because we prefer peace to avarice, and because we would prefer to enjoy our paternal rights and this great patrimony which we have been left by our venerable predecessors and ancestors with your illustrious daughter Katherine, our very dear cousin, than to acquire guilty treasures in sacrificing to the idol of iniquity, and to the disinheritance of the posterity of the crown of our realm, which would not please God, to the eternal prejudice of our conscience.

Given under our privy seal in our town of Southampton, upon the coast, 28 July.

Since Henry's invasion aims were overall to emulate his hero and ancestor Edward III and his great victories, the Battle of Crécy and the siege of Calais, Harfleur would serve as the ideal target. Quick to reach from Southampton, he could use cannon and other siege weapons, largely as developed by his father, to besiege and take the key castle and town of Harfleur and then march towards Paris or Rouen or Calais knowing that a major Crécy-type confrontation would be inevitable en route.

An important end result of success in France would, in Henry's eyes, be a wave of glory and unification of all the factions at home. After so many unsettling years of civil war, the magnates could unite against a single common enemy, and the veterans of past wars, bound to be rusty and out of practice, could be reminded of past invincibility. He must have experienced great hope and pride as he planned and implemented his great invasion plans and through the spring of 1415 watched the war effort gather strength.

Unlike Richard II who was implacable in his desire for revenge once he identified an enemy, or even a likely opponent, Henry took pains to forgive wherever feasible. As soon as he was crowned he had knighted various young nobles, including the sons of those same magnates who his father had executed for treason. The most important of these was the young *Edmund Mortimer* who was the nominated heir of Richard II and, as the rallying point for all likely anti-Lancastrian conspirators, had been imprisoned through his childhood by Henry IV and then spent his teen years in the friendlier atmosphere of Prince Hal's household. On being crowned, Henry had restored all the Mortimer lands to *Edmund*, and he remained a close and loyal supporter for the rest of his days.

To keep Parliament relatively happy at this time when alarming levels of tax were needed, those faced with the greatest levies were those very magnates, barons and knights who could expect to make the most from a successful French campaign by way of plunder and ransom.

As an accomplished practitioner of PR, Henry was keen

to ensure that the entire populace of his realm were aware that his stated motives for going to war were just, legal, moral and deserving of their wholehearted support. To this end he ordered that county sheriffs read aloud in marketplaces the full justification for his great endeavour. Proof of Henry's public relations success was that, over the four years of his French campaign, levels of taxation were to exceed even those at the beginning of Richard II's reign that had sparked off the Peasants' Revolt. Yet Henry got his money with scarcely a mutter from people or Parliament.

When Henry first made up his mind to launch a major invasion of France, he would have consulted his experts, men such as my kinsman *Admiral Geoffrey de Saye*, the victor of the great sea battle of Sluys. However efficient his army, Henry would need an equally capable navy. At his accession the entire Royal Navy consisted of only six ships. That was still the case in 1413 so, like Margaret Thatcher suddenly needing to dispatch a task force to the Falklands in the 1980s, Henry had to take over privately owned merchant ships and form his own shipbuilding enterprise.

Southampton proved to be the ideal spot for his new ship-yard, being situated on the edge of a ready supply of wood from the New Forest. Aiming for his projected D-Day of July 1415, Henry's new navy had twelve vessels ready with some 1,400 civilian ships chartered for the invasion period from various British and foreign ports.

The artillery on these ships was not impressive, for they sported no more than half a dozen cannons each, and these crude and clumsy weapons were inaccurate, slow to load and lethal to their crews when blown loose from their plat-forms by enemy action. So the offensive capacity of medieval warships depended on squads of marine commandos with grapnel hooks, scaling nets and hand weapons to act as boarding parties, while from the high rigging and masthead crow's-nest, longbow snipers could pick off enemy sailors one by one. Fire arrows were used to impressive effect on tarred wooden ships, as was Greek fire, a chemical which, once ignited, could not be easily extinguished with water. Small defensive towers were often erected fore and aft to cope with counter-attack by enemy crews.

Early in 1415 Henry sent his shipping agents to Holland to hire some 600 ships of at least twenty tons, safe in the knowledge that John the Fearless (who could easily have forbidden the Dutch to allow the English the naval means of attacking France) would not intervene. The agents were clearly successful in their ship-hiring mission since, by the end of May 1415, eight weeks before the intended invasion date, 1,400 Dutch and Flemish fully crewed ships arrived in or off Southampton, together with a squadron of specialist Dutch siege gunners.

While the ships were gathered together from foreign ports, Henry ordered that any and all ships of over twenty tons docked in English ports were liable to seizure by way of a sort of 'national service' or, to use Boy Scout language, 'to do their duty to God and the King'. This was highly unpopular, and indeed often ignored by fishing vessels since the fishing season was then at its most profitable.

Once the ships from Holland left their home ports, Henry had to start paying them and, while they waited in Southampton, feeding their crews. So with all the other vast expenses involved in the campaign to be considered, Henry must have been highly stressed by any event that looked likely to delay him from setting out for France.

In early summer Henry, ever keen on educational establish-
ments in England, such as those of his erstwhile chancellor,
my kinsman *William of Wykeham*, wrote a special message
to the authorities concerned with enforcing recruitment for
the army, telling them to leave university students and teachers
well alone. Not long after this missive was issued, a series
of complaints reached Henry from the good citizens of
Cambridge appealing for his help because 'certain scholars
of the university have made riots and unlawful assemblies
there and are striving day and night to continue to make
them to the disturbance of the people and in breach of the
peace'. This sounds very similar to modern grumbles about
'Bullingdon Club Hooray Henries', and cries of 'Bring back
compulsory national service.'

Much more serious for Henry, and occurring in midsummer when he least needed any interruption to his imminent invasion plans, there came like a thunderbolt from heaven
the so-called Southampton Plot.

My kinsman *Roger Mortimer*, who, having committed
adultery with Queen Isabella, wife of Edward II, had then
used a red-hot poker to dispatch King Edward, had sired
generations of *Mortimers, Earls of March*, ending up in
Henry's day with *Edmund Mortimer*, the great-great-
grandson of Edward III's second son. Since Henry himself
was merely descended from Edward III's fourth son, *Edmund*
had more right to the throne than Henry. Because Henry
had always treated *Edmund* through his formative years with
friendliness and respect, *Edmund* had always, at least openly,
shown only loyalty to the king. So imagine Henry's shock
and anger when, on the worst possible day in terms of his
invasion plans, he was visited by young *Edmund* who blurted

out a tale of a conspiracy led by their mutual cousin (yet another grandson of Edward III), the Earl of Cambridge.

The plot, which *Edmund* betrayed, appeared to involve placing him, *Edmund*, on the throne, halting the invasion, helping Oldcastle with the Lollard cause and linking with other anti-Lancastrians in the north, Wales and Scotland. Two or three of the plotters, including Henry's trusted ally and treasurer, Lord Scrope, were close to the throne, which would surely make Henry realise that he could trust no one and that he would risk treachery should he leave England for even a short absence. But his mind was made up and his determination to go ahead with the invasion was increased by the thought that the French might well be involved in the plot in order to prevent the invasion taking place.

Mortimer saved his own skin by betraying those who had plotted to put him on the throne, but Henry had his cousin Cambridge and his chief cronies beheaded with only the briefest of legal processes, and to ensure a quick guilty verdict at the hastily set up Star Chamber trial in Southampton he added the fictitious charge that the plot involved the murder of himself and his three brothers. He included my kinsman, *General Sir William Clinton*, on the Star Chamber board.

Determined that nothing at home would halt his plans, he began his initial campaign tactics on enemy territory by ordering raiding parties from the English garrison at Calais to create mayhem and pillage in the countryside around Boulogne, thereby giving the impression that he was about to land his army there. As a result, the dauphin sent out a small force from Paris to deal with the raiders from Calais.

Thanks to the long truce agreed by Richard II and continued after a fashion by Henry IV, round one of the Hundred Years War had ended. But now, with this first chess move at Calais, Henry V was announcing the imminent start of round two.

Fair stood the wind for France

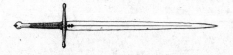

King Henry V, Britain's most revered military leader in his own day and down the long years to our present time, left London for the south coast on 16 June 1415.

As with every other great warrior figurehead from Genghis Khan to the Duke of Wellington, success comes with choosing good generals, good captains and suitable specialist forces. From that first trip down to the Southampton assembly point, it was clear who Henry's main men would be, for they rode beside him: his elderly uncle, the Duke of York, and his father's long-time military leaders, *Sir John Cornwaille* and his stepson, *John Holland*, whose sister was *Elizabeth Fiennes*.

Also in this royal cavalcade rode two others of my kinsmen who had long served with Henry on his Welsh campaigns: brothers *Roger* and *James Fiennes* from Herstmonceux Castle in East Sussex. These two brothers had often during their past service fought beside their illustrious cousin *Richard Beauchamp, the Earl of Warwick*, a royalist hero of the Battle of Shrewsbury and a senior diplomat of the king.

HENRY'S ROUTE to AGINCOURT

ENGLAND

Herstmonceux
Hastings
Boulogne
Calais
Guisnes
Ardes
St.Omer
Fiennes
Agincourt
Maisoncelles
Anvin
St.Pol
R.Authie
Frevent
Leucheux
Abbeville
Pont St.Remy
Forceville
Eu
Albert
Peronne
Dieppe
R.Bresle
Crouy
Arques
Pequigny
R.Bethune
Amiens
Fouilly
Bethencourt
Fecamp
Montvillier
Harfleur
Rouen
Honfleur
R.Seine
Vernon
St.Denis
Mantes
Paris

0   25   50
Miles

John Holland was not, on the face of it, an obvious favourite of the king's, bearing in mind that Henry IV had, only fifteen years previously, had his father, another John Holland, executed for his part in the Epiphany Conspiracy of 1400. Not holding the sins of their fathers against them did not always work, but in this case, the king received a lifetime of brilliant service from the younger *John Holland*.

Although the months of June and July were to see a frenetic hive of activity preparing for the invasion, this was certainly not because the overall plan had been a precipitate decision on Henry's part. Since birth, as Prince Hal, he had learned from his father about the English claims, whether legal or not, to the throne of France and since his coronation he had slowly but surely collected funds for the invasion. Early in 1413 he had worked with the arms experts in the Tower of London to develop siege weapons and to amass all the basic materials needed for a prolonged campaign abroad.

Mrs Thatcher had to react quickly in the 1980s to respond to the Argentinian threat to the British Falkland Islands, but then her relations with the treasury and with Parliament were a great deal more straightforward than Henry's.

I studied Henry's years of planning and preparation for his great foreign campaign with a sense of familiarity, for between 1972 and 1979 I had a parallel challenge to face. My wife had proposed an attempt at the first surface circum-navigation of earth − 52,000 miles without flying one metre of the way and involving the first ever crossing of both Antarctica and the Arctic Ocean. We had no income, other than irregular pay from the Territorial Army, and we needed a total of 1,900 sponsors of often specialist equipment, an ice-strengthened ship, a resupply ski-plane and fifty-two volunteers with skills such as marine chief engineer who would work for three years with no pay. Every little piece of a huge administrative task had to fall into place and, like Henry's, the whole enterprise must bear in mind insurmountable seasonal obstacles if we failed to keep to a tight time schedule, especially the start date.

At least a year before Henry's intended departure time of July 1415, he contacted the few specialist agents who dealt in artillery. By Christmas 1414 he had amassed 10,000 stone cannonballs of the right diameter bore for the great cannons his agents collected from castles all over Britain. Not at all certain that enough cannons of the largest known bore would be accrued from existing stock, Henry approached foundries, placing orders and warning foundry bosses to collect ample brass, bronze and iron items from which to fashion new cannons. Chemists who manufactured gunpowder, and they were few in number, were told to get busy and were forbidden to sell to any buyer other than the crown.

The chronicler John Strecche recorded some of the items on Henry's ordnance list as 'hauberks, helmets, shields, corselets, bucklers, lance-heads, gauntlets, plate armour, swords, bows, many thousands of arrows, casks full of bowstrings, axes, saws, wedges, hammers, forks, mattocks, hoes, spades, caltrops, and other tools for felling and splitting wood and mining walls'.

On Monday, 29 April 1415 the brothers *James* and *Roger Fiennes* travelled up to London from their Kent castle on orders from the king to sign up for the coming invasion. They were told exactly how many men they must each provide, whether men-at-arms or skilled archers. Looking down the lists they noted that their cousin, *Lord William Clinton*, a senior general of great campaign experience, was required to provide forty men-at-arms and twenty archers. Both *Roger* and *James* would have to produce seven men-at-arms and twenty-four archers.

They also noted that their names had three alternate spellings in the royal records, being Fleuez, Fenes and Felebert. But then other misspellings on the lists included: Germy for Geryne; Redsham for Rodsam; Haythorpe for Hagthrop; Wylton for Wyton; Wyn for Wyner; and Phithian Palm for Richard Fythian. There was also a listed Hertonk van Clux, a Jathakell and a Kethynok. This tendency for sometimes making wild spelling errors may well have long since sent people up cul-de-sacs when trying to trace their ancestors.

Records from the indenture seals of that day indicate that the elder *Fiennes* brother, *Roger*, would be able to claim £1,086 for his expenses once he and his men, with a relevant number of horses and fully equipped, clothed and armed for battle, presented themselves at the muster in Southampton. Younger brother *James* was detailed to lead his men as a 'lance' or small section of infantry in the division to be commanded by the king's youngest brother, Humphrey, Duke of Gloucester. *Elizabeth Fiennes*'s brother, *John Holland*, was listed as taking twenty men-at-arms and sixty archers.

Modern army infantry formations have altered in such a way that no exact parallels can be made, but there were rough equivalents to corporals and sergeants who were called ventenars and they controlled twenty archers, with centenars in overall control of five ventenars and all their men like the centurions of Roman legions.

Nearly half of Henry's army was supplied by noble families, and a preponderance of these was from the great (and traditionally troublesome) northern lands of the Percys, the

Umfravilles and the Nevilles. Many came from Ireland and they had a reputation for wild clothes, language and behaviour. By far the most skilled of the vital archer contingent were from South Wales, followed in order of reputed accuracy by archers from Cheshire and, for some reason, Lancashire.

Scottish troops at the time were being sent to help the French against the English soldiers, and mercenary bands of Welsh soldiers, like Genoese crossbowmen, worked for whoever paid them.

The number of serving soldiers on their way to Southampton that June totalled some 10,000 men, of whom 40 per cent were mounted longbowmen, 35 per cent archers on foot and 25 per cent mounted men-at-arms prepared also to dismount and fight on foot. Because no serious fighting had taken place since 1395, a great many of those awaiting transport to France had never fought before or had become pretty rusty at their chosen military skill.

The months of June and July in 1415 were hot and the harvest was good. The rains stayed away and waited in the wings for when they could make the most impact on the coming war. Midsummer's Day was feted as always with flowers around the doors of the houses of rich and poor alike and, in the evening, soldiers and tradesmen heading south joined in the village festivities. They danced and cheered the local mummers who, dressed as dragons, chased naked village boys all painted black and screaming in mock terror until they'd had enough and hid behind their parents.

The dusty coastal roads and the narrow footpaths were edged by lovely wildflower-filled fields where fat and dirty sheep grazed. These lanes were plagued by ruts, deeper than we would now put up with, in which heavy-laden war carts pulled by shire horses easily snapped their axles and were hauled out of the way by cursing soldiers carrying their own loads of war gear.

Merchant ships were also headed for Southampton waters filled with stout, banded casks of red wine from Gascony for Henry's armies, which they would need in great quantity in the months ahead.

Not far north of Southampton where the lanes from Dover in the east converge with those taking London traffic south, *Roger* and *James*'s men met up with the brothers at a pre-arranged inn. The ventenar of *Roger*'s group was a ruddy-faced man named Robert Prinkle, an opinionated sheep farmer in normal times but bearing a facial scar from a Welsh campaign. As *Roger*'s ventenar, he was on double the pay of his nineteen men. He touched his brow to both the brothers and, when asked, gave them the Herstmonceux news and gossip. His men had caught two deer poachers from the neighbouring estate of Sir Nicholas Pelham the week before and had beaten them to 'living pulp'.

A man from *Roger*'s stables, named only Bensell, handed over a note with the Fiennes wolf-dog seal from *Roger*'s wife, the little sister of the illustrious warrior *John Holland*. She was worried that *Roger* had left his favourite surcoat at home, the one that had so often brought him good luck in Wales. Should she send it to him?

In fact, *Roger* had, regretfully but on purpose, left it, his 'coat armour', a light silk over-garment emblazoned with his heraldic arms, due to an order from Henry that every soldier of every rank should wear an over-garment with the red cross of St George clearly displayed front and back in order to avoid confusion in battle. Too many good men on previous campaigns had been killed by what we now call friendly fire. In the heat and crush of close-quarter battle with friend and foe all mixed together and sword blades thrusting, axes slashing and cavalry lances seeking chance targets, it was all too easy to mistake ally for enemy. And archers on a flank aiming at bodies of men up to 200 yards away could easily send a deadly arrow barrage into a group of allied mercenaries instead of the opposition.

A common ploy of wounded soldiers, lying amid corpses, once they knew that their own side was losing the day, was to remove a dead enemy's surcoat and wear it in the hope of avoiding a slit throat from the inevitable death squads and scavengers at the battle's end. Henry, therefore, expressly proclaimed the immediate execution of any enemy caught wearing the cross of St George emblem.

French spies anywhere in England that summer would not have found it difficult to conclude from the hive of activity on roads all over England and Wales that Henry was about to invade France from Southampton.

Wherever armed men on their way south, from the northern borders to the Welsh Marches, met in roadside inns, their conversation naturally involved their thoughts about the immediate future and the French forces that they expected to confront very soon. Those who had campaigned in France before or who had listened over dinner to tales of Edward III's glorious victories in the previous century would have argued heatedly about where best to land the invasion force. But, with regard to this vital piece of information, Henry had, in Chaucerian terminology, kept his lips as tight as a nun's private parts.

The longer the gathered force had to wait on the coast, the bigger the administration and supply headache for Henry's ordnance officers. Herds of cattle and sheep blocked roads as they bellowed and baaed their agitated way to Southampton Common and other open fields where some 12,000 troops were encamped by mid-July.

In designated camps, different war needs arrived daily, including thousands of war lances, millions of arrows, many tons in weight, often with differently fashioned arrowheads for various types of target, saltpetre and sulphur for gunpowder and high-tech bowstrings.

Add to these obvious items the tons of more mundane wares, such as many thousands of horseshoes of assorted sizes with nails plus saddles, bridles, horse armour, halters and equine medicines of the day; specialist haulage oxen with heavy traces, cooking utensils as well as tents large and small. Ample medical supplies were vital, for disease and dysentery were common killers, especially where, for weeks at a time, armies defecated in their thousands around a besieged city.

Back at the Tower of London, an urgent message was sent by the king for yet more bows and arrows. The job of the Keeper of the King's Arrows, since early 1413, had been to replenish the stock of both items that had been depleted by Edward III during the years of Crécy and Poitiers.

At the same time, royal authority was given to the ships' masters of the seven main invasion ships then moored at the Tower's wharf to use force if necessary to find crews for their ships. This was the first recorded instance in English history of what came to be known as the 'press gang'.

As well as the soldiers, there were horses to feed, over 20,000 of them and probably many more. As French diplomats and English conspirators continued to cause last-minute delays, Henry must have been highly anxious because each new obstacle to departure was costing him a fortune and taking him ever nearer to the closing date of the invasion season.

One hundred and thirty years previously, *Roger*'s direct ancestor, *Ingelram Fiennes* of Martock in Somerset, had a son named *William*, whose grandsons *Robert* and *John* had their English estates confiscated by Edward II for giving sanctuary to his greatest enemy (and later murderer) *Roger Mortimer*. *John Fiennes*, who became the chief of the noblesse of all Artois, had a son *Robert* who, although Constable of France at the time, tried hard to claim back much of the Fiennes inheritance in England.

As *Roger* inspected his men on Southampton Common, his cousin *Robert Fiennes* left the family castle, Château Fiennes, in the village of Tingry, where both he and his late uncle the Constable of France had been born and which had withstood sustained attacks by the English and by rival French nobles over the previous few decades. Today only a single tower and piles of weed-covered rubble remain, for many of the houses in the nearby village of Tingry were built out of stone from the ruined sections of the castle walls after Robert the Younger's descendants abandoned our ancestral home.

The elder *Robert* had regaled his nephew with many a tale of how he and his men had frequently outwitted the English, and how Bernard Duguesclin, his successor as constable, also his great comrade-in-arms of many years, had continued to regain from the English most of what, at the time of Crécy and Poitiers, they had lost.

But *Robert* knew that the recent bitter civil war between the Burgundians and the dauphin's Armagnacs, allowed to continue unabated by the mad King Charles, had so diluted the royal French army that all the hard-won lessons of his uncle's and Duguesclin's time in charge had been forgotten.

Robert, as seigneur-to-be of the local militia of Tingry and Fiennes, was awaiting the imminent call-up from the king in the face of ever more alarming reports about the size of the English invasion fleet. Most of his men felt sure that Calais, the English-held fortress town some nine miles north of the castle, was the most likely port for the English invasion.

Had he been alive, the elder *Robert* would doubtless have wished that he, and not his young nephew as yet with no male heir to carry on their lineage, was about to lead the regional defence force against the invader, whether their king was to raise a meaningful main army or not.

At Southampton meanwhile, as Henry decided which conspirators, most of whom were related to him in one way or another, to execute and which to forgive, the seemingly endless supply of war materials creaked their way to the coast.

Verbal communications between British people were not as simple as today. There were many Welsh soldiers who had spent five years fighting against the same English soldiers that they were now fighting beside. But the two languages were unintelligible to each other, and even those Welsh who spoke English did so with dialects and expressions that required a great deal of gesticulation to render them intelligible. Likewise the dialects of the northern English and the Anglo-Irish groupings were largely double Dutch to their overlords and generals who were mostly Anglo-Normans.

The language that the gathering horde, no matter which part of the British Isles they came from, did understand as they waited in their camps, trained at the various martial arts, or sorted out old village feuds, was the language of food, wine, pay and the local availability of paid sex. Once they reached France, the source of their food would depend on both well-defended resupply lines from England and on local plunder. At least while still in England, the troops were kept happy on a ration of a daily gallon of ale, salted meat and dried fish with loaves of rough bread from bakers all over the south-east.

One merchant who is specifically recorded as a meat supplier to the army's Earl Marshal, Earl Mowbray, was the butcher of Petworth. I spent my teenage years in Sussex eating meat from Mr Speed, the local Petworth butcher whose meat was, in the 1950s, often described as 'the best in all Sussex'.

In the 1960s while fighting Marxist insurgents in the south of Arabia, I would leave the safety of my regiment's headquarters coastal compound for month-long periods patrolling both desert and heavily forested regions. My unit had six Land-Rovers, a water tanker and a three-ton lorry with stores. My sixty men had eight machine guns, one mortar tube and fifty rifles. I learned to take twice the amount of bullets and mortars that I was entitled to, with a similar excess of defensive items such as trip flares, anti-personnel mines and illuminating flares.

My administrative needs were chicken-feed compared to

Henry's, and when working out the mathematics of what he would need for a probable series of great medieval battles, the mind boggles at the work involved. Henry's version of our rifles was, of course, the longbows, and they did not just grow on trees; nor did the shafts of his arrows.

It has been estimated by experts that the British army longbowmen, most of whom were Welsh, shot, at the Battle of Crécy alone, 300,000 arrows, and that is not including the many that were recycled, having been plucked during the battle from dead or dying horses and men.

The highly prized bowyers who made the bows, the fletchers who feathered the arrow shafts, and the arrowsmiths who made the various types of arrow heads must have worked like demons in order to fulfil Henry's orders for his archers.

Bowstrings, like the bows themselves, were prone to breakage or loss in battle and replacements would be needed on long campaigns.

The wood for most longbows was imported from Italy, and yew was favoured due to its elasticity and ability to regain its shape over months, even years, of usage. Yew staves for bows were typically seven feet long, and master bowyers kept their methods of turning raw staves into the finished products as trade secrets, and their apprentices were sworn on oath to 'disclose nothing'.

English yew trees were despised by most archers of Henry's day. The reason why many yews are today found in church graveyards goes back to Saxon beliefs in the sacred nature of the yew tree and to the more practical fact that yew leaves are poisonous to grazing animals and so were best enclosed, as in churchyards.

It is always assumed that bow staves originate as branches,

but the best staves were split off from felled tree trunks. At each end of the stave the bowyer would screw on a nock made from the sawn-off tip of a cow horn with grooves to take the bowstring. Supplies of longbows and crossbows were kept in the Tower of London at all times, but not in sufficient quantities for major campaigns. When Henry, in his teenage Prince Hal days, had fought the Welsh, he had learned a great deal from them about archery, and by 1406 his generals had decreed that all arrow shafts should be boiled, and that arrowheads should be made of pointed steel. Each arrow needed three ten-inch-long goose feather flights, which were fixed in place with surgical precision using waxed silk thread or glue prepared to many secret recipes.

One medieval formula for arrow glue stipulates: 'The root [of the common bluebell flower] is bulbous and full of a slimie glewish juice which will serve to set feathers on instead of glew.' An alternative comprised a mix of various weird chemicals, including azafetida, better known as devil's dung due to its powerful stink.

At the same time as Henry's ordnance officers worked their magic to centralise hundreds of thousands of arrows (each of which will have taken at least thirty minutes to fashion as a deadly weapon), bows, bowstrings and quivers, recruitment of expert archers was also under way.

Over a century before Henry's day, his ancestor Edward I lost a great many men to the arrows of Welsh guerrillas, so he offered Welsh archers a third more pay per day of service in his army than they would get in their own. This worked well and Edward soon developed the trained longbow formations that were to revolutionise confrontational battlefield tactics for the next two centuries.

The better pay structure obtained by generations of Welsh archers soon produced a middle-class status, which set them above that of peasant. While this was true in England and Wales, it did not apply in France, where strict class structures remained in the military hierarchy of nobles on horseback and in full armour and the lightly armed riff-raff infantry on foot, whether using bows or blades.

Because during most of the Hundred Years War the Scottish army fought for the French and against the English, they were apt to develop their own weaponry along continental, not British lines, with the result that their longbow was designed with different curvature principles that never matched the power and distance capabilities of the British version. When, in 1424, King James I decreed an 'archery only' law similar to that in force in England to apply in Scottish villages at weekends, in order to increase archery skills, it failed to work due to the Scots' 'fanatical devotion to futeball and goff'.

Edward I and his successors came to recognise that the longbow could only be used with full power and accuracy by true professionals whose muscle structure, like that of modern-day bodybuilding trophy winners, is only achievable through years of hard work. So, to obtain sufficient depth of expertise throughout the kingdom, English laws forbade any weekend sports at all other than archery.

Henry's war-gaze needed to be omni-directional. To leave his own existing kingdom in order to add another far larger one to his realm was a very risky business and he was fully aware of the dangers. There were four main areas of likely trouble which were, in order of severity: at home in England, Wales, Scotland and Ireland. He did his best to deal with each.

At home, as demonstrated by the current Southampton Conspiracy, Henry's own cousins would be likely to seize their best chance to usurp his throne while he was absent, and the man most likely to be chosen willy-nilly to succeed him would be the descendant of *Roger Mortimer* and *Margaret Fiennes*, *Edmund Mortimer of the March*. So Henry kept the compliant *Edmund* close by his side at all times.

Henry clearly believed that *Edmund* had merely been a pawn in the conspiracy plot who had decided that his bread would be better buttered by spilling the beans to the king, and so he had betrayed his puppeteer-conspirators, one of whom, Lord Grey, described him as 'the hog', and another *Mortimer* cousin who disdainfully called him a 'simpleton'.

Henry's next move to ensure the minimal likelihood of home-based trouble in his absence was to dampen the Lollard underground movement's ardour to end his rule. To this end a fine example was set by Europe's number one heretic, Jan Hus, when early in July the European papal court, the Council of Constance, identified the Lollard teachings of John Wycliffe as heretical and all memories of him were condemned. On this basis the bishops then intoned to Jan Hus the dread words, 'We commit your soul to the Devil.' He was led out to a nearby field where, in front of a stake and nest of fire kindling, he was offered the chance to recant his heresy.

'I am no sinner,' he shouted, so they chained him to the stake and lit the fire.

Adding tar to heat the burning pyre as his screams mounted, his killers ensured that every last remnant of his body was turned to ash, even pulverising the bones and skull until they, too, were ash. Then the ashes, once cold, were dumped in the nearby River Rhine. This was all done to ensure that no martyr's relic could be used by his Lollard disciples to foment further anti-clerical troubles.

In England Henry sent a letter to the Mayor of London instructing him to keep alert for Lollard plots, but it was in Cambridge that the Lollard leader, John Oldcastle, surfaced for the first time since his escape from the Tower. Wrongly believing that Henry had already set sail, he broke cover to spark off his long-delayed uprising. Too late did he realise his mistake, and many of his regional leaders were caught and tortured to reveal their leader's whereabouts. Adept at escape and able to hide in the homes of many loyal Lollards, Oldcastle was not, in fact, burned alive until two years later.

As a further safeguard against heretic troublemakers, Henry recruited his own version of a *Dad's Army* or Home Guard. Every man not summoned to join the campaign for family reasons or due to old age must expect to defend the realm if called up by the regional sheriff. Even the clergy themselves were ordered by their bishops to attend training musters complete with weapons, and this included all parish priests and monks from monasteries. After all, the main enemy of the Lollard Protestant reform movement was the established Church, so who better to know how to defend themselves against likely aggression when the real army was abroad? Subsequent records show that, in the diocese of Lincoln alone, 4,000 able archers were enrolled from the clerical ranks and, in England overall, this Church army exceeded the numerical strength of the professional host in Southampton.

To cut down the number of powerful men who just might harbour grudges against him, Henry announced an order that summer to all county sheriffs that pardoned any person owing debts to the crown as from the date of his coronation.

To safeguard the English borderlands with Scotland and Wales, Henry ordered regional magnates to maintain alert local forces against rebellion or invasion.

As for Ireland, never an island that had attracted his presence, Henry dealt with the likelihood of any trouble by posting his arch-Doberman there in the shape of Sir John Talbot, as King's Lieutenant.

Talbot was ruthless to the point of sadism, or at least unnecessary severity, throughout his time as governor there. Any Irishman, whether of Celtic or Anglo-Norman origins, who caused, or appeared likely to cause, trouble was summarily executed, and their children, on the principle of 'like father, like son', were sent to the homes of families assessed by Talbot as being loyal to the crown. Older adult sons of rebels were not afforded this generous treatment, but were sentenced to death with their father. The cruelties of Talbot, as with those of subsequent notorious English invaders – Cromwellian Roundheads and twentieth-century Black and Tans – remain for ever damned in Irish annals and ballads.

Finally, Henry instituted a spy system throughout the kingdom to spot and identify miscreants on the move. Any stranger in town, whether seen on the street by local citizens or visiting an inn or a tavern, was to be questioned as to the motive of their journey. If their response was unsatisfactory, such persons were to be subjected to further questioning by sheriffs and, if then suspected of mischief, they must be imprisoned.

The other side of the imprisonment coin caused by Henry's dire need for professional soldiers was the fact, recorded in many chronicles, that 5 per cent of his army consisted of convicted murderers who were released from life imprisonment.

The vast majority of these men had, before committing their crime, been professional soldiers with the military skills and experience so badly needed for Henry's campaign. Their pardons were conditional on continued military service for the crown.

The language problems of this hybrid army's leaders were rendered even more confused with the arrival of Gascon mercenaries, who Henry hired as crossbow specialists, and by gangs of Irish cannon-fodder troops who wore scant or no armour, often fought barefoot, but were known for their ferocity with short swords and daggers. Against heavily armed enemies they could move with ninja-like speed, expertly aware of every tiny weak spot in different types of armour, especially the sights of visored helmets.

There are very few records of women fighters in Henry's army, although wives often accompanied husbands on medieval campaigns, even to the Holy Land. In theory, if a man indented for service and was then killed, his wife inherited his military responsibilities, but she could, in turn, persuade or pay some male to take her place.

Henry was a lover of music and paid musicians to join the campaign at the same daily rate as a man-at-arms. They played for the royal group's pleasure whether during a siege or when camped on long marches. They were also the key to achieving disciplined reactions during the heat of battle, when most shouted commands were inaudible. So the distinctive rattle of drums or the strident notes of trumpeters served to announce the vital commands as to retreat or advance, which could easily influence the outcome of a battle.

Drummers known as knackerers each wore two small drums slung low over their crotch, and this is thought to be why, in slang language, testicles have been called knackers ever since. Other instruments in Henry's military band included clarions, horns and English bagpipes to help inspire and embolden his troops in the face of the enemy.

Like the musicians, the various medics and surgeons who attended Henry's army were paid the same as the men-at-arms, whose wounds they would try to patch up. Henry had his own personal surgeon, and at least forty named medics of varying professional grades who went everywhere with the army. These doctors were trained physicians and were considered to be the topmost medical authorities. Beneath them were the surgeons who cut off limbs and generally did the manual jobs with knives, saws and plasters.

To obtain a doctorate in medicine, some surgeons spent a dozen years of full-time study. These physicians and qualified surgeons of both sexes were bitter opponents of the numerous quack doctors, many of whom were women, who described themselves as barber-surgeons and whose treatments were based largely on folklore and suspicion. One report sent by physicians to the Lord Mayor of London stated that: 'some barbers of the city who are inexperienced in the art of surgery do often take under their care many sick and maimed persons . . . whereof they are often worse off at their departure than they were at their coming. Because of the experience of these same barbers, such people are often maimed, to the scandal of such skilful and discreet men as practice the art of surgery.'

In some cases, the medical opinions of even the most respected physicians relied merely on outmoded medical treatises and astrologically based guesswork.

Seeing on television the appalling injuries sustained by

soldiers of the twenty-first century in places like Afghanistan must act as a powerful damper to teenagers who might otherwise contemplate an army career. Likewise, the dreadful wounds of soldiers from Henry's many Welsh campaigns, and of older men from the civil war, must have made the prospect of facing similar disfigurement a poor prospect in Henry's day. Why go to France for some unintelligible royal inheritance claim? Unlike a true crusade, such a campaign as Henry's did not promise an assured pathway to heaven. Better, surely, to stay at home with loved ones and tend to the farm and the harvest. There was no current plague in England, but foreign journeys, by all repute, risked horrible disease and dysentery.

Henry's ancestors had slowly worked at answers to this ever-present recruitment problem by raising their armies on a contract basis rather than the old unreliable semi-feudal system which encouraged mass desertion, often in mid-campaign and especially at harvest times. Henry's contract system relied on a number of magnates with military records undertaking to enlist specific numbers of men-at-arms, archers with horses, armour and weapons for specific periods to be produced at an agreed muster point, at which time their leader would be paid back all his expenses to date. The king would then be responsible for providing return transport.

Apart from the incentive of regular pay for each soldier for each day served, there was the additional personal potential for rich plunder and even, given luck, a sum of ransom money by capturing in battle a wealthy noble. Even after sharing the ransom with his unit captain, his relevant boss and possibly the crown as well, there might still be enough left for a simple soldier and his family to upgrade their home comforts considerably.

For professional soldiers who lived from campaign to campaign, there was always the chance of improving their personal body armour by stripping corpses after a victory. And, of course, the excitement beforehand for those who craved the adrenalin of battle and in the years to come of holding audiences captive back home with tales of derring-do.

By late July thousands of ships jammed the coastal waters around Southampton and Portsmouth, including rented vessels from Holland, Venice and Genoa, by far the biggest fleet ever to congregate off Britain and some twelve times the size of the Spanish Armada. The army that would have to fit on board included 10,000 soldiers, a number that was near enough one-tenth of the entire population of post-plague male England, and 25,000 horses of three different types for different purposes.

Loading the horses was a tricky, time-consuming business requiring men who had dealt with horses all their lives. First, horses, most of which had never been in knee-deep water before, were swum out alongside a ship with harnesses around their bellies. A crane rope would then be attached to an upper hook on the harness as near to the mid-point of balance as possible, and the horse, legs lashing the air and eyes saucer-wide, would be swung on to the deck to be tethered to strong points.

The costs of the campaign were monstrous and far beyond what early estimates had suggested. Henry was driven to pawning the crown jewels, court silver and even cutlery, for he had learned on his early Welsh campaigns that a well-paid soldier is a happy soldier and unlikely to desert.

As July mellowed into August, Henry's planned departure date had slipped. The area around Southampton Common was becoming unhealthy: the local population, initially excited at the military presence and in some cases profiting by it, had become tired of the dirt, the theft and the menace to their womenfolk. And nobody was more keen to get going than the king.

Having seen to the executions of the chief conspirators, Henry made his will. I note that the order of his favoured beneficiaries named in the royal will listed his grandmother, *Joan Fiennes*, the direct descendant of my ancestor *Ingelram Fiennes*, immediately after the Holy Roman Emperor, two of his brothers and the four senior bishops of the realm.

To a thunder of drums, great cheering from the ships and the shoreline, the fleet left England on the afternoon of 11 August. This was all at the will of one man, a king in pursuit of glory who had deceived himself into believing that his was a divine mission, indeed a crusade. The irony was that the specific mission of his 10,000 Christian warriors was to kill fellow Christians.

In Shakespeare's words:

> For so appears this fleet majestical,
> Holding due course to Harfleur. Follow, follow! . . .
> And leave your England, as dead midnight still,
> Guarded with grandsires, babies, and old women.

Parallels with the great invasion of D-Day 1944 abound. Henry had kept the geographical aims of the campaign to himself and his closest advisers. He had led the French to think that his intended landing point would be at Boulogne, just as the Germans believed some 530 years later.

The reality, which Henry now laid before the captains of

his navy and army, was that the fleet was to make a landfall on the low beaches of Normandy at the mouth of the River Seine, the gateway to Paris. The French castle that guarded the mouth of the great river, Harfleur, was close to the north side of the Seine's estuary and would need to be invested before any further advance inland could follow.

After this siege there were many possibilities, but Henry's prime aim was to retake the whole of Normandy, which he considered to be English by right since the days of William the Conqueror. Afterwards, if victorious in Normandy, the long march south to Gascony and Bordeaux would be a fitting end to a great campaign.

Henry summoned his council of war to board his ship by unfurling the royal flag. His army generals and all the great military magnates were present as Henry revealed his plans for the initial landing which, according to his fishermen spies of the previous week, would be unopposed by French defenders.

The two men selected by the king to lead the initial reconnaissance patrol inland from the beach were the brother of *Elizabeth Fiennes, John Holland*, and his stepfather *John Cornwaille*.

II

The actions of the tiger

The great armada was blessed with good weather for the three-day crossing.

Two days into the voyage, the lead vessel, with the reconnaissance group of *John Holland* and his stepfather *John Cornwaille* on board, nosed into the Seine estuary and dropped anchor, not on the southern side where the gently sloping and forested coastline offered good landing conditions, but off the craggy, and initially hostile-looking, chalk shoreline of the Cap de la Hève. Henry's spies had clearly done their homework, for an inlet, the Bay of Sainte-Adresse, offered adequate lee shelter for the fleet.

Although the two *John*s were ignorant of the nature of the French defences awaiting the English invasion, they had heard rumours that a reception force of several hundred soldiers under the Constable of France (who had succeeded *Robert Fiennes* and Bernard Duguesclin), a famous general named Charles d'Albret, was known to have set out for the Seine estuary to prevent any landing by the English.

With mugs of ale, *Cornwaille* and *Holland* discussed the details of their reconnaissance mission, exactly who they would take with them and whether they should move on foot, horseback or a mixture of both. *Holland* was friendly with *Thomas Wykeham* and his seventeen-year-old son *William*, both keen soldiers, and they were delighted and proud when *Holland* invited them to join the landing patrol that night.

Thomas was the grandson of the great architect and erstwhile *Chancellor of England, William of Wykeham*. He was also the grandfather of *Margaret,* the heiress of the Wykeham fortunes who had married my ancestor *William Fiennes*. *William*'s uncle, *Roger Fiennes*, was in turn married to *Elizabeth Holland*, the sister of *John*.

So the four men who led the invasion foray's first move on French soil were all interrelated. The *Wykehams* had always been loyal servants of the Lancastrian kings, but *Cornwaille*, although still in his mid-thirties, had been imprisoned in the Tower by Henry IV for marrying the king's sister, who was also *John Holland*'s mother, without royal permission. At the time she was already twice-widowed, but had fallen for *Cornwaille* when watching him win an impressive tournament victory.

In the years before the Harfleur episode, *Cornwaille* had won numerous jousting titles against Europe's best and, once back in Henry IV's favour, had fought valiantly on all the king's campaigns. In 1404 he had beaten off a French attack on Blackpool Sands near Dartmouth. (I have been involved with today's owner of that estate on various polar expeditions.)

Like *Cornwaille, John Holland* had a less than perfect record with royalty, in that supporters of Henry IV had executed his father for treason because of his part in the

Epiphany Rising of 1400 and had sent his head to the king in a basket.

The fact that *Cornwaille* and *Holland* were now being trusted by Henry IV's son with the most prestigious of tasks either indicated that past family sins were completely forgiven, or that such a dangerous mission was potentially a poisoned chalice.

It was agreed that *Holland*'s entire force, since all were battle-hardened, would form the vanguard of the silent patrol totalling twenty men-at-arms and sixty archers. Henry had knighted *Holland* two years before, and he stated in public that he approved of the young knight's military potential, calling him 'brave and high-spirited, though young'. Following the treason and execution of his father, who was the half-brother of Richard II, young *John* had been brought up by his mother and, following her remarriage to *Cornwaille*, he received from his stepfather the healthy sum of £41.50 per year as pocket money.

Just before joining the fleet, *John* had been selected for the tribunal that sentenced the Southampton plotters to death. He was at an exciting time in his life, but also an expensive one. He still relied on *Cornwaille* for most of his income, and the latter had stressed to him the importance of ransom money. Once, in 1404, when counter-attacking a French raid close by Dartington, where *Holland* was born, *Cornwaille* had purchased from another English knight the prisoners he had captured on the Devon beach. This investment had subsequently proved to be extremely profitable.

Cornwaille also stressed to his stepson that speedy payment by relatives for their captured kin was an important factor because, by the strict rules of chivalry, prisoners must be kept in the style of living that they would be used to back home. And that could prove very costly for their captor if ransom payments were slow.

Four weeks before leaving England, *Cornwaille* had received a missive from one of his senior squires at a separate camp in Southampton, one John Cheyne, warning his boss that he had been forced to write begging letters to rich friends promising personal belongings in return for cash. One of his hoped-for creditors, Sir John Pelham, was the hostile Kent neighbour of *Roger Fiennes* of Herstmonceux, *John Holland*'s brother-in-law. It was a small world.

An old friend of *Cornwaille* and a fellow Knight of the Garter, Gilbert Umfraville, also joined the scouting party that night with ninety archers. His direct descendant, Simon Umfraville, was my next-door neighbour for many years in south London.

Small boats took *Cornwaille*, *Holland* and Umfraville with their men on their silent reconnaissance mission, which they completed within twenty-four hours.

They were observed the following day by monks in the monastery of Graville above the beach, but no hostile troops were seen at any point between the landing beach and the outskirts of Harfleur town, which lay some three miles inland from a forested ridge. No obstacles, other than earthen ramparts erected just above the gently rising shingle beach, were spotted. There were areas of salty marsh, but there were ways around them. When reporting the patrol's findings to the king, *Holland* expressed surprise that, despite the obvious defence works above the beach, there was not a soldier in sight.

Meanwhile, on the far coastline of the estuary, the constable's army watched the English disembark, unopposed, over the next three days of fine weather, in the knowledge that there was no way they could reach the other bank in time to stop the landing. The constable had quite simply chosen to defend the wrong side of the Seine. He must have been gnashing his teeth with frustration.

Over the next three days and nights, the king slept very little, such was his personal zeal to supervise every aspect of the landing process. The watchword was, 'more haste less speed', for everyone was fully aware that a French army might yet appear and catch the English with their trousers half down.

Eight weighty cannons were hauled up the shingle and over marshy zones on heavy wagons with man-size wheels, each towed by twenty great pack-horses. Advance troops established a beachhead on high ground above the beach and erected the army's first tented camp there.

Local farmers anywhere near Harfleur would be lucky if they managed to hide anything edible, drinkable or of any value over the next few weeks. They would also do well to hide their womenfolk. Henry's men, after their months of enforced boredom at Southampton and their cramped time on the crossing voyage, were all set for the thrill of plunder and pillage.

Eight days after arriving at the landing beach, the entire army, once all 1,400 ships were unloaded, moved inland from the hill of Graville to their siege positions around the nearby town of Harfleur, some forty miles downriver from Rouen and a further eighty miles from Paris.

By capturing and taking over Harfleur, the English would be able to control one of the main river arteries of France, and at the same time would deny its usage to the French navy and pirates as the perfect spot from which to attack

English posts and merchant ships. French armies sent to support Welsh and Scottish uprisings during the reign of Henry IV had all set out from Harfleur.

Today, due to centuries of shifting sand, Harfleur has long since lost its viability as an active port and business has shifted further west, so that the old town is a mere industrial suburb of Le Havre. In 1415, however, the port and its town bustled with business. Fishermen and pirates, smugglers and wool merchants, salt-sellers who dredged the nearby estuarine marshes, and boat-repair yards made for a great potential source of plunder and influence, and the Normans and the French had sensibly spent a great deal of money on the town's defence works.

For a start, a very substantial fortified stone wall, two and a half miles long, surrounded the town with only three entry gates. This entire wall was protected on its outer side by a substantial seawater moat. At each gate a drawbridge crossed the moat and each of these boasted a massive iron portcullis and, at even intervals along the walls, twenty-six guard towers were flagged with colourful banners and manned by crossbow men.

Henry sent his eldest and most warlike brother, Thomas, Duke of Clarence, to cut off the far side of the town from any reinforcements that the French, he knew, were bound to send now that they knew that his clear intent was to take Harfleur. The troops he assumed would be the first to arrive were those of the constable, once they had crossed the Seine from the west.

The duke's force signalled to Henry just as soon as they were in position to the east of the town. They had, en route, captured a caravan of wagons taking cannons, gunpowder and crossbow bolts into Harfleur. The town was now surrounded on all sides, for the Earl of Suffolk's force had headed west, while the main army remained to the south and the fleet to the north.

Henry's heralds rode up to the town's northern gate and demanded that the garrison commander hand over the town to the King of England who was, they stressed, the rightful ruler of all Normandy. The commander said, 'Non', or words to that effect.

The town garrison normally numbered 100 soldiers with help available from armed citizens, but only four hours before Clarence had reached his blocking position, a very capable French army officer, Sire de Gaucourt, had slipped 300 professional soldiers through the eastern gate and had taken personal command of the town's defences. He was also confident that the dauphin (since the king was having one of his mad fits at the time) would send a massive relief force in the very near future in order to counter-attack the English.

Henry's artillery, mostly Flemish mercenaries, trundled their cannons, twelve feet long with twenty-four-inch-calibre barrels and capable of firing 800-pound stone cannonballs, as close as they could to the walls of the town's main defensive barbican. This massive tower protected the main gate and crouched across the outer side of the moat.

Pouring tar over the gun-stones prior to igniting and firing them resulted in an impressive rain of comet-like fireballs smashing into the bastions or flying over the town wall, destroying buildings and killing citizens within.

For good measure, the catapult men used chemical warfare by lobbing over the walls the rotting bodies of French soldiers killed during brave sorties against the cannon crews, along with great balls of maggot-infested offal and entrails from the English field kitchens.

Henry reckoned that a few days of bombardment by day and night would be enough to bring de Gaucourt begging for a surrender deal. But he was wrong, for the plucky defenders worked round the clock to make good each new area of destruction with rubble, stanchions torn from ruins in the town, and any other materials available. Every now and again groups of mounted men-at-arms would sally out of town to gallop at the gunner crews and sometimes managed to destroy the cannon frames and kill the gunners.

Henry, therefore, ordered the many Welsh miners he had brought for that purpose to dig tunnels under the walls with the intention of lighting fires under their very foundations to cause them to collapse: a well-tried siege tactic of the day.

De Gaucourt deftly matched this move by setting his own mole units to dig counter-tunnels with which to disrupt the English saboteurs and dispatch them with crossbow bolts.

As each day passed by, the danger grew of a French counter-attack by a relief force, as did the spread of disease. The sun beat down from a cloudless sky. Those besiegers working within effective cannon range of the walls were themselves at risk from crossbow snipers dotted along the walls, so they had to wear their mail and plate armour. Even when not having to work, the heat could be unbearable.

Henry, no doubt, needed to exhort his men. Shakespeare certainly thought so! He wrote his famous peroration that included the lines:

> Once more unto the breach, dear friends, once more;
> . . . Then imitate the action of the tiger:

Stiffen the sinews, summon up the blood . . .
Now set the teeth and stretch the nostril wide;
Hold hard the breath, and bend up every spirit
To his full height!

Centrally prepared rations were past their prime, including fish, and drinking water from the local streams was often polluted. Diarrhoea was soon rampant with no closed latrines and buzzing storms of flies to spread bacteria. Within three weeks the dreaded bloody flux, dysentery of a virulent and potentially deadly strain, was incapacitating Henry's men in droves.

Henry was to lose more of his men through sickness than through the fighting at Harfleur. Over 1,000 would need to be invalided home with ravaged bowels that turned all ingested food into uncontrollable floods of a foul-smelling mixture of dark blood and runny mucous. The bacterium responsible was shigella 1, which breeds on human faeces, and once in the digestive system, whether through faecal-infected water or food, it will kill within a week some 10 per cent of its victims through debilitating dysentery, kidney failure and septicaemia.

The Harfleur environment of the siege force provided ideal shigella breeding conditions: great heat, low-lying marshland, stagnant water, swarming insect life, thousands of horses drinking and defecating in the same area as thousands of humans. All the cattle, sheep and pig carcasses and offal from the many camp kitchens were dragged into nearby marshy tidal creeks, as were many of the shigella corpses, where feral dogs, crabs and gulls feasted on them, and then in their turn defecated into waterways which at some point were liable to be used as drinking water by thirsty soldiers.

From every tent, sunken gun pit and catapult crew shelter

came the foul stench of the inmates' frequent and sudden faecal splurges which soiled the floors of their living and eating quarters and the clothes they wore.

Two of Henry's war councillors and long-time friends, the Earl of Suffolk and the Bishop of Norwich, died. His senior commander, his brother Thomas, Duke of Clarence, and *Edmund Mortimer* were also seriously ill.

Nonetheless, the constant bombardment by Henry's heavy cannons backed up by traditional mechanical artillery with weird names, such as mangonels, bricoles and springalds, wore down the barbican's walls to the extent that, with his own ammunition supplies running low, de Gaucourt realised that he could not hold out much longer if not relieved.

On 16 September Henry selected *John Holland* and his brother-in-law *Roger Fiennes* to lead their men on a sudden assault of the crumbling bastion under the cover of a shower of fire arrows from 1,000 longbows. This commando-type raid was entirely successful and forced the French out of the barbican, over the drawbridge and back into the town.

The fall of the barbican was key to de Gaucourt's imminent defeat and, realising this, he sent messages to negotiate with Henry. The latter's terms of surrender were, however, too harsh for de Gaucourt to accept and still retain his honour. So the fighting resumed. Shakespeare well summarises the choice faced by the captain of every besieged city in those days. Surrender or else!

> Therefore, you men of Harfleur,
> Take pity of your town and of your people,
> Whiles yet my soldiers are in my command . . .
> If not, why, in a moment look to see

> The blind and bloody soldier with foul hand
> Defile the locks of your shrill-shrieking daughters;
> Your fathers taken by the silver beards,
> And their most reverend heads dash'd to the walls,
> Your naked infants spitted upon pikes . . .

An angry Henry, by now extremely worried about the passage of time, ordered every cannon and catapult to be fired without a break at the north gate, which was immediately behind the conquered barbican. The resulting damage and the sheer collateral destruction caused inside the town had the desired effect, for de Gaucourt now agreed on surrender terms. If not relieved within three days, he agreed to an immediate surrender of his town.

By then de Gaucourt had received word from the council of the citizens of Harfleur that they could take no more. They also knew that if the town was taken by force rather than yielded through negotiation, the ultimate fate awaited every man, woman and child in Harfleur in the form of an official massacre. This ultimatum, clearly stated to de Gaucourt by Henry at the very beginning of the siege, was the common practice of medieval warfare, as at Crécy and a hundred other such sieges.

My kinsmen and their relatives were lucky at Harfleur. *John Holland* emerged as a true hero of the campaign and has made it into military histories in the present day, as has his stepfather and comrade-in-arms, *John Cornwaille*.

Not so lucky was *James Fiennes* who contracted a (luckily mild) bout of dysentery, but was cared for by his seventeen-year-old apprentice *William Wykeham* whose camp, being on higher ground than most, was virtually unaffected by the bacteria.

The only fatality in the family was *William's* father, *Thomas*, who was killed by a crossbow bolt, a more romantic death than those who died as a result of the shigella bug.

Although *James*'s big brother *Roger* and his men had, with *John Holland*'s group, joined the Duke of Gloucester's force, the two brothers had always been close, and *James* treated *Roger* more as an uncle rather than an older brother.

While waiting for the three-day period of the surrender terms to expire, there was an unearthly silence as both sides preserved their ammunition and waited with bated breath for the first distant sound of the drum beats that would herald the imminent arrival of a relieving force from the French army.

Captain Robert Fiennes left Fiennes Castle on receiving a royal summons to report to the dauphin with his militia force from Tingry, many of whom had fought for his uncle in the days when he was constable.

Robert, a man of some forty years with the swarthy skin of his father and uncle, was proud of his physique and his fitness. He despised the dauphin who, at only nineteen years old, was obese, slack-jowled and, as was well known, led a dissolute life of wine and women, while his cousins, the great dukes of France, fought for influence and the favour of his father, the oft-mad king.

However, *Robert*'s loyalty lay with the throne, not with any particular wannabe ducal occupant thereof, so he bowed low to the podgy prince when he reached the temporary royal court at Vernon, about halfway along the main road from Rouen to Paris. He had left his men encamped in a field outside Rouen, where many similarly sized regional forces had already arrived to form a fairly large army.

A few hours after *Robert*'s arrival, a fanfare announced the arrival of an old friend of his, William de Léon. The two men hugged briefly, but de Léon was in a rush for his audience with the prince. He had been sent by de Gaucourt from Harfleur with the urgent mission of appealing to the dauphin to send the army to relieve the town immediately as the only way to avoid an ignominious surrender.

From a respectful distance, *Robert* watched de Léon's audience with the prince, who gushed charm, but his royal shoulders moved up and down in a classic Gallic shrug, his hands spread wide and upthrust. There was not, he explained, a large enough force as yet, and there was no point in him sending a half-ready army that would not be sure of crushing the English siege-force.

De Léon made further pleas that the dauphin should personally lead the French force currently at Rouen at least to within sight of Harfleur, since it might delay the surrender long enough for more regional troops to arrive. But the prince would not budge.

A contemporary French chronicler wrote: 'The French troops [at Rouen] did as much damage to the poor people as did the English. The weather was as fine as anyone could remember during the vintage, but nevertheless not one of the nobles of France came forward to fight the Englishmen there.'

Robert may have felt ashamed of his royal leader's inaction, but there was nothing he could do about it. He could hardly take his own small contingent to Harfleur with any hope of altering the situation there, so he pledged his troops' support with the Master of Rolls back at Rouen and awaited the next move against the English. He would not have long to wait, for Constable d'Albret and the great French Marshal Boucicaut were soon to arrive in Rouen to put an end to the dauphin's inertia.

D'Albret has been blamed for the fall of Harfleur by many French historians, but unfairly so, since his only error was to select the wrong part of the Norman coastline at which to wait for the English to land. Once he realised that he had guessed wrongly, he had a difficult catch-up game to follow, and this he did extremely well as Henry was soon to find out.

De Léon's return to Harfleur with the news that no relief army would arrive by the agreed time must have been a great disappointment to de Gaucourt and his men who had tried so hard to hold the town. The chronicler monk of St Denis wrote of their efforts: 'It ought to be remembered how often they repeatedly made daring sorties against the enemy, and how with their utmost strength they drove back every attempt to gain entry into the town through underground mines dug out in secret. Without any doubt, these men were worthy of the highest praise for their endurance of every adversity: even as the roofs of the buildings were crashing in around them, they remained continuously in arms, sustained by the most meagre rations and spending their nights without sleep.'

The formal surrender of the town began with de Gaucourt, himself now sick with dysentery, having, by the precise terms of the previous arrangement, to lead some seventy of his chief knights and town burghers on foot through the battered gates and up the steep hill to the English camp's headquarters and the royal tent.

The route was lined by English and Welsh soldiers and, to rub in the humiliation of the defeated, the ritual of the surrender ceremony stated that the French wore only shirts and trousers with rope nooses around their necks as they walked through the ranks of their victors.

Behind this gloomy line of supplicants, the citizens of Harfleur awaited their fate with apprehension.

On his knees before King Henry, de Gaucourt handed over the keys of the Harfleur gates, while on the battered ramparts of the barbican, the flag of France was replaced by that of St George.

Henry later toured the shattered town and proclaimed that all clerics and all rich merchants could keep their homes in return for massive ransoms. Likewise for de Gaucourt's surviving knights. But the poor, the sick and all their families must take what they could carry and leave town. Two thousand of these already half-starved exiles were given an escort through the British lines, but on their way to Rouen they suffered robbery and rape by their fellow countrymen.

Henry's original grand plan of a speedy and all-conquering march south via Harfleur and Paris to Gascony and Bordeaux was now clearly out of the question, due to the unexpected time taken to capture Harfleur and the lack of manpower resulting from the dysentery epidemic. He needed a new master plan, for he could hardly head back home after merely besieging a single town, even one as strategically important as Harfleur.

His first move was to send de Gaucourt to the dauphin with a personal challenge to a royal duel, the result of which would decide who should rule France upon the death of mad King Charles: his eldest son, the dauphin, or his cousin King Henry of England.

Henry gave the dauphin eight days in which to send his response before he, Henry, would take his army south from Harfleur. He did not state his specific geographic target, but the dauphin would no doubt guess that Paris and the French throne were at the top of Henry's wish list.

By deciding the issue of inheritance to the throne by personal trial-by-battle, a great deal of Christian bloodshed would be avoided, and this chivalric option to a full-scale battle between two armies was an accepted standard practice right up until the time of the Battle of Waterloo in the nineteenth century.

The dauphin, however, fat and no warrior, sensibly declined the offer to joust, thereby forcing Henry to follow a more difficult route to glory.

The capture of Harfleur was in itself a highly worthwhile prize, sitting as it did astride the riverain highway to Rouen and Paris and being an excellent seaport, second only to Calais. In London proclamations were made to entice rich merchants to set up businesses in Harfleur in return for free mansions and various other long-term perks. Fishermen, victuallers and wine merchants were all sent royal orders to sustain the garrison that Henry had to leave at Harfleur if its speedy recapture by the French was to be avoided.

A quarter of Henry's entire army was sent back to England with dysentery. The king also had to leave 900 of his men to man the new Harfleur garrison, so a full-scale battle with a much larger French army would risk a wipeout of his now reduced force.

While awaiting the dauphin's reply to his recent battle-challenge, Henry was not idle. He had his Dutch gunners set up cannons on the walls of the town and put his carpenters to work to repair damage to the defences. He appointed four senior barons to command operations in Harfleur, one being *Lord William Clinton*, the grandson of my kinsman *Geoffrey de Saye*.

There was now no time before the onset of winter to besiege another major city such as Rouen, so Henry decided to take his remaining men on a forced march from Harfleur to Calais through Norman lands that he considered to be part of his own realm and extended kingdom. He would then return home from his secure naval base at Calais, having shown the world that he could move through Normandy at will, just as his great-grandfather, Edward III, had done in the great days of Crécy. His route would be the same, close to the coastline and crossing the wide estuary of the River Somme, as Edward had done, by way of the Blanchetaque ford. Such a march would cock a snook at the French army and, provided the dauphin failed to raise a force equal in size to Henry's, there was even the chance of a confrontation against a smaller force that Henry and his archers would stand a good chance of winning. Thence a victorious return home.

When the eight-day period stipulated for the dauphin's response to Henry's battle-challenge was up, he marched out of Harfleur. His brother Thomas, Duke of Clarence, was no longer leading the vanguard, for he had been sent back home, apparently with dysentery, although some rumours suggested that he had argued strongly with Henry against the Calais march through fear of being cut off by the Somme and by superior French forces.

Other magnates and knights had also advised Henry not

to take the considerable risk of an overland dash to Calais because various spies had reported stories of two major French hosts already on the move to cut him off. Henry, who had clearly made up his mind on the overland route to Calais, risk or no risk, ignored the advice of his council and gave orders to ensure a speedy rate of advance.

Although no detailed maps existed with sufficient detail to enable a stranger to plan and follow a given route in a foreign land, there were always local guides to be found who could be paid or threatened into leading the way to a named town or feature, such as a river crossing point.

From Harfleur to Calais was a distance, under normal travel conditions, known to take eight days at the speed of a marching and pack-carrying soldier. So Henry ordered that every man must set out with eight days' rations. If food was available to plunder en route, so much the better, but that could not be counted on and would only slow down the rate of progress. In order to cut down the risk of further delays en route, the majority of soldiers would ride and minimal carts would be towed, since there was no need for heavy siege gear.

Knowing the men's potential and partiality for plunder and rape, Henry had his marshals proclaim a set of ordinances that threatened immediate execution for any man caught harming any unarmed person or stealing anything other than food to be had in passing.

Since the time of the dauphin's failure to respond to de Léon's appeal for a force to relieve Harfleur, the dauphin had not been idle, and Henry's personal battle-challenge had riled him. He had no wish to be branded the royal coward that he clearly was, so he sent out envoys from Vernon to every regional magnate and knight virtually threatening them with treason if they did not attend a national muster at Rouen without delay and with a full contingent of knights and men-at-arms.

When *Robert Fiennes* and his troop had arrived at Rouen, the scant turnout from the majority of regional lords had forced the dauphin to get tough. His message, rushed out to all non-attending magnates, was uncompromising:

Our adversary of England . . . has taken our town of Harfleur owing to the neglect and delay of you and others in not punctually obeying our orders . . . As the defence of our kingdom is the concern of all, we call upon our faithful subjects for aid to . . . drive the enemy out of our kingdom in disgrace and confusion.

You will proclaim these our orders in the most public manner that no one may plead ignorance and that under pain of being reputed disobedient and having their goods confiscated, they fail not to come to our assistance, sufficiently armed and mounted. Should any difficulties be made in obeying these our commands, you will enforce obedience by seizing on the lands of such as may refuse placing foragers within their houses and by every other means . . . Should there be any neglect on your part, we will punish you in such wise that you shall serve as an example to all others.

Whereas previous exhortations had achieved a pathetic response, the news of Harfleur's capture by the English sparked an immediate and countrywide rush to defend the motherland. Even the diehard feudists of the Burgundian and Armagnac factions temporarily joined together against the English menace.

Many of the dauphin's leaders knew their history of the previous English invasion and guessed without difficulty that Henry would make for Calais by way of coastal lanes. They also knew that he would have to cross the Somme, as Edward III had done, at the old tidal ford pioneered by Roman legions at Blanchetaque. As a result, Constable d'Albret had rushed ahead with a force not much smaller than the entire English army and had reached the far side of the ford in readiness for Henry's arrival there. Elsewhere, bridges over the Somme had been destroyed so that the English would have no choice but to turn back to Harfleur or turn inland to find some other crossing point which would, of course, take them away from Calais and into the arms of an ever-growing French army far larger than their own. Things were at last looking good for the dauphin as troops from all over northern and central France converged in great numbers on the Rouen muster point.

Bands of Genoese crossbow mercenaries were already at Rouen, and by the time the 7,000-strong English force left Harfleur, over 40,000 French soldiers were ready to give chase. With their mood set for a major battle, they started out in their thousands to hunt down the English.

12

Fiennes to the fore

With many thousands of horses, Henry's 7,000 soldiers and their support echelons headed east-north-east out of Harfleur on 8 October 1415. Calais, their goal, was 150 miles and several river crossings away to the north-east. So long as there were no unexpected obstacles and no major clash with the enemy, the English had every reason to believe that their eight days of rations would see them safely to their goal.

Unfortunately, the French army, far greater in number, was able to set out at the same time and, in some cases, earlier than the English in order to block the way to Calais merely by destroying bridges and fords. This was easily done by sending king's messengers on fast horses to local mayors with the relevant orders to raise local militias and block all river crossings. Then, once trapped, the English could be crushed and the Harfleur debacle avenged.

All went well for the English on their first day's march and, on the second, the Béthune River which reaches the coast at Dieppe was easily crossed at Arques. When confronted by the garrison commanders of the castles that overlooked key bridges, Henry threatened destruction unless he was allowed to pass by. There were minor attacks and some cannon fire from castle walls, but few deaths and virtually no delay. Large quantities of bread and wine were on three occasions sent by local authorities keen to encourage the English out of their area as soon as possible, since nobody and nothing was safe while an invading army was camped on the doorstep.

At Eu on the River Bresle a sizeable French cavalry squadron did attack, but they were beaten off and the river was quickly crossed. By the fourth night the English had managed eighty miles with ease and were camped in high spirits, except for the few hundred soldiers slowly recovering from dysentery who were marching in soiled trousers that caused raw and chafing crotches.

I know this unpleasant condition only too well. On polar expeditions we call it crotch-rot, from which I have suffered for hundreds of miles of man-haul sledging on the Antarctic continent. With no washing facilities for three months and frequent bouts of diarrhoea, I soon became raw between the legs. Henry's soldiers cut the backs out of their brais (underwear) to stop the bloody flux rotting the cloth.

By far the biggest obstacle on the whole journey was the River Somme with its long and wide estuary beginning at the Blanchetaque ford.

At their camp some thirteen miles short of Blanchetaque, the English were over halfway to Calais and on schedule. But, unbeknown to them, the professional army of France's greatest warriors, including Constable d'Albret and Marshal Boucicaut, had force-marched from their initial position at

Honfleur with the specific aim of blocking the Blanchetaque crossing and forcing the English inland and into the arms of the main French army.

Some seven miles from the ford on 13 October, *John Holland*, brother of *Elizabeth Fiennes* and leader of the army's advance guard that day, captured one of the constable's staff, a Gascon servant who guilelessly told his captors that the Blanchetaque ford was held by 6,000 troops who had hammered sharp stakes into the crossing's muddy tidal bed.

Henry summoned his immediate advisers to a prompt meeting which, after a two-hour-long debate, decided not to attempt a clearly suicidal Blanchetaque crossing, which his own cavalry spies had speedily confirmed to be blocked, nor to turn back ignominiously to Harfleur. Instead they would turn inland and follow the Somme's western bank until a viable unopposed crossing point could be found or until trapped by the French army.

Already weary but, until that point, buoyed up by the sight of the white chalk cliffs of the Norman coast leading them ever closer to Calais, Henry's soldiers had been cheerful and fairly certain that their limited food supply would last. That armies march on their stomachs is an understatement. I have seen the change of mood caused when food resupplies fail to be airdropped during desert warfare, even among my most equable soldiers.

However, Henry's men soon grew sullen. The bridges at Abbeville, the first town they reached after the Blanchetaque disappointment, were destroyed and at the next village, for the first time, they saw large bodies of French soldiers on the far bank making mocking hand gestures and jeering. After that, as they marched along their bank, they were observed and counter-marched by their enemy and would-be killers on the opposite river bank. And every bridge they came to had been rendered impassable.

This deadly game of cat and mouse inevitably had a negative effect on English morale. In one village, where for some reason the normal scorched-earth policy had been ignored, the leading troops found numerous wine barrels which they drank in great quantities until Henry ordered the hanging of anybody caught with wine, other than his knights. This caused further sullen resentment and open grumbling, particularly in the ranks of the unmounted who were especially tired and often badly blistered from the chafing of shoes, backpacks, armour and personal weaponry. To curb mounting indiscipline, Henry had a man hanged in front of all the army for stealing a religious ornament from a church.

On the eighth day from Harfleur, when they should have reached Calais, they were still some forty miles away and heading further from safety with every passing mile. To balance the hanging, Henry showed his gentle side by handing two very sick soldiers over to a local French noble who, in return for the payment of two fine stallions, agreed to have the men looked after.

The anonymous contemporary *Gesta* chronicle recounted:

Our provisions had run out, the enemy who had craftily hastened on ahead and were laying waste to the countryside in advance, would force us – who were already hungry – to suffer a really dire need of food. And, at the head of the river, they would with their great and countless host . . . overwhelm us for we were few in number, fainting with a great weariness and weak from lack of food. I looked up in bitterness to Heaven . . . without any other hope but this, we hastened on in the direction of the head of the river.

At the town of Corbie a sudden cavalry attack managed to capture one of Henry's royal banners and, in the resulting skirmish to retrieve it, two French soldiers were taken. Interrogation revealed that a new French cavalry tactic was to ride down English archers with heavily armoured squadrons specially trained for the purpose.

Henry at once gave orders that every archer in the army should carry a six-foot stake, sharp at both ends, at all times. Facing forward at 45 degrees, the idea was to impale any charging horse at chest height.

The river after Corbie curved around in a great bend, and Henry decided to cut straight across this loop and thereby save his tired troops a dozen or so miles. On the other bank the French had to follow the river's crooked course, so Henry's men gained ground on them, arriving at the village of Neslé well before the French advance guard.

Either through one of his mounted patrols or from the mouth of a local farmer, Henry was told that a couple of fords crossed the river not far from Neslé. A quick reconnaissance showed that local people had broken up the midpoint of each ford, but they were unguarded.

Sending an advance holding force of archers under *John Holland*, *John Cornwaille* and *Roger Fiennes* to the far bank to dissuade local yeomanry from opposing the crossing, Henry ordered the speediest possible repairs to both fords using doors, fences and all other suitable materials from nearby farms to provide firm footing for men and horses. By the following dawn every man, animal and cart was over the

Somme and heading north towards Calais, a distance of some
100 miles with no major geographical obstacles en route.

Robert Fiennes and his men waited in their tented camp at
the head of the Somme, as bidden by Constable d'Albret
and in readiness for the arrival there of the English army.

As a soldier of twenty years' standing and the heir to his
uncle, the ex-constable *Robert Fiennes*, *Robert* knew all the
military leaders in 1415 on first-name terms. He had fought
alongside Marshall Boucicaut and Raoul de Gaucourt,
recently of Harfleur fame, during a vicious war against the
Turks nineteen years before.

On the night of 19 October, two of *Robert*'s cousins from
the Amiens region, *Philippe* and *Guilbert d'Auxy*, called at his
tent. *Philippe* was a *Lord of Dampierre* and *Robert*'s paternal
grandmother was the late *Isabel of Dampierre*, the *Countess
of Flanders*. Another visitor that evening was Robert de Waurin,
great-grandson of Alix, *Robert*'s own great-grandmother. De
Waurin was Sénéchal of Flanders and an old friend of *Robert*'s.

The Auxys and de Waurin had their own troops ready for
battle and the four men were all keen to polish their family
reputations by being in the front line when their army came
face to face with the English invaders. *Robert* had, in his
youth at Fiennes Castle, met many of his father's Anglo-
Norman friends and was no doubt wondering whether any
were in King Henry's army.

Soon after midnight the entire French army stirred suddenly
as news reached Constable d'Albret of the surprise crossing

of the Somme by the English. Instead of waiting for Henry's men at the head of the river, the entire French army was now to head north with all speed to catch up, overtake and then annihilate the invaders.

The estimate of de Waurin, having listened to various rumours, was that the English army totalled some 7,000 men, whereas the French host was at more than double that number and still growing as knights from further afield arrived on the scene.

That night the two armies were camped a mere seven miles from each other.

Constable d'Albret, at a ceremony witnessed by some 40,000 French troops, officially unfurled the great red flag, known as the Oriflamme, the sacred banner of France. This action signified the specific decision of the king and his commanders that no prisoners were to be taken in the ensuing battle. Then, to the sound of blaring trumpets, the clicking and swishing of plate armour and the whinny of excited horses, the pride of France headed north for a date with death.

Early on 21 October King Henry led his men north past the grim walls of the castle at Péronne, where the French army leaders had held councils of war not many hours before. In pouring rain and in full battle dress, the tired and hungry English marvelled at the evidence of the enemy's recent presence. They observed a huge area of mud and the hoof marks of horses so numerous as to inspire terror in the minds of men about to face almost certain death. The *Gesta* chronicler recorded: 'We found the roads remarkably churned up by the French army as if it had preceded ahead of us by the thousand . . . We raised our eyes and hearts to heaven crying out with voices expressing our inmost thoughts, that God would have pity on us and in his ineffable goodness, turn us away from the violence of the French.'

Other records show evidence that many of the English were extremely frightened at this time, as though the weeks of sickness, hunger, lack of sleep and now the incessant rain soaking their heavy unsuitable clothes had worn down their normal sangfroid. Many may well have wished only to desert, but they knew that, in this hostile land, their only faint chance of staying alive was to remain with their army.

Between Péronne and Calais there were eighty miles and five or six minor rivers to cross. Both armies, with the French leading, were heading north up the muddy main road, but at the first opportunity Henry took a side road that paralleled the French route just a few miles to the west of it.

The Duke of York led the vanguard troops at a blistering pace, fought off several French harassing raids and just managed to cross the various rivers before French patrols were able to destroy the crossings. The duke was an impressive leader, especially bearing in mind the desperate state of his soldiers, who could genuinely be described as starving.

Although the archers had cut through their loose underclothes to enable the waves of dysentery to splash to the ground as they marched, the men-at-arms, encased in armour, had no such relief. The mind boggles at the embarrassment and lowering of personal morale that such circumstances must cause.

By diverting from the main road along which the French host was heading, Henry avoided the obvious danger that the likes of Marshal Boucicaut, Constable d'Albret and the overall royal commander, the Duke of Orléans, would select a suitable blocking position and sit waiting for the British to plunge into a well-positioned trap.

For their part, the French commanders may well have assumed that Henry's diversion from the main route clearly indicated that he wished to avoid confrontation, wanting only to escape to the safety of Calais by outpacing the French. So they, too, hastened their progress with their far fitter troops on a better road, and they aimed for a known area of open fields where they knew the English route would converge with their own.

Not waiting for the arrival of various lords, even dukes with their large retinues, Boucicaut's force raced ahead of the English and chose what appeared to be a perfect position in open countryside between the two small villages of Agincourt and Tramecourt, some nine miles to the south of the forest and village of Fiennes and blocking the road to Calais.

Behind the French position open fields stretched away northwards towards the coast, on either flank were thick woods, and to their front the field fell away fairly sharply to a small valley that the English would need to cross, should they dare to advance against their more numerous enemy.

The fields all around the French had recently been ploughed with deep shears, as was normal for a winter wheat crop, and heavy rain had softened the soil. A more experienced overall commander than the Duke of Orléans might have chosen a different location, but, from a purely blocking point of view, it was ideal.

Henry approached the area of the French position on 24 October. Scouts had already reached a ridge top overlooking Tramecourt and made their report. Henry halted his army in the village of Maisoncelles.

Four knights, all related, met that evening in a cow barn on the outskirts of the village. King Henry was housed in a local property. The men of the army were all around the village, keeping quiet, by royal order, so that any suspicious night movements by the French would not be missed. Bonfires were kept burning, the better to see any French patrols or sudden attacks, and a lucky few could keep warm as they stoked the flames. The rain was incessant through the long night and served to dampen and distance the sounds of the French host less than a mile away who were clearly under no noise restrictions.

Two of the knights in the barn were my cousins, *Roger Fiennes*, thirty-one years of age, and his brother *James*, ten years younger. They had already checked with their ventinars that their men were as comfortable as possible in their tents. They were the lucky ones compared with many hungry, shivering soldiers with blistered feet, dysentery, raw crotches and pack-bruises, who had no shelter but the apple trees in the village orchards.

The other two knights in the barn were Roger's brother-in-law, *John Holland*, the hero of Harfleur, and Roger's mother's third husband, *John Cornwaille*, who treated *Holland* like his own son.

A fifth member of the group who, like *James*, was part of the Duke of Gloucester's close protection group who travelled with the king, was another royal favourite, *William Wykeham*, the heir of Henry IV's *Chancellor William of*

Wykeham. *William* was only seventeen, but his uncle, *Thomas Wykeham*, had been killed at Harfleur so he had taken over the family standard and led his archers on towards Calais, befriending the *Fiennes* brothers en route. This led, twenty years later, to the marriage of *James*'s son to William's daughter and heiress, resulting in the Fiennes family inheriting Broughton Castle which we still own today, and of which my great-grandfather was the eighteenth lord.

The five men discussed the pending action and their king's plans. All were to be in the central body of the English front line and grouped about the royal standards. They may have talked also about the small differences in their armours, which were close beside them in the barn and would soon be donned with the help of their pages, currently asleep at the far end of the barn. *Holland* had met the Duke of York that evening and had heard first-hand why they had camped in Maisoncelles. For some time the duke had led the advance troops towards Calais and had done a brilliant job of navigation, discipline and speed. He was the last remaining grandson of King Edward III and a warrior of great experience.

One of the duke's forward spies had moved ahead of all the others and, reaching high ground after crossing the River Ternoise at Blangy village, had suddenly seen the French army in all its impressive might and with the sun-glint off countless helmets, armours and lances.

Like many specialists in King Henry's army, his forward patrol horsemen were trained to report with accuracy and in detail and never to exaggerate what they observed. Like medieval heralds, they could recognise the colour and symbols on many of the more important dynastic standards and, from them, were able to deduce the strength of the whole force.

During the Cold War in Germany, when I was a captain of a reconnaissance unit trained to watch for advancing Soviet forces, all my men were endlessly tested on identification of different fighting vehicles, and we were thus able to deduce which major Soviet formation was approaching.

However, the Duke of York's scout was not at first inclined to accuracy, gulping forth the words, 'Quickly. Be prepared for battle, as you are just about to fight against a world of innumerable people.'

Including the multitude of pages, servants, cooks, carpenters and other non-soldiers, the total number of Frenchmen reported by English eyewitnesses, including the Duke of York's spies, averaged out at some 50–60,000 men, and many military historians, playing with the various recorded data, have since revised those figures down to 30,000, or even 20,000, soldiers. The recorded quotes of those who watched the French advancing across the valley below included: 'Their numbers were so great as not even to be comparable with ours . . . filling a very broad field like an innumerable host of locusts.' And Shakespeare describes the scene:

> The poor condemned English,
> Like sacrifices, by their watchful fires
> Sit patiently, and inly ruminate
> The morning's danger; and their gesture sad,
> Investing lank-lean cheeks and war-worn coats,
> Presenteth them unto the gazing moon
> So many horrid ghosts . . .

Before the cold gleam of daylight spread over the sodden trees and tents of Maisoncelles, Henry sent out orders to get ready for battle. The order for silence still held. The smell of woodsmoke as fires died down vied with the foul body odour of the soldiers scurrying through the gloom to the whispered orders of their sergeants.

The five men in the barn, unable to sleep, were keen for action, any action, to break the dread anticipation of waiting for death or worse. After donning their full battle armour with assistance from their pages, they bade each other God's blessing and went to the camps of their men.

I remember only too well the stomach-churning fear of pending action when outnumbered in enemy territory and cut off from any support. In the 1960s I took some twenty heavily armed Omani and Baluchi soldiers deep into the Marxist-held mountains of Dhofar on a mission to kill or capture two senior Marxist commissars. We moved for ten hours in darkness through deep valleys and over plateaux held by terrorist groups. A single wrong move could end in ambush, cut-off and death in those pre-helicopter days. I have never felt such a deep, primordial fear again, but I have been reminded of it in reading many accounts of that night in Maisoncelles.

That King Henry managed to maintain his army as an effective fighting force capable of a highly professional performance against superior numbers of well-armed soldiers on a battlefield of *their* choice suggests that he was a highly successful leader of men.

Football managers can affect their team's performance against more talented opposition by their oratorical skills. A convincing gift of the gab is surely what enabled King Henry to spread his aura of confidence, like some medieval form of chemotherapy, to prevent the cancer of fear from spreading on that awful morning and from fatally affecting the aggressive willpower that his men were about to need if they were to save themselves in the great battle to come.

What message did Henry come up with to do the trick? Shakespeare put words in his mouth that have made him and the battle famous over six centuries and has Henry encouraging the fearful before dawn:

> Walking from watch to watch, from tent to tent . . .
> . . . he goes and visits all his host,
> Bids them good-morrow with a modest smile,
> And calls them brothers, friends and countrymen . . .
> With cheerful semblance and sweet majesty;
> That every wretch, pining and pale before,
> Beholding him, plucks comfort from his looks . . .
> Thawing cold fear.

The chronicles of Titus Livius and of the monk of St Denis and of Juvenal des Ursins specifically stress that the low morale of the English soldiers was boosted by their king's harangue on the eve of the battle as he toured their campfires and tents in the rain to instil his own beliefs into each miserably cold, hungry and fearful man. The specific message that he forcefully promoted included references to the Battle of Crécy, fought very close to Maisoncelles, being won by men like themselves with the same skills and against superior numbers. He reminded his men that their folks back home and 'all England' were praying for their success, that the glory of victory would last all their lives, and that God was on their side fighting for a truly rightful cause.

He stressed that the French were so arrogant and confident

of winning that they were boasting how they intended to cut off the two key active fingers from each archer they captured. This is said to have been the origin of today's V-sign, meaning 'Up Yours'. Whether or not that is true, Henry certainly stressed it and would have impressed on his archers that aggression, rather than pessimism, was key to overcoming an enemy intent on emasculating their great and unique skills with the longbow.

Records going back over 200 years show that it was standard practice in Europe to execute any captured archer without question, in the same way that the Gestapo, in the Second World War, executed special operations agents. And a century prior to Agincourt the Scottish rules of battle on capturing an archer were to cut off his right hand and gouge out his right eye.

The English writer Thomas Walsingham recorded that Henry's men, on hearing that the enemy intended to sever two of their three bow-fingers, were filled with anger and 'forgot all their misfortunes, exhaustion and weakness'.

Henry also emphasised that he intended to die or to win the day. Under no circumstances would he allow himself to be captured and held to ransom in order to evade death. Nor would he hold back surrounded by a protective curtain of knights. His men could not expect the safe option of surrender and ransom, so neither would he. He would wear his crown and his full kingly regalia for all to see and he would fight at the battle-front. This was, of course, designed to avoid the rank and file thinking, It's all right for the toffs but not for us.

Henry knew that his men were superstitious, so he stressed that that very day was highly auspicious, for it was St Crispin's Day and, exactly a year before, the French had tortured and massacred British bowmen captured at Soissons. Now was the time for vengeance. And as for fearing the sheer size of the enemy force, the men should remember that their great longbow skills had often proved the key to success against superior numbers.

Over in the French camp my cousin *Robert Fiennes* greeted his cousin the *Count of Dammartin*, his neighbour the Sire of Ardres, and another cousin *Bertrand de Bournonville*. His ancestors in the Fiennes family over the previous three centuries had married into all three families and kept close ties with them. All were pleased with the way that certain regional lords had joined the national army, despite their mutual antipathy.

Neither the French king nor his son the dauphin was present to decide on the tactics best suited to the imminent battle. But Charles, Duke of Orléans, had just arrived and, at twenty years of age, was a suitable royal figurehead, despite having no battle experience.

Robert's veteran friends, Marshal Boucicaut and Constable Charles d'Albret, agreed with *Robert* that the best course of action was to avoid open battle with Henry, but to hem in his army, attack his supply lines and weaken his already hungry, enfeebled men into submission and surrender by fatally slowing their progress towards Calais. That way would avoid the carnage that all three men knew could be the result of an open confrontation with Henry's longbowmen.

However, a great many regional lords had congregated at Rouen and were slavering for the glory of what looked like an easy victory over the inferior English force. So Boucicaut, d'Albret, *Fiennes* and other veterans of previous confrontations with the English were outvoted and their policy of cautious attrition was overruled. Instead, as though the bitter experience of Crécy and Poitiers, sixty years before, had never happened, the council decided on a traditional deployment.

And so, chatting in their tent the night before the battle, the great marshal, the constable and the veteran son of the previous constable, unlike the excited host all around them, were definitely not full of the joys of spring. Not only were they unhappy with the principle of confrontation, but they suspected that the very location selected for the battle was a potential death trap that would, through its narrow front between two woods, cause their forces to be dangerously constricted. As they talked, the music and laughter of their army camped in the orchards of their host villages of Tramecourt and Agincourt was evidence that the overall mood was one of extreme confidence of an imminent and historic victory, plunder, glory and ransom.

Boucicaut summarised the danger of the selected battleground. The width of the open fields between the two flanking woods was such that the numerical advantage of the French could not be fully used. Instead, many fine troops would merely have to wait uselessly behind their own front line until, once the latter were dead or dispersed, they could then join the fray.

That evening many thousands of horses were being led or ridden around the fields on soaking wet ground by pages or grooms, especially in the dark fields of the prospective battlefield down towards the silent camp of the enemy in Maisoncelles.

Heavy rain continued through that long night, increasing

the misery of the many men without the shelter of a barn or tent at both ends of the great muddy field overlooked by the castle of Agincourt.

Robert Fiennes had, earlier in the day, walked down the field between the villages and had noted that, although the available space between the two woods where the army would form up was some three-quarters of a mile wide, it narrowed down to less than half a mile at the point where, he estimated, the armies would actually clash. And this would see the bigger force seriously compressed. He also noticed that his feet were sliding about as he walked, due to the mud in the field's deep furrows. He remembered his uncle's many repeated warnings that mud was the great enemy of cavalry and of heavy armour.

Boucicaut and d'Albret were in agreement that, however well they commanded their own divisions on the morrow, they were worried that such a large army should have nobody with experience in overall charge. This they felt was the greatest danger they faced in the coming fight. *Robert* looked at his shoes and the muddy trail of footprints behind him and was not so sure.

Staring over towards the other side of the field, *Robert* could clearly see the confines of the English army 1,000 yards away. He may have wondered if any of his English cousins were camped there.

13

A family at war

Throughout the long, sodden night new bands of French soldiers arrived on the edges of the sprawling camp to be greeted by chaos and disorganisation. No signs. No stewards. How to find the main command post? Who was in charge to give detailed operational instructions? Where exactly was the enemy and where on the battlefield were they to station themselves?

Charles d'Albret and Marshall Boucicaut did their experienced best to find out exactly who had arrived, who might arrive soon and to tell each group leader where on the battlefield to deploy at dawn.

Conspicuous by his absence was John the Fearless, Duke of Burgundy, who had sent the king assurances that he would arrive with his army in the near future. But, as was generally suspected, he was still focused on taking Paris and, in due course, the throne, and not on defeating Henry, with whom he had hopes of a mutually beneficial alliance, or at least a non-interference pact. Nonetheless, he had hedged his bets by allowing some Burgundian regional forces to join up with the national army.

The other great magnate who had failed to arrive, along with his 10,000-strong army, by itself the size of Henry's entire armed might, was the Duke of Brittany. Neither King Charles nor the dauphin was present, which was surely a considerable relief to d'Albret and his Armagnac allies, since they had every reason to fear that the Duke of Burgundy might join up with Henry if he thought he stood a fair chance of killing or capturing both the king and the dauphin in a pitched battle, and then following this with a victorious march to Paris and the French throne. No doubt he also had a Plan B in place to get rid of Henry thereafter.

Overall then, d'Albret was the military leader of a huge army with many regional leaders but with no royal figurehead. Facing him was a far smaller force of weakened, sick and hungry invaders desperate to escape back home via Calais. His opponents' two great assets, d'Albret knew well, were their longbowmen and their uniquely capable warrior-king.

The greatest military powers in Europe, probably in all the world, shook themselves dry like two tigers as the rain stopped that dawn, and then moved out to face each other as would two sporting teams. But the winners would be those who proved more efficient at killing other men, not at kicking a ball. And the victor's desired reward would be the throne of France, not some silver chalice.

D'Albret's old friends and fellow veterans, *Robert Fiennes* and Gilbert Lannoy, neither of whom was deeply committed to Burgundians or Armagnacs, helped him sort out the deployment problem in the small hours before dawn. Gilbert had a history of many campaigns, often fighting under the direct command of *Robert*'s father. These included raids on English coastal towns (one of which was Pevensey when *Roger Fiennes* was sheriff there), and battles in the Prussian crusades and against the Moors in Spain. He had fought for the Duke of Burgundy, but was loyal to France alone when it was threatened by invasion.

Robert and Gilbert followed the deployment plan agreed by d'Albret, Boucicaut and the Royal Council more or less as designed and agreed the previous fortnight in Rouen when the army was still a mere half of its current size. But their attempts at deploying the various groups of men-at-arms, archers, crossbowmen and lance-bearing cavalry were governed by the distance between the two forests that flanked the designated battlefield.

French records vary as to the exact numbers involved at Agincourt, but most reckon on 30,000. There were, according to the originally agreed French plan, to be 4,000 archers and 1,500 crossbowmen, with 8,000 men-at-arms all on foot in the front line (vanguard) with, on either flank, some 700 mounted men-at-arms. Behind them would be the main line-up similarly divided, and behind them again the remaining groups as rearguard.

Every county in northern France had sent an armed contingent and each town provided as many armed men as they could spare. Although only four ducal members of the royal family were present, there were at least 1,000 glory-seeking knights, lords and minor aristocrats, all itching to make their reputations as warriors and none prepared to start the battle in any position other than on the front line. There would, after all, probably be no English knights left to kill or capture if you were deployed anywhere but on the front line – such was the overall certainty of victory by the Frenchmen who had observed or heard about the numerical difference between the two armies. Therefore, any self-respecting or would-be knight was damned if he would allow himself to be relegated behind the front line.

There would never be a finer example of the saying 'too many chiefs and not enough Indians', because the direct results of allowing all the nobles to fill up the front line meant in many cases separating them from the men they should have been leading and, worse still, having to place the archers and crossbowmen behind the entire front line, including the shock cavalry squads on each flank.

The rearguard, which was expected to grow in size hour by hour as late arriving militia continued to appear, would be commanded by two of my kinsmen, the *Count of Dammartin*, whose ancestor *Agnes de Dammartin* had married *William Fiennes I*, and the *Lord of Ardres*, whose ancestor *Adèle* had married *Eustace Fiennes* (the son of *Count Eustace of Boulogne*). The latter had brought with him many men from the border regions of Boulogne.

The latest plan for the opening French move was that an elite force of 2,000 of the best cavalry men available would charge from either flank of the front line and mow down the English archers on either flank of *their* front line to annihilate them before their deadly firepower could effectively get under way. Since these veteran French horsemen were chosen from various host bodies, this again lessened the effectiveness of their original units.

Various chronicles relate that those groups of men whose leaders, and in most cases their most experienced veterans, were removed, were relegated to a mishmash of leaderless groups in the immense rearguard. Thus bereft of leaders, these men were not likely to prove useful in the struggle to come. For an army drawn from all regions of a country where a sense of national patriotism had only recently, and as yet only partially, replaced regional patriotism, the key ingredient that was sadly missing was the presence of the King of France.

Another big difference between the two armies was that of class structure. The French nobles despised the soldiers as peasants, a lower form of life which, out of uniform, they could and usually did have nothing to do with. 'Upstairs Downstairs' ruled supreme.

Chivalry and most of its medieval rules originated with the French aristocracy. Many were imitated in England, but to a lesser extent. British archers, whether from Wales, Cheshire or Lancashire, were from the peasantry, for which reason the French aristocracy avoided raising specialist bowmen of their own. Indeed, when King Charles VI, in a sane moment, suggested after Calais that the French army should start recruiting and training archers, he was threatened with deposition by a powerful group of horrified French nobles.

A French chronicler with the great name of Pierre Cochon (Peter Pig) described the English archers that he observed at Harfleur thus: 'All with bare feet . . . dressed in scruffy doublets made of old bedding, a poor iron skullcap on their heads . . . That was all the armour they possessed.' The further down the social ladder a soldier was, the less protection he had from the horrific spear, sword, arrow and poleaxe wounds of medieval warfare.

When an aristocrat lost to an opponent in battle, he could beg to be ransomed rather than die. Peasants had no such option. There were many recorded cases of badly wounded soldiers on the battlefield taking the armour and surcoat from some nearby aristocratic corpse and donning it to avoid being knifed as worthless when the post-battle scavenger bands arrived to check the wounded and decide whether they should be killed or ransomed.

Far from treating his archers as an underclass, Henry gave them the respect they deserved and increased their ratio against that of men-at-arms on his successive campaigns. And he fully appreciated their dual-purpose ability – first as bowmen, then, on running out of arrows, as light-clad, close-range killers with hand weapons. In addition to the archers each regional retinue would bring to a given campaign muster, Henry often took on semi-professional groups of skilled archers hired from Wales, Cheshire and Lancashire. He rated them by their remarkable skills, so vital to his military results, rather than by their generally lowly birthright. Shakespeare echoed this by having Henry's pre-battle soliloquy include the words:

> We would not die in that man's company
> That fears his fellowship to die with us.
> This day is call'd the feast of Crispian . . .
> We few, we happy few, we band of brothers;
> For he today that sheds his blood with me
> Shall be my brother; be he ne'er so vile,
> This day shall gentle his condition.
> And gentlemen in England now a-bed
> Shall think themselves accursed they were not here,
> And hold their manhoods cheap while any speaks
> That fought with us upon St Crispin's day.

What Henry felt towards those mercenary English archers (about 100 of them) who had hired themselves out to the French Duke of Bar, and so fought for France that day, was never recorded. They were placed with the French archer contingent in the rearguard and therefore probably never loosed off an arrow all day.

The monk of St Denis recorded that when the city of Paris offered the assistance of a fully armed force of 6,000 citizens, the scornful response from Jean Beaumont was, 'The help of mechanics and artisans must surely be of little value, for we shall outnumber the English three to one.'

The pro-French priestly chronicler Pierre Cochon wrote: 'The French thought they would carry the day given their great numbers, and in their arrogance had proclaimed that only those who were noble should go into battle. So all the men of lower ranks, who were enough to have beaten the English, were pushed to the rear. In addition, there was a great divide between the parties of the Duke of Orléans and the Duke of Burgundy.'

In order to fit all the bickering dukes and knights and all their top retainers, together with their pages and banner-men, into the central vanguard in the front line as well as the elite cavalry squads on either frontal flank, all the archers and crossbowmen were relegated to the rearguard to be called up when needed.

Veterans d'Albret, Boucicaut, *Robert Fiennes* and others must have shaken their heads in disbelief at this last-minute compromise made entirely to boost the egotism of the various magnates and knights and for fear that, otherwise, slighted group leaders might simply take umbrage and leave with all their men.

But common sense and the voices of experience were as naught against the latent animosities of the magnates whose mutual hatred was greater than their fear of the reputedly weak English invasion force. So why had they eventually come together in the days immediately prior to the Agincourt battle? Self-interest and public relations are surely the reason.

When Henry first arrived at Harfleur, he had correctly calculated that the ongoing French civil war between the two main ducal factions of the Duke of Burgundy and of Orléans (the Armagnacs), as well as numerous hostilities and jealousies between other regional magnates, would mean comparatively light opposition to his invasion.

The Armagnacs, based in Paris, had recently recaptured various cities previously lost to the Burgundians. But many Parisian citizens actually favoured the Burgundians, so the Armagnac leaders around the throne feared that, should their army march north to relieve Harfleur, the Burgundians (who were known to have had 'secret' talks with Henry) would attack in order to take Paris and the throne.

Equally, when the Duke of Burgundy received the king's summons to join the national army against the invader, he feared that such a mainly Armagnac army might speedily deal with Henry and then be used against him.

The resulting stalemate, which helped Henry by giving him the time needed to take Harfleur without interruption by a French relief force, had begun to dissolve when his very success at Harfleur so alarmed the French that patriotic groups responded when calls to war from the king in Rouen were sent out to all parts of the realm. Very soon over 14,000 soldiers had converged on Rouen ready to attack the common enemy. Armagnac regional knights, keen for glory, had then joined up, which in turn sparked many Burgundians and previously Anglo-friendly Brittany lords to head for the kill.

So, all of a sudden, the French army had more than doubled in size. Modern revisionist historians, keen as always to attack their predecessors' records, simply utilise the initial smaller size of the French army and suggest that such was still the French strength at Agincourt.

The Oriflamme was traditionally only to be unfurled when the king was present at a battle but, at Agincourt, his royal relatives would have to suffice. It was now a Frenchman's duty to attend the fighting, a matter of honour which, if ignored, would be a stain for ever on the family escutcheon. So even the Duke of Burgundy's younger son and two of his brothers joined up, albeit at the very last minute.

Among the French commanders, my kinsmen included *Sir Robert Fiennes, the Count of Dammartin, the Lord of Ardres, Ingelram de Bournonville II*, and *Philippe d'Auxy (Lord of Dampierre)*.

Among the English field commanders were *Roger* and *James Fiennes, John Holland, John Cornwaille, William Wykeham* and *William Clinton*, the self-styled *Lord Saye*.

Robert Fiennes and his Tingry men-at-arms all dismounted and joined those of Gilbert Lannoy in the centre of the main French force lined up behind the jostling front line of banner-waving, heavily armoured warrior-lords and their pages.

After an hour had passed and the various knights were satisfied with their front-line positions, many were helped by their valets to recline and take breakfast. There was no movement from the English front line, now clearly visible some 700 metres away, which, as far as *Robert* could see, looked like a single front-line formation, no more than four soldiers deep and with no back-up forces. This compared with the French front line which was at least thirty men in depth and with many thousands of reserves behind the main battle group, of which *Robert*'s men were part.

Roger and *James Fiennes* were camped in different parts of Maisoncelles but both shared the same family crest on their lance pennants.

James, having checked with Prinkle three hours before dawn that all the men were ready to move out with the Duke of Gloucester's contingent when the signal was given, called for his page to help him into his armour.

James's page went by his surname of Cade and was in his mid-teens. His father was a senior member of the staff employed at Herstmonceux Castle by *James*'s elder brother *Roger*. Over the past two months Cade had become quite slick at putting *James* into his armour, taking him out of it and cleaning it when not in use. He was in charge of the three horses required to carry all *James*'s equipment. *James*'s armour had to be donned in a specific order. For more on the arming of an English man-at-arms, see the appendix on page 291.

Without the weapons, *James*'s armour weighed forty to fifty pounds, which was a reasonable and manageable weight for a trained warrior, and meant he could mount and dismount if he had to without help from his groom or page.

I noted, when studying the source locations of the magnates' coat armours, that Henry's veteran friend and great warrior, Sir John Fastolf, a good friend of *James Fiennes*, had his and his men's coats manufactured at his Wiltshire estate of Castle Combe, the very village where in 1965 with friends and army explosives borrowed from an SAS demolition course, I blew up a concrete dam built by 20th Century Fox in the interests of conservation. Caught by the police, I was heavily fined and put on local police probation for six months.

Another coincidence that occurred during research was that Thomas, Lord Camoys, the great Agincourt knight who commanded the left wing of Henry's vanguard, was buried in the churchyard of the tiny Sussex village of Trotton. It was there when I was sixteen and best man at my sister's wedding that I fainted during the service and came to immediately beneath the lifelike funerary brass of Lord Camoys and his wife.

James Fiennes, while being armed by Cade, caught up on the camp gossip including the fact that the king had spent the night in the pouring rain visiting soldiers shivering under bushes and had moved them into better shelter. Such actions won him his men's love and respect.

In the sodden silence that follows the drumming of a downpour the armed groups came together in the field beyond Maisoncelles' last orchard, and Henry's favourite knight, the veteran Sir Thomas Erpingham, began to position them, all 7,000, into straight lines, four men deep from the edge of the Agincourt wood on their left flank to that of the Tramecourt wood on their right. Most of the archers he formed up on either flank, but small groups were also placed strategically along the front line.

The French could be seen through the slowly clearing

ground mist 1,000 yards away to the north, also arrayed between the two forests.

The great field separating the two armies had been recently ploughed and was soaking wet. Many of the men were cold, shivering and coughing up phlegm. Those with dysentery still lingering relieved themselves where they stood in line, swearing or mouthing prayers.

The central line-up of steel-clad men-at-arms was commanded by Henry assisted by his brother Humphrey, Duke of Gloucester, *John Cornwaille*, *John Holland*, the *Fiennes* brothers and other such veterans with their contingents. The left-hand side of the line-up was under the command of Lord Camoys and the right under the king's uncle, the Duke of York.

On either flank were ranged the massed archers, 5,000 in all. Many were bareheaded and barefoot, the long march having torn up their leather shoes. And seldom in the history of war can so many have smelled so bad.

The king, having attended three separate masses, rode down the long line of men, English, Welsh, Irish and even the odd Gascon. All eyes followed Henry and, beside him, Sir Thomas Erpingham, veteran of fifty years of war, as grey and grizzled as an old Moses.

As the king rode slowly down the front line, and so that every man could hear him, he repeated his words of encouragement, the text of which, unlike Shakespeare's imagined and brilliant rendering thereof, was recorded by his chaplains. Henry specifically urged the men, as he had himself been taught by his spiritual adviser, Friar Fromyard, to take no credit for victory in battle but to realise that God decides the outcome of all things. This was the teaching of my direct ancestor, *Emperor Charlemagne*, going back thirty-nine generations. He, too, had always heard mass before every battle.

The king rode a small grey horse and his legs hung down with no stirrups. His armour was mirror bright and his helmet was crowned with a richly jewelled golden battle crown. Three high banners were held by banner-men riding great white horses with his royal crests and the flags of both England and France. Once in his battle position he would be a clear and unambiguous target for the glory-seeking knights of France, a sure way of encouraging the French front line to converge centrally, giving the English flank archers their best possible targets.

'Now is a good time,' he said for all to hear, 'for all England prayeth for us. Therefore be of good cheer and let us go to our day's work.'

By nine o'clock all ground mists were gone. The French lines were described by the king's chaplain: 'The number of them was really terrifying . . . with its forest of spears and the great number of helmets gleaming in between them and of cavalry on the flanks.'

According to the *Gesta* chronicle, a knight close to Henry, Sir Walter Hungerford, expressed his wish that the English army was at least another 10,000 men stronger, whereupon Henry rounded on him with the words: 'That is foolish talk. I would not have one man more than I do for those men with me are God's people. The Almighty with these few is able to overcome the opposing arrogance of the French who boast of their great number and their own strength.'

Henry then sent his horse to join the thousands of others in the baggage train in Maisoncelles. Those pages and grooms considered too young to fight were in charge of the many carts, collapsible tents and the general mass of supplies which, as soon as the battle commenced, would be at the mercy of the already lurking and armed villagers eager for plunder. Henry had assigned four dozen soldiers as guards but, once his back was turned, these men crept back to their units either through a desire to fight or because they feared death should the baggage train be attacked by superior numbers.

The sharpened stakes that the archers had carried on the march were now hammered into the mud ahead of each man, with the specific aim of impaling a charging horse. Each archer carried a leaden mallet with other hand weapons of choice hanging from hooks on his quiver belt. After his stake was in place, he used his dagger to resharpen its point.

With both armies now ready for the killing to begin and a great many individuals on both sides desperate not to show their terror to their comrades, the rules of war dictated that he who attacks a sound defensive position will risk losing the action. So each side poised at either end of the wide muddy space between the two dark forests nursed the hope that the other would make the first move.

D'Albret was fully aware of Henry's predicament. The English aim to reach the safety of Calais was blocked by an overwhelmingly superior force that was increasing in size every hour. Henry's men were desperately tired, hunger-weak, cold and many were still debilitated with dysentery. They had marched for 250 miles in the last seventeen days. The last thing Henry needed now was delay.

Nonetheless, a diplomat to his toes, Henry sent out his heralds to meet their French counterparts in the midst of the ploughed field. Their horses could be seen to slither as they approached each other.

French chronicles later summarised Henry's reason for this last-minute parley as his weak position and fear of defeat. So, they opined, he offered to give back Harfleur, Calais and all his prisoners in return for a free passage to Calais. This conflicts with English records, which state that Henry actually offered to give back Harfleur and renounce his title to the French throne in return for Aquitaine, Ponthieu and marriage to Katherine, the French king's daughter.

Whatever the facts, both sides quickly rejected each other's offer and returned to the business in hand. The stalemate then continued as d'Albret and Henry both willed each other to make the first move.

The dense lines of French men-at-arms received a last-minute order to shorten lances in readiness for very confined combat. Then many sat down and ate whatever food they carried or drank from their wine carafes.

Due to the jammed-together presence in this front line of so many magnates and knights shadowed by their pages, many a noble would have found himself next to sworn enemies who, even recently, may have fought each other in the civil war. But this was no time or place to argue, so reconciliations, however temporary, may have resulted in the shaking of steel-gauntleted hands in the hope that no opportunistic sword thrust from behind would occur in the fight to come.

Those English with dysentery exacerbated by the dreadful apprehension of watching and waiting (which would turn the stomach of the boldest) used their daggers to cut away their underclothes to ease the passage of their dung.

The minutes ticked by. All of a sudden a new banner arrived in the French front line, blowing fitfully in the morning breeze and twice the size of all the others. A murmur went up from the English, most of whom knew its meaning. Blood-red with no escutcheon, it was the Oriflamme which, unfurled, told the enemy that there would be no quarter given and no prisoners taken.

I am glad that I was not there. I have waited in ambush with small groups of Arab soldiers, sometimes for two days and two nights, expecting heavily armed opposition, and the waiting was always the most difficult time, even though I was never hungry, cold or sick, like Henry's men.

At around eleven o'clock King Henry conferred with his veteran advisers, and all agreed that, risky as it would undoubtedly be, they must make the first move, as every hour of waiting was debilitating the men both physically and in terms of morale.

So Henry sent orders for the baggage train to move up to the immediate rear of the army in order to avoid isolation and pillage, whether by villagers or by raiding patrols from the enemy. Then he gave the order for every man to kneel, pray and kiss the ground. Their lives, this symbolic act acknowledged, were in the hands of God. Next the marshal of the army, Sir Thomas Erpingham, threw his long baton twirling high into the air and shouted to the archers, who wrestled their stakes out of the mud.

Henry raised his sword and cried out, 'In the name of Almighty God and Saint George. Advance banners.'

All 7,000 men moved forward screaming their battle cries at the release of hours of pent-up emotion, frustration and fear. And behind them, the squad of drummers and trumpeters sounded the Advance to Contact.

As steadily as possible and keeping in as straight a line as the muddy field allowed, the 5,000 archers and 1,000 men-at-arms advanced a total of 700 metres to within easy longbow range of the French. At any time during their advance, had the French cavalry charged from both flanks, the archers would have been at their most vulnerable with no stakes to protect them. But, with many of their own leaders bunched up and on foot in the proud, banner-waving front line, the French cavalry, made up of many leaderless contingents, failed to grab their opportunity until after the English had consolidated at their new position and the archers had repositioned their protective hedgehog line of stakes.

Once thus protected, the eyes of every archer turned to the lonely figure of their marshal who screamed a single word of command (recorded by French historians as 'Ne strogue', but, in fact, probably, 'Knee-stretch'), at which 5,000 archers raised their longbows and the battle began.

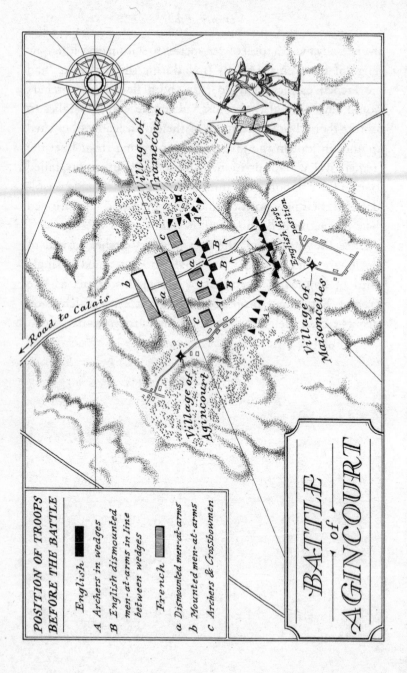

POSITION OF TROOPS
BEFORE THE BATTLE

English

A Archers in wedges
B English dismounted
   men-at-arms in line
   between wedges

French

a Dismounted men-at-arms
b Mounted men-at-arms
c Archers & Crossbowmen

Village of Tramecourt

English first position

Village of Maisoncelles

Village of Agincourt

Road to Calais

BATTLE
of
AGINCOURT

14

A Vaste Multitude Yielded Up in Death

I remember my first experience of bullets cracking by, kicking up the dust as I ran, bent double in order to present a lesser target, towards the enemy. I could not see them among the rocks 500 yards away, but I could see the bright flash of their rifles. The man running beside me, a sergeant, cried out as he crumpled and fell with a 7.62mm bullet in his thigh.

Most of all I remember the whine and crack as hundreds of high-velocity bullets passed by and overhead. That was Arabia in 1968, 553 years after Agincourt, but when I study the deadly mathematics of the medieval longbow, I can easily sympathise with the French men-at-arms, whether mounted or not, who faced the lethal arrow storms of Henry's skilled archers, for they must have been very afraid.

Each Frenchman bent his head and closed the visor on his helmet. Above the screams of the wounded men and horses, the trumpeters of d'Albret sounded the agreed call for the carefully planned charge of the elite cavalry squadrons on

217

each flank of the front line to crush the archers, the key to winning the battle.

Because the speed and simultaneous impact of 1,000 horsemen with lances and swords on any front line had a shattering effect, discipline of horses and riders was the key to success.

D'Albret's sensible plan for an initial killer-charge by 1,200 cavalrymen against the English archers, had it been correctly conducted, could have been decisive. But for various reasons it misfired, lacking discipline, close formation, speed and, therefore, any impact on contact. Instead, there was lethal chaos.

The French had been caught by surprise at the sudden advance of the entire English line-up. Many of the horsemen on either flank at the time were simply not ready for battle, having gone off for a snack or to exercise their horses behind the rearguard. So when the two flank cavalry leaders trumpeted the call to charge, only some 450, instead of 1,200, men were ready to respond. And when they did charge forward, they were hampered by the sticky clay ground immediately ahead of them which had been churned into a quagmire the previous night by grooms walking their horses around. So the full headlong gallop of a traditional cavalry charge, such as that by my own regiment, the Scots Greys, at Waterloo exactly 400 years later, proved impossible.

The mounted knights who did immediately respond to the charge order, in ragged lines rather than the required serried ranks, were under concentrated arrow attacks from ahead and from small groups of archers who Henry had hidden in the woods, a trick he had learned from Welsh guerrillas many years before.

Arrows thudded into horses and riders, and arrows that struck helmets head-on, although not always penetrating the steel, were still able to cause blunt trauma and knock a rider off his horse or even kill by a brutal point-loaded bruising of the brain, despite no actual breaching of the headgear.

As the shrill screams of the warhorses mingled with the war cries of both armies, injured horses plunged to the ground, catapulting their riders into the Picardy mud where they sank into the water-filled furrows recently ploughed extra deep for the sowing of winter wheat.

Some knights did reach the stake lines of the archers, where their horses were impaled and their owners dragged off by lightly clad archers who then clubbed them to death through their hinged visors with their lead-headed mallets.

Some horses spotted the stakes just in time to swerve or rear up, thus unseating their riders, then headed back in terror to their own lines. In doing so, they crashed into the slowly advancing columns of dismounted French men-at-arms. The French fell like flies, the second and subsequent ranks tripping over their bodies. Some, desperate to see more clearly where to tread, raised their visors and were hit by arrows in their eyes or mouths.

Strangely enough, very few of the knights involved in this initial cavalry charge were killed, captured or even wounded when compared with all other men-at-arms subsequently involved in the battle. Various historians, seeking an explanation for this conundrum, have noted that many of the knights involved were known enemies from the two rival factions – the Armagnacs and the Burgundians – several of whom had killed each other's close relations in the recent past. Thus, at Agincourt their anti-English zeal, once they sensed the suicidal nature of the action, turned about and then they furtively retired from the battlefield in order to save themselves for future inter-factional battles. A French chronicler, listing those who shirked the fighting, wrote that they 'failed to do their duty, for they fled shamefully and never struck a blow against the English'.

The immediate result of this complete failure of the cavalry to neutralise the English archers was to allow the latter unfettered target practice at close range on the subsequent advance of the massed French men-at-arms.

Once d'Albret, Boucicaut and the other divisional leaders realised the extent of the failure of the initial cavalry attack, they signalled a mass advance by the entire vanguard, but this only exacerbated the problem of the fallen who, struggling to haul themselves out of the sludge, were now knocked flat by the new arrivals who, in turn, tripped, so that a great many drowned in the wet mud beneath other bodies even though no English weapon had touched them.

The English had placed their stakes at the narrowest part of the battlefield where the flanking woods were at their closest. The French front lines had begun their advance from a considerably wider frontage and so, as they moved forward, they became compressed. Those knights who had sufficient vision through their sights to see the detailed layout of the English battle line, headed for the great banners of the magnates, where glory and ransoms were most likely to be had. This led to an even worse traffic jam.

At this crucial point of the action, 5,000 archers were able to aim accurately at easy targets while they themselves were under virtually no missile attack at all, other than the very occasional cannonball (which was later recorded to have caused only a single casualty). Since virtually every French archer and crossbowman had been relegated to the rear lines behind the knights and their retinues, they could only aim speculative fire over the heads of their front ranks, with every likelihood of striking their own men-at-arms.

Nonetheless, the French vanguard bravely continued their clumsy but inexorable advance until a body of some 8,000 heavily armed men-at-arms, having clambered over the heaps of dead and dying men and horses, reached the thin English lines, screaming their war cries and thrusting their shortened lances at Henry's men.

Once the two sides were locked in close-quarter combat, the archers could no longer fire indiscriminately. Also, since they had been loosing off their arrows at a rate of 1,000 every second, they would have quickly run out of ammunition. Messenger boys were tasked with ferrying new supplies of arrows to the archers, both by pulling used ones from corpses and by fetching resupplies from the baggage train arrow-carts.

Once the close fighting began, the English were forced to retreat under the slash and thrust of French steel. One factor at this key touch-and-go point of the battle that saved the day for Henry was the compressed mêlée of the Frenchmen which obstructed their ability to wield their weapons as effectively as their less densely packed opponents. Despite this, groups of skilled French knights, many of them invincible in the joust, forced their way to the royal banners.

The Duke of York was killed, supposedly smothered in the press. A dozen French knights who had vowed to kill or capture Henry himself managed to smash the crown on his helmet before the royal protection squads of *John Holland* and *Roger Fiennes* counter-attacked and saved the king.

The king's brother, Humphrey, Duke of Gloucester, fell with a sword thrust in the groin before his close protection knights, one of whom was *James Fiennes*, could assist him. The king rushed at once to stand astride his brother's writhing body and swung his battleaxe, while *James*'s men surrounded and killed the three French knights responsible for the attack.

Seeing that the English men-at-arms were beginning to fall back and fearing imminent defeat at the hands of the next great wave of Frenchmen, thousands of archers, out of arrows and wearing virtually no armour, grabbed their daggers, mallets and poleaxes and rushed to assist their armoured but retreating comrades.

The *Gesta* chronicles, written by a veteran reporter of many battles, described the scene:

> O, deadly war, dreadful slaughter, mortal disaster, hunger for death, insatiable thirst for blood, insane attack, impetuous frenzy, violent insanity, cruel conflict, merciless vengeance, immense clash of lances, aimless arrows, clashing of axes, brandishing of swords, breaking of arms, infliction of wounds, letting of blood, bringing on of death, hacking up of bodies, killing of nobles! The air thunders with dreadful crashes, clouds rain missiles, the earth absorbs blood, breath flies from bodies, half dead bodies roll in their own blood, the surface of the earth is covered with the corpses of the dead, this man charges, that man falls, this one attacks, that one dies, this one recovers, that one vomits forth his soul in blood . . . cruelty reigns, piety exults, the brave and the strong are crushed and mountains of corpses are piled up, a vast multitude is yielded up in death, princes and magnates are led off as captives.

The counter-attack by the archers turned the tide of the battle against the French, many of whose leaders were attempting to surrender in the face of certain death. But their bloodlust up after their long march, stalked and fearful from Harfleur, the archers were in a killing frenzy and for a while took no prisoners. Chronicler Titus Livius recorded: 'The English took no prisoners until victory was certain and apparent.'

When each successive rank of the French men-at-arms arrived at the heaps of the slain, they clambered over the steel-clad corpses and those screaming for help, only to be met by mallet-swinging Welshmen who hammered them back down or on to the death-pile. And those who, realising the hopeless situation immediately ahead, turned around to retreat found that they could not do so due to the thousands of new, still battle-thirsty French arrivals pressing forward.

These included *Robert Fiennes* and his men from the Fiennes and Tingry districts who had mustered at Fiennes Castle and travelled some thirty road miles to reach the battlefield. They had then been sent by *Robert*'s old friend, Marshal Boucicaut, to join with the armed groups of Gilbert Lannoy and Geoffrey de Boucicaut, the marshal's younger brother. They were positioned on the French left flank under the command of the Count of Vendôme, and when the trumpets had sounded their wing of the army had moved off together, their battle cries diluting their fear.

Robert had heard all the gossip about how weak the English were, but he had fought them before and his uncle had many times told him tales about the 'dark rush of killer arrows' at Crécy. So he had not been surprised when the cavalry charge had failed and when, on moving forward, he had to clamber and stumble over hundreds of French bodies. In the crush of the advance, he had glimpsed the bright banners that he recognised as those of the English Duke of York, the specific target of the Count of Vendôme, whose front squad included *Robert*'s men. As at last he closed with the enemy, he slammed down his visor.

The fighting was fierce when Vendôme's men clashed with York's. *Robert* killed Englishmen, both men-at-arms and archers, but at some point of the advance, while sensing victory, he was wounded and fell among heaps of dead and injured Englishmen.

Robert, whose wife of twenty years had died, was engaged to be married to the Lady of Ardres. He wished to have children, for his uncle, his hero, had none, and so it was his grave responsibility to continue his line, the blood of *King Pepin of the Franks* and of the great *Emperor Charlemagne*. True, there were his English Fiennes cousins, but by their foreign allegiance they were, in Robert's opinion, no longer true Fiennes blood, so he had to produce sons before he could die. But even as these thoughts must surely have been uppermost in his mind, other wounded men, French and English, fell on or crawled across him, so I can only presume from existing chronicles of Agincourt, the records of prisoners taken and registers of death, what then happened to *Robert* and others of my family that day.

What is recorded by chroniclers and witnesses on both sides is the highly unfortunate chain of events that followed the hand-to-hand fighting in which the Duke of York was killed, and the unplanned onrush of the archers with hand weapons which prevented the massed French columns from breaking through the thin red line of the British and giving instant victory to d'Albret's men.

Too late to protect the Duke of York but significant in terms of turning the tide of the battle, *John Cornwaille* personally disarmed and captured the Count of Vendôme.

At the moment when, to their amazement, the English saw the French front line beginning an overall retreat all along the corpse line between the two forests, their attitude towards those Frenchmen who begged for mercy altered. Sensing a remarkable victory, bloodlust turned to thoughts of plunder and a once-in-a-lifetime chance of great wealth. Locate a still breathing Frenchman with expensive armour and, better still, a coat of arms, and take him prisoner before anyone else did, and you could, overnight, change your family fortunes for ever.

Combat between individuals gradually broke off as the French began to retreat, slowly and wearily dragging their steel-encased bodies through the deep mud, as the pressure from men behind them also lessened. French trumpeters sounded the retreat, Englishmen of all ranks took prisoners – over 2,000 of them – and headed back with those who could walk, their helmets removed, towards Maisoncelles and the English baggage train.

Somewhere under layers of the dead and the slowly suffocating, never to be retrieved, lay the proud symbol of France, the Oriflamme, which that very morning had been unfurled to show the English that no quarter would be given, no prisoners taken. Truly an example of counting your chickens before they are hatched.

Like so many ants teeming over and feeding off festering cadavers, the British archers, many barefoot and bareheaded, searched the piles of corpses for signs of the wealthy wounded. Literally hundreds were found, including *Robert Fiennes*,

Marshal Boucicaut and the royal figurehead of the French army, Charles, Duke of Orléans.

With Henry's men certain of their victory and engaged in taking prisoners, those French who had been part of the fighting, and others who had fled without participating in any action, forced their way back through the still massed lines of the rearguard men-at-arms, many of whom were mounted and ready to advance fully armed and more than enough in number to defeat the British, whose archers were mostly out of arrows. Fortunately for Henry, this threatening horde was mainly leaderless since their knights had, as previously noted, gone off to gain glory in the front line.

The designated overall commander of the mixed forces of the rearguard was my kinsman, the *Count of Dammartin*, who was doing his best to keep various contingents of the rearguard from deserting.

Then, seemingly out of nowhere, thundered Antoine, the Duke of Brabant, with a small mounted contingent. His brother, the Duke of Burgundy, John the Fearless, had never turned up and Antoine, although too late for the main battle, was still in time to take part in a late victory and save the family honour.

Henry's scouts, observing the sudden commotion of Brabant's arrival and of a stirring of *Dammartin*'s massed cavalry squads, warned Henry of an imminent attack.

At more or less the same time, according to some chroniclers and eyewitnesses, another planned attack from behind the English army was reported. So Henry was suddenly confronted with the prospect of simultaneous attacks from front and rear, with the added perilous ingredient of 2,000 French prisoners in armour in the epicentre of his own army groups. At any moment a hard-won British victory was liable to become a disastrous failure. So Henry reacted with ruthless military common sense by ordering the immediate execution of all but the most noble and valuable of the prisoners.

Was Henry justified in making this cruel order? With hindsight, arguments can be made for and against him. Certainly the event has been used over the centuries as a stain on his character.

From my own military experiences, on an infinitely smaller scale than Henry's, I would, in his shoes, have played safe and ordered the killings of the prisoners, rather than risk adding a further danger at a time of apparent peril. After all, had a bloody defeat followed, Henry would doubtless have been criticised by those same detractors for having been lenient on the prisoners and, as a result, helping to cause the death of many of his own men. If the battle had been renewed, nothing could have stopped the 2,000 prisoners from retrieving helmets and weapons from the dead.

When fighting Marxist guerrillas in the Dhofar Mountains in the 1960s, my small ambush force would rely on silent and unseen penetration into the mountainous enemy territory, the quick ambush of an enemy patrol and immediate escape to the safety of the desert before being cut off. (No helicopters back then!) My dilemma, and it occurred several times, was what to do with goat herders or lone farmers who came across us by chance? If I let them go, they could easily tell the enemy, and we would be surrounded. If we took them with us as we advanced to our ambush site, they could easily scream out warnings to the enemy. So to slit their throats quietly was clearly the most sensible option.

The fact that I risked my own men's lives by failing to kill such individuals could have had most regrettable consequences. But I was lucky; I knew of SAS patrols at the time in the Radfan Mountains of nearby Yemen where failure to silence local shepherd boys had led to the subsequent ambush and death of the patrols.

King Henry could easily have endangered his own loyal soldiers by failing to kill his potentially dangerous and numerous prisoners while there was still time to do so. As it was, his killing order was initially disobeyed because the prisoners' captors were naturally disinclined to kill their 'golden geese' so soon after having secured them, and with the tantalising prospect of future wealth. So Henry had to give specific orders to a nearby esquire, Sir John Bernard, to command a group of 200 archers with daggers and swords to execute immediately all but the most important prisoners.

According to the chronicles of a French eyewitness: 'All those noblemen of France were there killed in cold blood and cut in pieces, heads and faces, which was a fearful sight to see.' English authors such as Sir James Ramsey have subsequently described the action as 'cruel butchery'.

There is an argument that Henry, a shrewd judge of men and their moods in wartime situations, could have deduced that the French would not be inclined to renew the attack after their severe initial setbacks. But he clearly recognised at the moment he announced the kill-prisoners order that the battle could still go either way. What were the thoughts that led to his decision?

The French had that very morning clearly stated their own intention to take no prisoners when they had unfurled the Oriflamme; the remaining French army still outnumbered Henry's host, so he would need every last one of his men for the expected renewal of the battle, and none could be spared for guarding 2,000 prisoners; on the other hand, the unwritten laws or mores of Christian lands, accepted by French and British, clearly expected the lives of Christian prisoners of war to be saved where feasible, especially when they were unarmed after giving themselves up.

Henry would surely also have done his homework on the feuds between the French knights, whose identities were known to him through their banners. He would, therefore, have known that, with all the main French commanders dead or captured, those with leadership potential left with the 8,000-strong rearguard were highly unlikely to wield sufficient influence over the disparate forces to order a worthwhile attack. Instead, if true to form, one regional knight would refuse to accept suggested orders from another, and no Burgundian would serve under an Armagnac, or vice versa. Gascons and Bretons would obey only their own leaders and follow their own banners.

Henry may well have suspected that this would work in his favour, but he would have been stupid to count on it. So he ordered certain knights to prepare their men for an attack from Maisoncelles to their rear, and others, the bulk of his force, to form a new thin line, with stakes where feasible, just behind the corpse line. Archers were told to replenish their arrow stocks from the field as and when they could, and a group of less wealthy-looking prisoners was detached from the main group and herded back towards the baggage lines to be executed.

Among the throngs of prisoners were two, both wounded but able to limp, who had been extricated from the piles of wounded near to the place where the Duke of York had been killed. Both looked, from the excellence of their armour, to be worthy of ransom. One was *Robert Fiennes* and the other Gilbert Lannoy. Along with a dozen other wounded and prosperous-looking prisoners, also retrieved from the death-heaps, they were led by a guard from the king's household staff to a barn on the outskirts of Maisoncelles.

When Henry's order to kill the prisoners was announced, persons unknown, whether on royal orders or not, set fire to the barn and blocked the entrance. *Robert*, Gilbert and another man managed to crawl behind a heap of tiles close beside a locked back door with a draught that saved them from certain death. Gilbert, who knew *Robert*, was later dragged out alive but seriously wounded and was subsequently ransomed to *John Cornwaille*. Later, when his family had paid the ransom and he returned to France, he told *Robert*'s family that *Robert* had still been alive behind the tiles but feigning death when the English had reappeared.

The various battle chronicles fail to agree on how many French prisoners were executed on the battlefield, but they do reveal the clear reluctance of Henry's men to obey the killing order, either due to their conscience or the dictates of chivalry or merely because they did not wish to waste good ransom potential. At least 2,000 prisoners did reach Calais a week or so later, so it is unlikely that more than 100 were killed by the time Henry repealed his controversial order.

It seems that soon after the Duke of Brabant's impetuous attack, an act of suicidal bravado with a small squad of his own men, a substantial body of mounted men-at-arms from *Dammartin*'s rearguard were motivated by two counts to save the honour of France. However, as their various groupings were marshalled into the necessary attack formation,

An army on the march with its baggage train.
Henry V had to bring from England massive amounts
of weaponry, food and other essential supplies.

Cannons were
important weapons
used during sieges
such as Harfleur.

Henry V looked more like an athletic monk than a soldier.

John Holland brother of *Elizabeth Fiennes* – effigy with his first wife Anne

John Cornwaille also a Fiennes kinsman (with his wife, Henry V's aunt Elizabeth), was step-father to *John Holland* – both men were selected by Henry to lead a scouting party when the army arrived in France.

Bertrand du Guesclin, successor to *Robert Fiennes* as Constable of France.

Marshal Boucicaut, the legendary French leader, was captured at Agincourt and died a prisoner of the English.

St Crispin's Day, 25 October 1415: the Battle of Agincourt, at which the French and English *Fiennes* faced each other. From King Henry's point of view, Agincourt was merely the opening round of his bid to gain the throne of France, which he believed to be his God-given right.

This visored bascinet, made in Milan, was designed to deflect attack from virtually every direction. Helmets of this type almost certainly saw action at the Battle of Agincourt.

Gauntlets, also made in Milan.

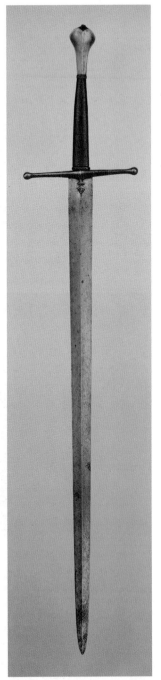

A two-handed sword, made of iron or steel and cord, 3ft 10in long, weighing nearly c. 6lb.

Henry ordered that every soldie[r] should wear the red cross of S[t] George in order to avoid confu[sion] sion in battle. The trumpeters (i[n] the background) announce the vit[al] commands during the battl[e].

Henry's troops, including his archers, were known for their skill and ferocity with short swords and daggers.

The spoils of victory – soldiers count their booty on the battlefield.

The murder of John the Fearless, Duke of Burgundy by
one of the dauphin's men, 1419. Henry V was able to
take advantage of the on-going civil war between the
Burgundians and Armagnacs.

The eight-year-old Henry VI of England is crowned King
of France in Paris, 1431. My ancestors *Lord Clinton*, *John
Holland* and *Roger* and *James Fiennes* were among those
who accompanied him from London.

Joan of Arc led the French army's relief of Orléans and
routed the English siege force.

In April 1450 the French won the battle at Formigny, and by August the only
remaining English-held town in Normandy was Calais.

Henry's archers loosed off enough arrows to dissuade the disorganised assembly, whose horses headed off in all directions, and thus the danger of renewed fighting evaporated.

At more or less the same time, news reached Henry that the attack from behind Maisoncelles by the Lord of Agincourt had merely targeted the royal baggage lines and had never been intended as a new battle front. In fact, three local barons, including Agincourt, had led a band of armed local peasants who had easily seen off Henry's few baggage guards and had carried off their plunder.

When news of the 'murder' of the unarmed noble prisoners spread through France, a witch-hunt followed to try to identify those responsible for forcing the English king into such an unchivalrous act. Strangely enough, most of the French chronicles blame, not Henry, but only those who forced him into a corner through their thoughtless actions.

The scapegoats, who were duly arrested and imprisoned, were the lords of Agincourt and of *Bournonville*, the descendants of my kinswoman, *Alice de Bournonville*, wife of *Conon de Fiennes*. Among the items stolen from the baggage train were the king's crown, a priceless jewel-encrusted cross, the state sword of England, and the Seals of the Chancery.

Once Henry's adviser and scouts confirmed that no further threat from the French existed, at least in the immediate future, and that the road ahead was, to all intents, open to Calais, a new search of the battlefield for wounded but revivable nobles ensued. For many of Henry's men this was what the fighting was all about – the ransom and the plunder.

A ransom market soon began as wealthy prisoners were identified. There were even ransom specialists like *John Cornwaille* who had developed their own contacts and agents for top-value prisoners, and within hours of the battle's end, *Cornwaille* and others were bargaining with each worthwhile prisoner's captor for immediate sales.

Meanwhile, the brothers *Roger* and *James Fiennes* and their brother-in-law *John Holland* had joined their ventinars to search among the several thousand bodies for absent members of their own 'lances'. Each searched the approximate area where they had fought.

Had tape recorders existed, there can have been no more heart-rending sound than the screams, groans, hymns, croaking prayers of confession and desperate cries for help from the dying. These were punctuated every so often by cries of sheer terror each time a battle scavenger prised open the visor of a soldier trapped under other steel-clad bodies, some with no wounds at all. Once sure that the owner of the visor was of no value, the battle scavenger would plunge his dagger into the eyeball or throat of his victim before quickly passing on to the next 'live' body.

There were those, sometimes trapped beneath three or more corpses, who had managed with a free arm to detach their helmet to avoid slow suffocation and who, upon seeing a man with a bloody poleaxe and a look of murderous intent approaching, would cry out that they were of noble blood and of great value; or simply that they were Christians and their killer would go to hell and be burned for ever. These 'carrot' or 'stick' entreaties both worked from time to time, while from the peripheries of every pile of corpses there crawled or limped desperate survivors heading for the cover of the nearby forest.

The chronicles state that many of those French knights who succeeded in reaching neighbouring French villages by way of the forest paths were murdered as soon as their surcoat escutcheons were noted as Armagnacs, because of the seething hatred in which they were held for the episodes of pillage, murder and mass rape that they had visited on the countryside north of Paris during the dauphin's campaigns against Burgundian lands.

The villagers of Maisoncelles, Tramecourt and Agincourt crawled vulture-like all over the battlefield. There were 10,000 French dead bodies to be looted and at least 600 English. Various chroniclers later cut these figures down to 3,000 French and a mere 200 English dead.

Lists of the known dead named over 1,400 French lords, knights and esquires, including *Robert Fiennes*, although my researches never unearthed whether *Robert* died in the Maisoncelles barn from which Gilbert Lannay was removed, or perhaps escaped to die later near by. Two other French *Fiennes* brothers who were killed in the battle were *Jean* and *Louis du Bois de Fiennes*, the sons of *Sohier du Bois de Fiennes* and *Lady Masie d'Azincourt*. A great many French, and especially Norman, dynasties, including our French line, were decimated at the battle, including families where five or six members covering two generations were wiped out.

Within twenty-four hours of the battle's end, the scavengers from the villages and many of Henry's soldiers, some of whom had carried on with their gruesome work through the night and in heavy rain, had stripped naked the living and the dead wherever good armour was to be had.

The nobility of France lay sprawled in the mud in a nightmare scenario, and, according to the chronicles, 'naked just like those newly born'. The Constable of the French army, Charles d'Albret, was found among the dead, and his great battle comrade, Marshal Boucicaut, was taken captive to England, as was the popular young Duke Charles d'Orléans, the nephew of the king.

The battle observers or heralds, French and English, like modern football referees, discussed the result of the battle and declared the English as official winners. After giving victory speeches and repeated statements that God, not he and his army, was responsible for the miraculous results, Henry slept the night in Maisoncelles.

The following day he ordered the English dead to be taken to a local barn to be burned along with any battle detritus deemed to be of possible use to the French but too heavy for his men to take to Calais. He ordered that the body of the Duke of York, the last of Edward III's grandsons and a large man, be boiled without delay and that his bones be then separated and sent back to his family in England.

Three days later Henry's victorious army camped at Guînes, some four miles past Fiennes on the road to Calais. That same day in the Fiennes family castle in the village of Tingry, the family were in mourning. *Constable Robert Fiennes* had died in the 1370s without a natural heir from either of his two late wives. *Robert*, his nephew, had, as a youth, been like a much favoured son to him. But *Robert* junior was now believed to have died at Agincourt and he, too, had no children. His cousins, the de Bournonvilles, came from a village halfway between Tingry and Fiennes and they inherited the castle and all the other estates of *Robert the Constable*.

Mahaut de Bournonville, named after her mother, *Mahaut de Fiennes*, now learned that her cousin *Robinet de Bournonville* was being blamed for the attack on the English baggage train at Maisoncelles, and thus for the killing of the French nobles, and that two of her brothers, Aléaume and Bertrand, were missing presumed dead. Two of her other cousins, Gaviot and Ingelram, were definitely known to have died at the battle and, by the testament of her father, *John de Bournonville*, the estates of the family would pass via the *St Pol* family to *Francoise, Dame de Fiennes*, and thereafter into the Luxembourg dynasty.

Mahaut invited Isabel d'Auxy, another cousin and long-time friend from the *Dampierre* family, to stay at the castle, for she was also in mourning. Six of her family had been killed in the battle. As the chronicler Pierre Cochon recorded: 'This was the ugliest and most wretched event that happened in France over the last one thousand years.'

But it was not the end of the Hundred Years War. From King Henry's point of view, Agincourt was merely the opening round of his bid to gain the throne of France, which he believed to be his God-given right. His current war chest funds were waning, so he would have to take his army back home, but he would be back to claim his French kingdom, given the two vital ingredients of the longbow and sufficient finances.

15

La Mort de Fiennes

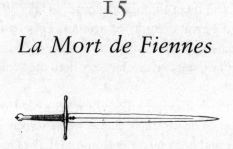

Henry's army followed the tracks north to Calais, their baggage carts jolting under the added weight of those soldiers too badly injured to walk. Behind them at the battle-field they left over 4,000 bodies stripped of their armour and in most cases of their identity too. All over northern France there would long be families who never learned the fate of their missing loved ones.

By far the greatest number of the dead had facial wounds that disfigured them even before their looks were altered by the rotting of their flesh, with the result that for months afterwards, if at all, families never knew whether their father or husband, brother or son was dead or perhaps a prisoner in England, where many died years later, their ransoms unpaid. One such, who Henry refused to release, was Marshal Boucicaut.

Quite why the English chose to kill with head rather than body wounds is not difficult to deduce, bearing in mind that the archers aimed at visors and that helmets came off their owners more easily than did their body armour.

One local eyewitness chronicler from a village close to Agincourt wrote: 'The King of England had 500 men well armed and sent them amongst the dead, to take off their coats of arms and a great quantity of armour. They had small axes in their hands and other weapons and they stabbed both the dead and the living in the face so that they might not be recognized.'

If the English had not killed those wounded who did not slowly bleed to death, their chances of survival would have in all likelihood been nil, at best minimal. Broken bones due to falls from horses, if only minor fractures were involved, could have been reset and splinted. However, skull fractures would have been untreatable, and deep arrow wounds were almost certain to cause fatal blood poisoning, not least because of bacteria on dirty underclothes beneath the body armour.

The finger of blame for the French failure at Agincourt would hover between the Armagnacs and the Burgundians down the centuries, and the brief truce in their dynastic struggle to defend France against a common enemy was soon cancelled. Each blamed the other for the debacle.

Because great numbers of horses had been taken from the English baggage train at Maisoncelles, many of those who had been mounted from Harfleur now had to walk, hungry and weary, with their crotches rubbed raw and their feet brutally blistered. The forty-five-mile journey took three days, and on the evening prior to reaching Calais, the victorious column passed through Fiennes Forest and directly beneath Mount Fiennes before camping in nearby Guînes.

Back at Agincourt during the week that followed the army's arrival at Calais, many relations and servants of those killed in the battle arrived to locate a specific corpse or corpses. Many who were identifiable, despite their missing armour and their facial wounds, were taken away for burial in their home churchyard until every plot was taken.

The majority of the dead, however, were left to rot or be pecked at by birds and gnawed at by dogs, wolves and rats until eventually three deep pits were dug and some 5,000 bodies were interred. Each pit was marked by a tall wooden cross.

Henry's royal party arrived at the walls of Calais to be met with a rapturous reception, especially from the English garrison and citizens, but nobody wanted several thousand hungry and potentially troublesome soldiers in their town, so only their leaders were allowed in. Too many past examples of looting and rape in many French towns by soldiers, usually French ones, were still fresh in the memory.

So the victors of Agincourt soon lost their post-battle sense of elation when, on reaching the walls of their long-sought destination, they found it to be far from friendly. The food, wine and women they longed for after so much hardship were not to be theirs, and life was just a sorry continuation of their hunger and suffering.

The ample quantities of food and wine that Henry had ordered from England for his army failed to arrive in time, so the men were forced to sell the prized loot that they had carried from the battlefield at rock-bottom prices to the town's canny merchants outside the walls. Likewise, many French prisoners were able to buy their freedom from their captors for far smaller ransoms than had they been taken to England.

Henry's ships arrived one by one in bad weather and, having taken soldiers on board with their prisoners, then made the return voyage in successive severe storms which, for many of them, took two or three weeks.

Henry realised that many of his men might still be hungry and desperate, so he extended their period of pay and gave each enough cash to pay ships' captains, when the ships duly arrived, to get themselves and their horses back home.

Of the thirty men that *Roger* and *James Fiennes* each took to France, only four of *Roger*'s and three of *James*'s failed to survive and return to farm life back in Sussex. *John Holland*, who had taken eighty men in his group, lost only eight. This was surprising since they had fought in the sector held by the Duke of York's squad and the duke had lost a quarter of his 370 men.

The insane King of France had lost seven of his nearest cousins, and King Henry's own stepmother, Queen Joan of Navarre, who attended the celebratory service held at St Paul's on Henry's return to London, must have had very mixed emotions as the victory music sounded. Although her stepson had clearly won a unique and unexpected victory, she learned that a huge toll of France's grandees had been killed. Among those magnates, and she had no way yet of knowing who had survived, were two of her own sons and two of her first cousins, all dukes.

Henry stayed in Calais long enough to arrange the ransoms of his royal prisoners and those who, out of chivalric regard to their word of honour, reported to him in Calais as promised following their capture and parole after the fall of Harfleur. While there he gave an audience to the three key fighters of his brother Humphrey of Gloucester's battle group at Agincourt, the brothers *Roger* and *James Fiennes* and *Roger*'s brother-in-law *John Holland*.

He awarded all three men honours that would make their fortunes. *Holland* became *Duke of Huntingdon, Roger* was given the custody of *Portchester Castle*, the gateway to Portsmouth harbour, for life and was promoted to senior captain of Henry's army. *James* was given the lordship of various estates in Normandy, including all those within the bailiwick of Rouen and Caux. Witness to this royal audience with the three men was the Captain of Calais, *Richard Beauchamp, the Earl of Warwick*, who was a third cousin of the Fiennes brothers.

The results of the battle gave a massive boost to the morale and European approval ratings of King Henry and his fighting machine.

Eighty years after Agincourt, an Italian visitor was recorded as saying: 'The English are great lovers of themselves . . . They think there are no other men than themselves and no other world but England. And when they see a handsome stranger they say that "he looks like an Englishman".'

A secretary wrote to the Venetian ambassador describing the English soldiery: 'They have a very high reputation in arms and from the great fear the French entertain of them, one must believe it to be justly acquired.'

Seventy years after Agincourt, the Italian Dominic Mancini wrote of English archers:

There are hardly any without a helmet, and none without bow and arrows; their bows and arrows are thicker and longer than those used by other nations, just as their bodies are stronger than other peoples', for they seem to have hands and arms of iron. The range of their bows is no less than that of our arbalests [crossbows]; there hangs by the side of each a sword no less long than ours, but heavy and thick as well. The sword is always accompanied by an iron shield . . . They do not wear any metal armour on their breast nor any other part of their body, except for the better sort who have breastplates and suits of armour.

Indeed, the common soldiery have more comfortable tunics that reach down below the loins and are stuffed with tow or some other material. They say that the softer the tunic the better do they withstand the blows of arrows and swords, and besides that in summer they are lighter and in the winter they are more serviceable than iron.

King Henry's own voyage home was marred by rough seas and, sailing at the same time, two of *John Cornwaille*'s ships were sunk with their cargo of soldiers, horses, prisoners and booty, never to be found.

Landing in a snowstorm at Dover, the royal group was greeted by the Archbishop of Canterbury and by the *Fiennes* brothers who were the sheriffs of Sussex and Kent.

A week later, Henry was welcomed to London by a great procession of the city's citizens and hugely elaborate festivities in honour of 'Henry the Fifth, King of England and France'. Everywhere he went, the king took behind him his chief prisoners, Charles d'Orléans, the Duke of Bourbon, and Marshal Boucicaut. The latter would die as a prisoner in England, and Charles d'Orléans was not released until 1440 when Henry's heir, officially the King of France, came of age.

The capture of Harfleur gave English sea captains and south coastal townsfolk some respite from predatory pirates and raids, and Agincourt enhanced England's reputation throughout Europe. But had Henry's expensive venture failed, as could so easily have happened (if, for instance, the French had raised the Harfleur siege, or they had prevented the English from crossing the Somme in their weary, hungry state), then Henry would have faced a very different reception back home. Had his army been massively defeated and his lines of retreat cut off, capture or death would have been inevitable. Those Southampton plotters who had escaped execution would then have been able to exonerate their dead co-plotters and proclaim that God, by punishing Henry, the Lancastrian usurper's son, had shown that He approved of their attempt to replace Henry with the *Earl of March* and his Yorkist heirs. Had this happened then and there, the disastrous civil war that was later to follow might well have been avoided. But then history is full of ifs and buts.

Henry V's key man in Parliament was his chancellor and uncle, Henry Beaufort, who had been his crucial supporter since he was merely Prince Hal. The fact that, for forty years, Henry's two royal predecessors, unlike him, had proved unpopular and ineffective certainly helped Beaufort raise the taxes so vital to Henry's ability to continue his war with France. But only on condition that the war was successful.

Henry was well aware of this fundamental rule that only successful tax-raising by a successful chancellor enables a warrior-king to wage successful campaigns and, in Henry's case, to achieve his overriding ambition to gain the crown of France.

In addition to praising Henry's initial Normandy successes, Beaufort stressed to Parliament that Henry was keeping his coronation promises at home to protect English trade, to preserve law and order, especially in the borderlands, to keep the peace between the magnates, and to avoid trouble with the Welsh, Scottish, and Irish. He had done well to date on all these counts.

In terms of suppressing heresy, which was necessary to keep the wealthy and influential Church faction on his side, Henry had done what he could to crush the ever lurking danger of Lollard resurgence. During his absence in France, the government had arrested and burned at the stake each and every Lollard foolish enough to announce their belief in the teachings of the martyr, Wycliffe. But the Lollard leader Sir John Oldcastle was still around and capable of sparking new uprisings, and, as such, he was Henry's only real and identifiably dangerous enemy at large on home territory.

Beaufort's task was to concentrate on raising a great deal of cash as quickly as possible to enable Henry to mount another attack on France while the shock of Agincourt was still sharp and the Burgundians were still at loggerheads with the Armagnacs. Unfortunately, the war effort had already cost the government dear, and Henry had pawned his crown and his royal jewels in order to underwrite the 1415 campaign. There was now a mountain of debt and the new, substantial ongoing cost of the upkeep of the Harfleur garrison, along with the provision of a sizeable navy to keep it supplied.

Nonetheless, thanks to the nation's post-battle atmosphere of triumphalism and Beaufort's successful PR campaigns, Parliament was unusually generous in imposing many imaginative tax-raising devices in order to pay off debts and provide funds, evidence of their wholehearted approval of Henry's aims to continue the war in France.

The Church, through the bishops' convocations, was also extremely generous to Henry's war chest, proclaiming its support for his French plans, which it depicted as the will of God with Henry acting as a mere instrument of God's aims to unite England and France under a single Christian king who could then conduct a more powerful war against the heathen.

This was spelled out in the clerical chronicle *Gesta Henrici Quinti* as: 'And may God of His most merciful goodness grant that, just as our king, under His protection and by His judgement in respect of the enemies of his crown, has already triumphed twice, so may he triumph yet a third time, to the end that the two Swords, the sword of the French and the sword of England, may return to the rightful government of a single ruler, cease from their own destruction, and turn as soon as possible against the unsubdued and bloody faces of the heathen.'

Henry put *John Holland* in charge of the navy, and *Roger Fiennes*, as custodian of Portchester Castle, was ordered to build up the harbour defences at Portsmouth, then as now the home port for the Royal Navy.

Despite Henry's precautions, the French carried out successful raids on both Southampton and Portland in the summer of 1416, and it took *John Holland* a further year and a major sea battle at the mouth of the Seine before Henry could feel that his merchant navy was truly safe in the Channel. *John*'s naval 'commando force' consisted of 350 men-at-arms and 700 archers.

Apart from honouring the likes of *Cornwaille*, *Holland*

and the *Fiennes* brothers, Henry also made sure that his gratitude to all those who had made his French victories possible was duly acknowledged. To this end he announced three new public holidays to honour three major Welsh saints as a thank you to all the Welsh archers whose skills had ensured victory.

On the French side, King Charles VI was increasingly prone to spells of insanity, and his eighteen-year-old son Louis, the dauphin, was not prepared to lead an army of those Armagnac forces not killed at Agincourt against Henry or against the Harfleur garrison because the greatest threat to his position as heir-apparent came not from the English, but from John the Fearless, Duke of Burgundy.

The duke, for his part, even though his two brothers had died at Agincourt, was not interested in vengeance, for his focus was fixed on the French throne. So a mere twenty-seven days after the battle he set out with his army to attack Paris, in the knowledge that Henry had eliminated most of the upper ranks of the Armagnac military leaders.

The young dauphin, sheltering in Paris, sent an urgent message for help to a highly capable military leader and royal magnate who had survived Agincourt, Count Bernard of Armagnac. The count responded at once, but fate beat him to it, for the dauphin died that week, to be succeeded by his seventeen-year-old brother, Jean, who happened to be of Burgundian sympathies and was married to the sister of John the Fearless. This sudden death resulted in John of Burgundy halting his advance on Paris while he tested the water to see if the new dauphin would kowtow to him, in which case a military attack on Paris might be unnecessary. This delay gave Bernard of Armagnac time to reach Paris and, as John of Burgundy was soon to discover, Bernard was to prove just as ruthless and capable as he was.

Henry found this highly reassuring. The semi-cessation of the French civil war, which allowed both factions to send forces to combat the English, was definitely over and Henry could, therefore, continue to play one side off against the other in his own ongoing plans to acquire the French throne.

By the early summer of 1417, Henry's newly expanded navy, a prerequisite of any successful French campaign, had gathered under *John Holland* in Southampton. *Holland*'s first move was to attack a French fleet of Genoese warships based in Honfleur at the western mouth of the Seine and almost opposite Harfleur. The ensuing naval battle confirmed the efficiency of the English navy and, soon afterwards, Henry landed his army of some 10,000 men, including both *Fiennes* brothers as divisional leaders and many other veterans of Agincourt, unopposed at the coastal port of Touques. His first aim was the conquest of Normandy.

Rather than choosing the obvious strategy of basing himself in Harfleur and thence heading south on the eastern side of the Seine to attack Rouen and then Paris, Henry decided to move south on the western side of the river and besiege the second most important city after Rouen, that of Caen some ten miles inland. He sent his brother, the Duke of Clarence, who had done well at the siege of Harfleur, to lead this siege.

Luck favoured Clarence because the patriotic French monks in Caen's great abbey, built by Henry's ancestor, William the Conqueror, decided to obstruct the siege by destroying their own abbey. One monk, who secretly objected to this plan, crept out of the city walls by night some two weeks after the start of the siege and bumped into none other than the Duke of Clarence sleeping in a garden. He begged the duke to assault the city walls speedily in order to halt his brother monks' arson plans. He could advise Clarence, he said, how and when it would be best to attack a poorly protected section of the city's defences.

Clarence reacted with speed and took Caen a few days later. Henry, by the chivalric code of the day, could have put all the inhabitants to the sword, since they had chosen to hold the city against him rather than yield at once. But, in pursuance of his doctrine that he was already King of France and therefore the inmates of Caen were his citizens and not the enemy, he harmed nobody and only exiled those citizens who openly rejected his claims to rule Normandy.

In writing this book as a devotee of Anglo-Norman history but not as a qualified historian, I have needed to check with great care the historical facts as recorded by modern military historians. This has not always been straightforward and the aftermath of the siege of Caen is an example of this problem.

Ian Mortimer's '*1415, Henry V's Year of Glory*' states: '*and such acts paved the way for grosser acts of cruelty in later years. In 1417 at Caen, he (Henry) gave orders for 1,800 men to be slaughtered in cold blood.*'

Ian Mortimer has BA and PhD degrees in history from Exeter University and an MA in Archive Studies from University College London.

Compare the description of the same event published some five years later by Professor Christopher Allmand, Professor of Medieval History at Liverpool University: '*The lesson must be that whilst acceptance of Henry's rule would be rewarded, opposition would be punished both by expulsion and by the loss of property confiscated for rebellion against him. Yet Henry was also acting with mercy . . . Caen had refused to surrender and its population was liable to such penalties. By the custom of his day, Henry was acting with considerable restraint in expelling only part of the population from the recently captured town.'*

In one book I consulted Henry had 1,800 people executed. In another he expelled a few from their homes and is considered relatively merciful. Wherever I have come across discrepancies of this nature, I have gone for the more proven version.

At the same time as Henry was besieging Caen, John the Fearless gained full control of the area north of Paris and east of the Seine, thereby locking up the Armagnac forces of the dauphin and preventing them from interfering with the English campaign to the west of the Seine.

Henry knew that he could never trust John and the Burgundians unless he was in some way helping the latter's anti-Armagnac struggle.

In May 1417 the Burgundian army took Paris, and a bloody series of executions of Armagnac leaders followed. The dauphin, Charles, escaped but, with the king mad and in Burgundian hands, John was now, to all intents and purposes, King of France. So, his unofficial alliance with Henry, whose aim was to be acknowledged as the true King of France, made no sort of sense.

However, while the dauphin's armies continued to lurk south of Paris and south of the great River Loire, it paid Henry to ignore Paris and eastern France, just as it suited John, at least for a while, to let Henry continue his thrust into southern Normandy, so long as the English kept to the west of the Seine and away from Paris. Nonetheless, it must

have been obvious to all three contenders for the throne of
France and the subsidiary Duchy of Normandy that no alliance between any two of them would be likely to last.

With a goodly part of northern Normandy now under his
control, Henry pressed on south towards the great city of
Rouen, the capital of Normandy. The walls of Pont de l'Arche,
close to the key confluence of the Seine and the Eure rivers,
confronted him, for he would need to cross the Seine at this
point in order to surround Rouen, which was situated on
the other bank.

In the 1960s in the British army during the Cold War, I
travelled the entire length of many French and German rivers
by canoe and participated in planned river crossings with our
sixty-ton tanks. Some rivers were a great deal easier than
others and, even today, I marvel at the enterprise of Henry
and his engineers in managing to get his entire army, complete
with heavy cannons and massive siege catapults, over the wide
and powerful stretch of the Seine at Pont de l'Arche.

John Cornwaille, who was partly in charge of the crossing
plans, took a bet with the incredulous French garrison
commander of Pont de l'Arche that once the town surrendered the crossing was feasible. He won the bet, but even he
must have had his doubts.

From the siege of Harfleur onwards the inhabitants of
Rouen were aware that Henry, in order to regain Normandy
from the French, must take their city. So they were well
prepared. Each citizen was required to keep a stock of food
sufficient for at least ten months' survival.

By the time Henry's army reached the city, all wooden
houses had been burned and all usable suburban shelters
destroyed where their proximity to the main city walls would

allow the English to observe and fire over the walls. And a thorough scorched-earth policy had been applied to all the surrounding countryside. This was, however, rendered fairly ineffective since the English controlled the river traffic on the Seine and so could be easily resupplied by waterway from Southampton.

The various English army leaders, including the royal dukes of Beaufort, Clarence and Gloucester and my kinsmen *Holland*, *Cornwaille*, *Beauchamp of Calais* and both *Fiennes* brothers, set up their armed camps around the city in readiness for a siege that Henry reckoned would last six months.

There were over 400,000 Rouen inhabitants in addition to the armed garrison, and over the following months many sallies in strength of armed groups issued out of the city gates without warning. So the siege forces had to be permanently on the alert.

Inside the walls the conditions slowly worsened as the months ticked by. All living animals and birds were consumed, and the cost of a cat or a rat became too much for even moderately poor folk, and many starved to death. The citizens hoped that a French army would, sooner or later, drive the English away. But neither the Burgundians from Paris nor the Armagnacs from the Loire ever appeared, so ten months after the siege began, desperate citizens started to seek dialogue with Henry.

To make supplies last longer, the garrison commanders forced the old and the poor and the sick in their thousands to leave the city, assuming that the English would have to feed them. But Henry did not let these human wrecks through his lines and they died in the no-man's-land at the foot of the walls of their own city. Henry was emphasising that the garrison's only option was death or surrender, and in mid-January 1419 Rouen at last opened the city gates to the English.

Immediately after the fall of Rouen, *Roger Fiennes* led the siege of Caudebec and accepted its surrender in Henry's name. He was made Bailli of Caux and Captain of Longueville, and he only returned to England alongside the king in 1421.

The *Fiennes* brothers continued to reap great financial rewards for their loyal service to Henry. He never forgot to repay his supporters or to execute those who betrayed him. An example of this, two years after Agincourt, was the eventual capture of the chief of the Lollards, Sir John Oldcastle. During Henry's days as Prince Hal, Oldcastle had been a close friend and co-fighter throughout the years of the Welsh wars. But, following his capture, Henry did not hesitate to order his death by burning at the stake.

Although on the face of it everything seemed rosy for Henry at the outset of 1419, he was aware that his takeover of Normandy, never mind of all France, was extremely slow. Rouen alone had taken the attentions of his entire army for some ten months. Back home he could not count on Parliament's continued generosity with tax-originated revenue to pay for never-ending war. And, to his south, along the west–east obstacle of the River Loire, the main army of the dauphin was being strengthened by Henry's old enemy, the Scots. He knew that he must speed up his overall campaign of conquest, and clever diplomacy might well prove to be the best way forward, especially marital diplomacy used as a means of leapfrogging the royal claims of both the dauphinists and the duplicitous Burgundians. Such a plan involved Henry marrying King Charles's daughter Katherine, and through her securing the throne of France on Charles's death. With this in mind, Henry sent his most able diplomats to Paris.

Meanwhile, he had an army of some 10,000 men in France, with at least a quarter of them kept pretty idle in garrisoning the ever growing number of Norman cities that fell to his successful sieges.

Increasingly important for an army working abroad were the attached specialists, and these included stone workers fashioning cannon balls from the Caen quarries, two dozen surgeons including two who dealt in 'nose problems', miners to help undermine city walls, armourers to repair plate armour and mail and fletchers to help speed up the great quantity of arrows needed after each engagement. Sulphur and cannon-balls were gradually becoming the key ammunition stores as siege-work took over from pitched battles. Nonetheless, historians have worked out that the number of arrows purchased by the king between 1418 and 1422, the key years of his French successes, was just under one and a half million.

Cooks, carpenters, musicians, grooms, priests and account-ants were all needed too. Coopers worked round the clock mending the wheels of heavily laden supply carts, and 5,000 horses were kept busy resupplying the army, its field outposts and the garrisons. As also were Henry's ordnance ships between Southampton and various stops along the Seine.

The French, for a year or so after Agincourt, organised raids on the south coast of England, especially on Southampton and Portsmouth where Henry kept his navy. *James Fiennes* was again ordered to bolster the defences of Portsmouth harbour, a job that kept him from full-time service with the army in France.

During the first few months of 1419 even the most difficult cities had fallen to Henry's army and the whole of Normandy was under its control. Now for the rest of France.

In May Henry's diplomats arranged a key meeting in the town of Pontoise, less than twenty miles north of Paris, between King Henry, the dauphin and John the Fearless. This meeting would hopefully seal a treaty for peace, marriage between Henry and Katherine, and the crown of France in due course for Henry. However, not only did this meeting fail to produce any agreement, but in July the Burgundians and the dauphin's followers agreed to cooperate against the English. Together, they agreed, they could throw Henry and his men right out of France.

When Henry learned of this he knew that he could never trust either group and that his diplomatic efforts must be backed up by a show of force. So, less than a fortnight after the truce between his enemies, Henry launched a surprise night attack, a pincer movement under the command of a Gascon noble and my kinsman *John Holland* which, despite the fact that *Holland* temporarily lost the way to the target castle of Pontoise, was a resounding success. The castle had long been under Burgundian control and was key to the control of the Vexin, the region just north of Paris.

Henry followed up this masterstroke with a speedy march led by the Duke of Clarence that brought the English army to the very gates of Paris within a month of the Burgundian–dauphinist proposal for a truce. The two French factions decided to meet in order to agree how they would jointly vanquish the English. This meeting took place south of Paris in mid-September, and the leaders met in the middle of a bridge, so little did they trust one another.

Exact details of what happened when the two leaders met are disputed, but the result was the murder of John the Fearless by one of the dauphin's men.

This horrendous royal murder had a direct effect on the succession chances of the three pretenders to the throne of King Charles VI. The Duke of Burgundy's son Philip was young, inexperienced and, luckily for Henry, ineffective. The dauphin Charles had, because of the murder of John the Fearless, which he witnessed even if he did not actually plan it, utterly disgraced himself in front of his nation. So King Henry was able to take immediate advantage of the ensuing French disarray. He was already in possession of much of northern France, he had as great a logical and legal claim to the throne as did, say, William of Normandy to the English throne when he invaded Britain, and he had a number of trump cards up his sleeve to please each of the other players.

The Treaty of Troyes that followed on 21 May 1420 was attended by the King of France, his daughter Katherine, Duke Philip of Burgundy and, on the English side, the king's brother and war leader, the Duke of Clarence, war heroes *Holland*, *Cornwaille*, *Beauchamp* and the *Fiennes* brothers. Henry's loyal uncle and chancellor, the Duke of Exeter, key to so much of Henry's ongoing approval ratings back in England, was there, as were all this favoured group a week later at the marriage of Henry to Katherine, who was eighteen years old.

Following the Treaty of Brétigny some sixty years before, the Treaty of Troyes was a highlight of the Hundred Years War, as seen from an English viewpoint. Katherine of France was now Queen of England and Henry of England was regent of France while the insane King Charles VI still lived. On his death, Henry and his heirs for ever were to be kings of France, and this was agreed by Charles VI himself when in a lucid spell.

A neat side agreement was that Henry, already the Duke of Normandy, would return that province to France once he was crowned king in Paris.

To the Burgundians the treaty meant that, although their duke would not rule France, nor would their hated enemy the exiled dauphin Charles.

To the dauphinists, their leader was the rightful monarch and, from their base to the south of the Loire, they would fight Henry until the English were thrown out of France.

16

Another Fiennes loses his head for losing the War

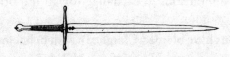

Henry's honeymoon was spent besieging castles on the Seine to the south of Paris. Then, leaving his brother John, Duke of Bedford, as regent of France, his brother Humphrey, Duke of Gloucester, in command of his army, Henry returned to England. He had last been there three long years ago and his absence had clearly not worked against him as news of his ongoing victories, along with the level-headed regency of his uncle Henry Beaufort, had kept him popular.

The current heir to the throne, Henry's brother Thomas, Duke of Clarence, was as busy as ever seeing military glory against the dauphin's forces. Hearing that the latter had gathered a sizeable army at the city of Baugé to the north of the River Loire, Clarence marched south hoping for a decisive victory.

Instead, in April 1421, Clarence found himself outmanoeuvred, cut off and facing a well-disciplined dauphin-led army, reinforced by a powerful Scottish force under the Earl of Buchan. Bold and impulsive as ever, and ignoring the advice of *John Cornwaille*, Clarence attacked the French without even waiting for his rearguard, including his longbow contingent, to catch up. The result was a disaster for the English with many of their best leaders, including Clarence, killed. The *Fiennes* brothers and *John Cornwaille* escaped with their lives, but *John Holland* was captured and imprisoned for the next three years until his stepfather, *Cornwaille*, managed to pay off his ransom in exchange for an important French count.

Historians have blamed Clarence's rash behaviour at Baugé on an inferiority complex, from which he was said to have suffered since birth, exacerbated by his absence from Henry's army on the battlefield at Agincourt – that 'band of brothers' that included most of his peers and comrades-in-arms.

Clarence's second-in-command, the Earl of Salisbury, who took over on Clarence's death, saved the remnants of Clarence's force from further upsets after the Baugé debacle, but the dauphinists' morale was considerably boosted by their first great victory over the English.

So important was the part played at Baugé by the powerful Scottish contingent that the dauphin took the unique step of appointing the Earl of Buchan as Constable of the French army. The late constable, *Robert Fiennes*, would no doubt have turned in his grave at this news.

In England Henry worked hard to counter the sense of disillusion and pessimism engendered by the Baugé disaster. Well aware that his ongoing debts were frighteningly large and that to demand greater taxes from Parliament would cause considerable dissent, Henry made do with private loans from known supporters. It did not help that the weather in England (as in all Europe) that year had produced a very hot, dry summer followed by a long, cold winter, with resulting pandemics and widespread hunger.

The good news in June 1421 was that Queen Katherine was pregnant. Henry appointed his highly effective brother, Duke John of Bedford, as regent in England and rushed back to France with his other brother, Humphrey of Gloucester, his army commander, backed up by my kinsman *Richard Beauchamp, Earl of Warwick*, and the redoubtable Salisbury.

A dangerous outcome of Baugé was that the Duke of Brittany, whose long-term treaty with Henry had provided a safe zone on Normandy's western flank, now made a new treaty with the dauphin and was, thereafter, a potential threat to the English.

As a teenager I studied French at a hostel in Blois on the River Loire and I spent many happy hours visiting the great castles along that river, which I canoed from its source to the sea. The great castle of Orléans is situated on the river's most northerly bend, and Henry arrived there with his army in September to find it so heavily defended that he withdrew back to the north as his resupply lines were too dangerously extended for a lengthy siege.

Back in Paris, he agreed with his ally Philip of Burgundy to besiege the dauphinist stronghold of Meaux, close to Paris and on the River Marne near to its confluence with the Seine. The defences of Meaux, making clever use of the river and a wide canal, rendered the city exceptionally difficult to besiege. Its garrison commander, known as the Bastard of Vaurus, was infamous for his dogged and ruthless nature. He had recruited his garrison from a motley band of soldiers who had good reason to hate and fear the English, and were thus unlikely to surrender at any cost. They included a substantial number of Scots as well as English and Irish army deserters.

Henry's army surrounded Meaux in October 1421 and, as with Rouen, took six long months to achieve the garrison's surrender. Flooding, enemy attacks on English foraging groups, disease, hunger and desertion were not helped by the ever diminishing support for the war, both in Burgundian France and back in England. At some point during the siege Henry himself fell sick. And his old friend, the Agincourt hero *John Cornwaille*, was badly wounded when his son, standing beside him, was killed by a chance cannonball strike.

Morale, at this depressing time, was greatly improved by news from Windsor Castle that Queen Katherine had given birth to a baby boy named Henry after his father. William the Conqueror was King of England and Duke of Normandy. Henry VI was born to be King of England and of all France. . . *Touché*.

The royal birth occurred in the nick of time, for Henry died, probably of dysentery, just eight months later in August 1422 on his way to help Philip of Burgundy attack a dauphinist castle on the Loire. Alert to the end, Henry rewrote his will, appointing the elder of his surviving brothers, John, Duke of Bedford, as regent of France alongside Duke Philip of Burgundy, and his brother Humphrey, Duke of Gloucester, as regent of England and guardian of the young prince. His uncles Henry and Thomas Beaufort, as well as my kinsman *Richard Beauchamp, Duke of Warwick*, were to oversee the young Prince Henry's education.

Only six weeks after Henry's death, King Charles VI died and, although the Treaty of Troyes, signed by both kings, clearly stated that the baby Henry VI of England was now the King of France, the majority of Frenchmen, including Normans, naturally felt that the dauphin Charles, despite his involvement with the murder of John the Fearless of Burgundy, should be their king rather than an Englishman.

So the dauphin set up an alternative kingdom of France based in Bourges and called himself King Charles VII, while English France was ruled with efficiency by the Duke of Bedford as regent with the Earl of Salisbury as his military commander.

In England, a Royal Council led by Bedford and Gloucester ruled Britain on behalf of the baby Prince Henry. His father had died at an inopportune moment, putting all his hard-won French territories at risk. His successor would have an uphill battle to maintain his gains.

From the start the rather ambiguous powers that Henry left to his brothers, Bedford and Gloucester, caused bitter dissent from and among other English magnates who, sitting on the Royal Council, soon gnawed away, with the assistance of Parliament, at the royal dukes' authority. Although the councillors were largely men of considerable experience and high standing, they, like many a coalition government before and since, soon became riven with rivalries and tensions that would in time prove disastrous to England's well-being at home and its ambitions in France.

My kinsmen from Henry V's reign were all at some point key members of the council or of the royal household during Prince Henry's minority. *Lord John Clinton*, a veteran warrior and councillor, was, like *Roger Fiennes* (the treasurer of the royal household), a direct descendant of the late Geoffrey Lord Saye and Lord Dacre (the two titles were intertwined). *Roger Fiennes*'s old Agincourt friends, his brother-in-law *John*

Holland, Duke of Exeter (when not in a French prison), and John's stepfather *John Cornwaille*, were also key councillors, as was their cousin *the Earl of Warwick*, the ex-Constable of Calais.

At this early stage of the regency, *Roger Fiennes* used his eminent position to support his beloved younger brother *James* who, like him, had done extremely well out of their heroics at Agincourt and during the late Henry's subsequent French victories. This fraternal patronage enabled *James* to establish a network of men with local power and influence in the Fiennes's home county of Kent.

By 1432 *James* had become Justice of the Peace in Kent, a position he was to hold until his untimely and gruesome end. Four years later, again with *Roger*'s help, *James* was elevated to the position of Sheriff of Kent, and in 1438 he became the Member of Parliament for Kent as well as Sheriff of Sussex and Surrey. He rose rapidly through the ranks of local society and to a position of power and influence at court.

In 1440 *Roger* handed over to *James* the impressive Hever Castle with much appended land and associated offices. As a quid pro quo, while serving as Sheriff of Sussex, *James* then returned brother *Roger* to Parliament. The sky would soon be the brothers' limit.

Roger showed his appreciation of his connection with his wife Elizabeth's brother, the *Duke of Exeter*, by officially mingling the Fiennes and Holland coats of arms.

Over the long years of Prince Henry's minority, the Bedford, Gloucester and Beaufort factions fought each other with increasing bitterness over various matters of policy. The young prince was naturally upset by the bad atmosphere between his three closest male relatives and often begged them to be friends. But the late Henry V's uncle, Henry Beaufort, whose influence as an éminence grise and senior statesman was powerful within the council, grew to hate Gloucester to the point where each man tried to arrest the other for treason. There were various reasons for the triangular power-play of the three royal cousins, but the ongoing war in France and the taxes involved were the main causes of disagreement.

Gloucester was heart and soul in favour of Henry V's dream of the dual rule of France and England by his son, as was, at least initially, Bedford, but Beaufort and, increasingly as the years passed, the prince himself were for peace even if this meant losing part or all of France.

When Bedford was doing a spell as regent in France, Gloucester's influence back in England naturally increased, as did his influence over the prince. And when Gloucester was away fighting the French, the opposite was true. At times over these regency years, Bedford acted as peacemaker between Beaufort and Gloucester, but never for long.

By way of increasing his support for his peaceful overtures to France, Beaufort enlisted the Pope's approval, and he was promoted from bishop (of Winchester) to cardinal.

John Holland, following the disastrous Battle of Baugé in 1421, had been kept a prisoner in France for three years, at which point his stepfather, *John Cornwaille*, arranged his ransom in exchange for that of the Count of Vendôme, and he returned to his old life as Gloucester's greatest supporter, both fighting under his command in France and in the Royal Council power struggles in Westminster.

For the first two years after Henry V's death, Bedford and his experienced field commanders oversaw a successful series of sieges in Normandy, including that of Crotoy Castle at the mouth of the Somme, a victory that helped to keep the allegiance of the Duke of Brittany. To cement his alliance with Philip of Burgundy, Bedford married his sister.

In August 1424 the first pitched battle for a long while involved Bedford's main army clashing at Verneuil on the Normandy/Maine border with the dauphin's forces supported by some 6,000 Scottish soldiers. At least 10,000 French and Scottish bodies were counted at the end of the day, which many historians reckon to be the zenith of English successes in the Hundred Years War.

Whereas Bedford's marriage to Duke Philip's sister helped the Anglo-Burgundian alliance, the subsequent marriage of Gloucester to the Duchess of Hainault and Gloucester's subsequent interference into Hainault affairs had the opposite effect of intensely annoying Duke Philip, as Duke Philip was the Duchess's heir.

By 1425, Bedford's armies in France were well commanded by my kinsman *Warwick* to the east of Normandy, by Lord Salisbury to the south and to the west by the Duke of Suffolk, a close friend and patron of *James Fiennes*.

Between their periods of French campaigning, the various magnates and knights returned to their English estates and, usually escorted by liveried groups of retainers, went to London to participate in the Royal Council and, when appropriate, Parliamentary sessions.

Travelling along country roads without an armed escort was not a good idea at that time, for crime throughout the kingdom was endemic and involved the higher echelons of society as much as the lower. Much of the crime was neighbour-on-neighbour, one group of retainers against another, and with some magnates hiring armed groups to attack coveted property, or even to kidnap and ransom the members or staff of some other landowner with whom a property dispute had escalated into a feud.

Serious offenders included my two kinsmen and Agincourt heroes, *John Holland* and *John Cornwaille* (aka *Lord Fanhope*). The former pursued a long legal battle against the Duke of Norfolk, and on one occasion carried on a bitter argument against the Earl of Stafford in Parliament after both men had arrived there with bands of heavily armed retainers. A special Parliamentary Bill was introduced as a direct result of this incident forbidding a magnate's servants from carrying a weapon in Westminster's precinct while Parliament was in session.

Cornwaille hated his neighbour Lord Grey to the point of disrupting the peace with a public affray, as was also the case in an ongoing feud between my kinsman *Richard Beauchamp* and the Duke of Norfolk.

As a consequence the Duke of Gloucester made *Holland*, *Beauchamp* and *Cornwaille* swear an oath that they would take any dispute in which they or their families became involved to the council.

Lord John Talbot, ex-Lord of Ireland and a senior general of Henry V in France, was about to become England's military supremo, but that did not stop him flouting the law in his native Herefordshire, the crime centre of England at the time. In one feud with the Beauchamp family, Talbot's brother was killed and the Duke of Bedford had to intervene personally to prevent a major family conflict.

Welsh and Irish immigrants were blamed for much of the trouble in the cities, and in 1422 it was decreed in Parliament that all Irishmen must leave England within six weeks unless they had visible means of support and a trade.

Prisons throughout the realm were full to bursting and warders had become afraid of their own prisoners, especially in the Tower of London.

The Lollard movement continued to be dealt with by the execution, preferably at the stake, of any known and prac- tising heretic. A brief attempt by various regional Lollard groups to stage a popular uprising in 1431 was quickly crushed by the Duke of Gloucester.

If examples of how not to behave are set by a nation's leaders, then the Protector Gloucester and the Chancellor Beaufort were showing the way, for relations between them grew increasingly strained to the point where their personal supporters, fully armed, faced off against each other at either end of Southwark Bridge in London. A massacre was luckily prevented by the cool head of the mayor, but high-level tensions between these two royal cousins, who to all intents and purposes fulfilled the role of the monarch throughout Prince Henry's minority, were to plague the nation for over a decade. When Bedford was back in England from 'the other kingdom' he was usually able to cool the tempers of his feisty relations and, in 1426, when the prince begged the two to be friends, 'they shook hands in token of their mutual love and accorde'.

This togetherness act was only skin-deep and the contin- uing discord between the two men was often in danger of paralysing the government that they were meant to head. Fortunately, there were enough influential and experienced magnates in the Royal Council to block the factions of both Beaufort and Gloucester from forming and directing policies without the council's general approval.

By 1428 Bedford's French regency had proved successful and Normandy was helping considerably to underwrite the costs of maintaining his armies there, so he and his senior generals, including Lord Salisbury, the architect of many victories during the post-Henry V years, agreed that the time was ripe to advance south into the Loire valley and to confront the self-proclaimed King Charles VII of France and his Franco-Scottish army. So in June 1428 Salisbury led a major expeditionary force with a mountain of supplies and siege weapons down to the city of Orléans on the River Loire.

No great excitement occurred to begin with and most of the English soldiers involved had already experienced the monotony of many city sieges over the last half-dozen years. The difference with Orléans came in the surprising shape of a pretty young girl dressed in shining armour who led the French army's relief of Orléans and routed the English siege force, many of whom, including Lord Salisbury, were killed in the battle and subsequent withdrawal. This was followed two months later by another humiliating defeat at the Battle of Pataye, again at the hands of a French army buoyed up by the divinely inspired and almost magical presence of Joan of Arc, a teenage peasant girl from eastern France who told of heavenly voices that had assured her of the defeat of the English at Orléans and of the subsequent coronation of Charles VII at Reims.

Joan's remarkable effect on the dauphin's previously ineffective forces can be explained by a number of factors that came together at the time, and although Orléans and Pataye were indeed the first English setbacks since the disastrous Battle of Baugé, they were not the decisive turning point in the Hundred Years War any more than was Agincourt.

Men were and are, when about to fight for their lives, inclined to heed superstitions and omens more than usual. This was as true in the First World War, when many British soldiers believed themselves watched over by the Angel of Mons, as at Pataye when they were greatly in awe of this new French guardian angel who infused such a great new fighting spirit into the soldiers that she personally led into battle. She clearly believed that her mission to get rid of the English was divinely inspired – just as Henry V had the same God-driven aim to rule France.

French soldiers were also far more inclined to follow her patriotism, which stood for the glory of all France and not merely for one faction. On top of all this and every bit as important in making an impact on the military results of the day was the recent sacking of generals who had originally been selected merely because they were court favourites and their replacement with professional veterans of the calibre of the late *Constable Robert Fiennes.*

Having fulfilled her two promises to Charles VII to relieve Orléans and have him crowned at Reims, a happy Joan told him that she had now done all that her 'voices' required of her and she was off back home. But Charles would have none of this and kept her at the forefront of his ongoing military campaign. The result was her capture the following year by a Burgundian force who sold her to the English. They, in turn, sensibly handed her over to a jury of ardent French Catholics in Rouen, who promptly denounced her as a witch and burned her at the stake.

The French knight Raoul de Gaucourt, who had held Harfleur against Henry V for so long and was thereafter kept a prisoner in England for many years, gave evidence in 1455 (by which time he was eighty-five years old) that enabled the Pope officially to reverse the witchcraft judgement on Joan.

To offset the political impact of Charles VII's coronation, the Duke of Bedford decided that the eight-year-old Prince Henry should be officially crowned in England and then in France. *Lord Clinton*, *John Holland* and the *Fiennes* brothers accompanied the coronation party to Paris, as did the prince's mother, Queen Katherine.

The hoped-for political benefits of young Henry's Paris coronation were, unfortunately, negligible, and this was rubbed in for poor Bedford when, only three days prior to the ceremony, the Duke of Burgundy concluded a truce with King Charles VII to last for six years. Bedford became utterly disillusioned with the whole business, especially when, soon afterwards, his wife Anne, the Duke of Burgundy's sister, died. Six months later he married again, this time to the Duchess of Luxembourg whose family was deeply distrusted by the Burgundians. As the English situation in France gradually deteriorated, it became apparent that the Burgundians were likely to turn against their former allies at any minute.

Differences of opinion between Beaufort, Bedford and Gloucester continued to prevent a well-thought-out military plan, territory continued to be lost to the French and in 1435 an attempt, at the Congress of Arras, to broker a truce only worsened the situation when the Duke of Burgundy did finally cement an alliance with Charles VII. The congress envoys on both sides failed to find a way to a compromise from their long-entrenched positions, and witnesses at Arras wrote of both the English and the French that 'their pride was only equalled by their obstinacy'. Soon after this futile attempt to achieve peace and a status quo, England's main representative in France, the Duke of Bedford, died. The Burgundian army, reported at the time to be 60,000 strong, then attacked Calais but made a complete mess of their siege and were seen off even before the arrival of a relief force under the Duke of Gloucester.

John Holland was made Admiral of England with the task of defending both Calais against further Burgundian attacks and the English south coast from French raids. These had again become likely since the French had retaken many Norman ports including Harfleur.

At this point in the Hundred Years War, with Bedford dead and his other two guardians, Gloucester and Beaufort, well past their prime, young Prince Henry was beginning to listen to other long-term and close members of the royal household, in particular *Roger* and *James Fiennes* and their patron, the Duke of Suffolk, all three of whom had sound reputations as French war veterans and were loyal supporters of the prince.

Henry was the third and last Lancastrian King of England. He was the only English king ever to be the rightful King of France, he was the youngest monarch ever to be crowned King of England and his reign lasted thirty-nine years. Sadly for him, he is remembered (with Shakespeare's help) largely because he lost all the French gains of his famous warrior-king father.

Aged sixteen, the prince declared that his own minority should end. He was ready to be king. His upbringing, like his father's, had stressed standard Christian beliefs alongside the divine right of kings. But whereas his father had translated his divine duties as being the conquest of France, the prince saw the ongoing struggle between the two nations as one of unnecessary bloodshed between Christians and cousins. He wished to end the long war by finding some acceptable peace treaty with his cousin King Charles VII, but after Bedford's death the war policies of the Duke of Gloucester were popular and for the next decade English and French armies continued to engage in conflicts like a series of chess games where neither side gained a conclusive victory.

In 1436 the French retook Paris, but great English generals, like John Talbot and my kinsman *Richard Beauchamp, Duke of Warwick*, continued to win or win back castles and cities elsewhere. Talbot's successor in 1439 was the Duke of Somerset who, having spent the previous seventeen years in a French prison following his capture at the Battle of Baugé, was certainly not a leader of tried and tested experience.

Set against the powerful Gloucester faction in the Royal Council who, ever loyal to the memory of Henry V, were determined to fight on in France, the Duke of Suffolk and the Fiennes brothers did all they could to help Henry bring the war to an end.

The formal head of the royal household after 1436 was the Duke of Suffolk, and the crucial financial post of treasurer, who controlled the king's military expenditure, was, from 1439, in the hands of *Roger Fiennes* with the intimate support of his hyper-ambitious brother *James* and his own two sons.

Roger, unlike *James*, was an honest, selfless servant of the king, but in 1441 he told Parliament of his inability to honour the royal household's mounting debts. That year he handed over his stewardship of the Duchy of Lancaster to Suffolk himself. That same year he was joined in the royal household by his old army friend from Agincourt days, *John Cornwaille*, who was his brother-in-law's stepfather (and the king's great-uncle).

Henry expressed his newly won authority by rewarding and patronising those men with whom he had grown up and who had protected him in his household. So *Roger* and *James* benefitted hugely. Henry's uncle Gloucester, on the other hand, because of his long years of royal bickering within the household and his bossiness towards young Henry, was gradually removed from his position of supreme influence. Nor did it help Gloucester when his second wife, Lady Eleanor Cobham, was a victim of vicious and un-attributable rumours accusing her of witchcraft and of plotting to kill the king.

Henry clearly believed that, due to his own ongoing attempts to limit Gloucester's influence, Eleanor was out for revenge. So Gloucester was powerless to protect Eleanor who was placed under a series of house arrests for the rest of her days and her marriage to Gloucester was annulled. Since Henry had no heir and Bedford was dead, Gloucester was next in line, and any child of Eleanor's would inherit the throne. So it is not hard to find a reason why *Fiennes* and Suffolk might invent sorcery rumours about Eleanor, knowing that Henry feared the powerful effects of witchcraft, as apparently proven by the successes of Joan of Arc. Indeed, Henry's step-grandmother Joan of Navarre, the widow of Henry IV, had in 1419 been falsely accused by Henry V of witchcraft and of plotting against him. He later forgave her, but Henry VI showed no such mercy and Eleanor was to die, still imprisoned, in 1453.

Gloucester's long-time adversary at court, Cardinal Beaufort, grown old and still detesting Gloucester, had handed his baton to the Suffolk/*Fiennes* clique who were determined to see Gloucester finished off, one way or another, and along with his demise, they hoped, would come the end of the Hundred Years War.

From his minority days, Henry had shown a keen interest in educational facilities in his country and, once monarch, he commissioned *James Fiennes* with the foundation and development of Eton College and of King's College, Cambridge, the two projects that provoked his enthusiasm above all else.

In future years when *James* was to become an object of national hatred, Shakespeare had him addressed in *Henry VI* with the words 'Thou hast most traitorously corrupted the youth of the realm in erecting a grammar school.' So much for Eton! To this day the original accounts for the building works at Eton can be viewed there. The very first such account is inscribed: 'To my right worshipful . . . and especal good master *James Fenys* squier for the King's body.'

In the early 1440s *James* acquired estates all over Kent, including the administration of all lands in Kent belonging to the Archbishop of Canterbury, who was quoted as telling his prior, 'havying consyderacion how the seid *James Fiennes* standing aboute the Kyng as he dooth, may dayly proufyte our church and us'. *James*'s influence at court also earned him retaining fees from a future contender for the throne, Richard, Duke of York, and from his own famous cousin, the *Duke of Warwick*.

Because his brother *Roger* owned the finest fortified manor in Sussex, Herstmonceux Castle, *James* was determined to build himself a home of equivalent acclaim. And in 1445, by which time he was the greatest landowner in Kent, he began the building of Knole Manor, near Sevenoaks, while he was still living in the nearby village of Seal. He later, when made a lord, chose as his title *Lord Saye and Sele*, and the *lordship of Dacre* was also his.

At this time, and without the involvement of his brother, *James* got together a group of local minor and would-be magnates who, through misuse of local bureaucracy intimidation and corruption, became a powerful mafia in much of Kent. *James* did not always get away with his chicanery and land speculation unnoticed. On one occasion, jurors on a royal commission charged that, at Kemsing, he had forced a prominent landowner to make an unprofitable exchange of property and had then kept both estates. And, after purchasing a substantial group of estates in the Romney Marsh area, he had the rightful heir arrested and coerced into sealing a release for the property.

Already the Constable of Rochester Castle, *James* was, in 1447, made Constable of Dover Castle and Warden of the Cinque Ports at a time when south coast towns were under considerable threat from French raiders and, at one point, from Burgundian invasion.

As part of *James*'s and Suffolk's plan to counter Gloucester's 'hang on to our French territory' policy, they supported a French-approved offer of marriage to Henry with a relatively minor French princess, the fifteen-year-old Margaret of Anjou, whose aunt was Queen of France. The only positive outcome of this marriage from the English point of view would be a two-year truce with France in return for yielding their claims on certain French provinces.

Gloucester was naturally fiercely opposed to the whole deal, and a considerable number of magnates backed him.

This confirmed to the Suffolk-*Fiennes* clique that the duke would finally have to be dealt with.

Their plan was to accuse him of treason on the grounds that some of his supporters had recently attempted to release his 'sorceress' wife Eleanor from prison, and that he, Gloucester, the heir to the throne, planned to have the king murdered. With Gloucester out of the way, Suffolk could then safely follow up the king's policy for peace with France without meaningful opposition.

Late in February 1447 Gloucester was duly arrested and charged with treason. The extreme shock of his arrest and imprisonment was responsible, according to his gaolers, for the mood of acute depression into which he sank. Four days later, from no known causes, he was found dead in the house of his imprisonment. Foul play was suspected and the fingers of guilt all pointed at Suffolk, *Fiennes* and their close ally, Bishop Aiscough, a royal councillor and the king's confessor.

According to the *English Chronicle* of 1460, Gloucester fell victim to a long-maturing conspiracy headed by Suffolk and *Fiennes (Lord Saye)* who, realising that the duke's behaviour stopped short of providing a basis for any judicial charge against him, resorted to malicious slander. Suffolk, *Saye* and Aiscough were undoubtedly at the centre of this conspiracy, and when, three years later, the Commons formulated their petition against Suffolk in 1450, they declared him to be the 'cause and laborer of the arrest, emprisonying and final destruction of the most noble, valiant, true Prince youre right obeisant uncle the Duke of Gloucestre'.

The Commons accusers, before arresting Suffolk and *Fiennes*, worked out that they had managed to persuade

Henry that his uncle was about to raise the Welsh in rebellion against him, a treasonable offence if true. The Commons were also aware that the conspirators' real reason for having Gloucester done away with was his ongoing and determined opposition to their policy of peace-at-any-price in France.

James, whether rightly or wrongly, was ever thereafter believed to have been directly implicated in Gloucester's death, even though they had served together at Agincourt and elsewhere. *James* certainly profited personally from it, since the very day after Gloucester's death, the Chancery received warrants signed by the king approving *Fiennes*'s petition for offices held by the late duke, and some weeks later he was appointed chamberlain of the royal household, which gave him control over access to the king. That summer he was elevated to Constable of the Tower of London during the minority of the Duke of Exeter whose father, his old friend *John Holland*, had just died. *James* was now second only to Suffolk as the most influential (and unpopular) of the king's advisers.

Not content with a mere knighthood, *James* sought a barony, and the king was happy to oblige. Inherited titles being more classy than the self-made variety, James found a roundabout way to obtain one. By a special writ on 3 March 1447 at a parliamentary session, 'after consideration of his eminent services performed beyond the seas as in this realm of England, advanced to the degree and dignity of a baron of this realm by the title of *Lord Saye and Sele* and to the heirs male of his body'. *James* selected the Saye bit of his grandiose new title from the family name of his ancestors, whose heiress, *Joan de Saye*, was his grandmother.

Henry's senior army general, *Sir John Clinton*, had a better claim to the title of *Lord Saye* but, being hard up at the time, agreed to sell it to *James*. So nobody, not even *James*'s elder brother *Roger*, could argue that James had not 'inherited' his title. *Roger* himself retired from his position as treasurer of the royal household in 1448 due to ill health, and he died two years later.

James, by 1449 when the war in France was still ticking along quite well for the English, thanks largely to the brilliant leadership of John Talbot, reached the pinnacle of his power through his appointment as treasurer of England, the man responsible for fuelling the army with its lifeblood funding.

In the autumn of that year the French army began to notch up an increasing number of successes, for their artillery technology, under cannon designer Jean Bureau, had improved alarmingly, rendering even the strongest English-held fortifications easy meat.

As I discovered when researching my book *Mad Dogs and Englishmen*, when the French captured the key town of Pontoise, they slaughtered 500 English soldiers in the garrison and ransomed their commander, *John Fiennes, the sixth Lord Clinton*, who had married *Elizabeth Fiennes*, the granddaughter of that *Roger Fiennes* who was treasurer of the royal household. Like his father before him, this *Clinton* styled himself as *Lord Saye*. But the exorbitant ransom that *John Clinton* had to pay to escape the clutches of the French (twice, because he was later recaptured!) crippled his finances and, to retrieve his fortunes, he sold the title of *Lord Saye* to the *Fiennes* family, where it had rightly belonged since one of the *William Fiennes*es of Herstmonceux had married *Joan de Saye* almost a century before.

Charles VII's main army, having advanced with comparative ease through much of Normandy, was about to lay siege to

Calais, so Henry, greatly alarmed and despite his desire for peace, put together a substantial new force under the command of *Roger Fiennes, Lord Saye* and another court favourite, Lord Rivers, all three being army veterans of many years. Nowadays it is difficult to imagine the likes of Chancellors Alistair Darling or George Osborne being sent off to Afghanistan in charge of a task force, and, as it turned out, no such counter-attack force was in fact ever mounted. Calais, nonetheless, survived as an English redoubt in France longer than any other town.

The financial demands of the long decades of war and the huge resulting debts culminated in 1449 with virtual bank-ruptcy, and so it was a bad time to be treasurer. Nevertheless there were many warrior-magnates who continued to dream of reversing recent defeats and regaining the glory days, just as there were a great many unhappy veteran soldiers returning from their stints in France and ready to voice their disgruntle-ment by blaming those who had failed them through lack of funding for their efforts and their sacrifices. Henry VI and his ministers had, in their opinion, shamefully betrayed Henry V.

Most of these veterans, on their return to home soil, landed in Kent and there spewed forth the bitterness of their feel-ings. And not only was the soldiery distressed at the turn of events in France, for popular resentment at the losses there was widely felt, as indeed was alarm, for many folk, espe-cially those in southern coastal towns, felt apprehension at the likelihood of invasion.

This was not all. In a world already ravaged by the Black Death, there had followed outbreaks of plague, killer famines, wet summers, sheep epidemics and poor wool prices. Private armies of disbanded soldiers, most, but not all, led by local barons, bullied and wrecked local economies.

Matters came to a head in January 1450 when public disapproval of the government focused on Suffolk who was specifically blamed for the marriage of the king to Margaret of Anjou, thereby causing the loss of the hard-won lands of Maine and Anjou. The Royal Council reacted out of self-protection by condemning Suffolk for treason because of the loss of Maine. Some of the other key council members had been increasingly aware that Suffolk was monopolising the king and thereby destroying the reality of a genuine collective council.

So Suffolk's rise to power was quickly terminated. The king, ever loyal to his favourites, managed to reduce Suffolk's punishment from execution to five years' banishment, but so hated was the duke that, en route to his exile in Burgundy, his ship was intercepted off Dover by a privateer manned by an anonymous 'group of sailors' with the dedicated aim of murdering him. After trial by a kangaroo court, the duke was put in a small boat and beheaded with a rusty sword by a sailor from Bosham on the Sussex coast. His body was left on a beach near Dover.

In June 1450 a great crowd from all over Kent came together at the town of Sevenoaks ready to march on London in order to confront the king and his hated ministers, especially *Lord Saye*.

History describes the murderers of Suffolk and their ringmasters' ensuing rebellion as the Peasants' Revolt. But they were from all parts of society and their leader, who called himself John Mortimer, was certainly no peasant. Because of a curious set of coincidences, I need to look at the background of Mortimer (or Jack Cade, as history knows him) before looking at his rebellion.

Documents that my cousin *Nat Fiennes* (twenty-first *Lord*

Saye and Sele) lent me in 2008 from the attics of Broughton Castle indicate a sub-plot behind Cade's killing of *James Fiennes*, which powerfully suggests a family feud between a group of *Fiennes* and *Dacre* cousins and their powerful kinsman, *Lord Saye*. Cade had worked for and lived with *Thomas Dacre Fiennes*. *James Fiennes*'s nephew *Richard*, who inherited Herstmonceux Castle from his father *Roger*, had married *Joan*, the heiress of the *Dacre* family, and hence the link between the two families.

Returning to the chaotic scenario in London in the summer of 1450, the loss of its French territory and ports was causing England, a country reliant on continental trade, lost markets and ever increasing levels of taxation. Since it was widely known that the king was weak, the target of popular wrath was the powerful and unpopular Suffolk/*Saye* faction that dominated the government.

While Cade was still rabble-rousing in Kent in May after Suffolk's murder, in which he may or may not have been implicated, news of his growing menace reached the king and his council and they recognised that Suffolk's exile had clearly not sufficed to assuage public anger. So Suffolk's two main allies, *Lord Saye* and Bishop Aiscough, were arrested with the full connivance of the king who, like the rest of his household, was desperate to find suitable scapegoats to save himself. *James Fiennes* was shut up in the Tower on the king's order 'dredying the malice of the peple'. The king then fled the city, leaving its defence in the hands of the mayor.

This abandonment of London by the cowed monarch of course encouraged Cade's men from Kent (and other rebels from Essex) to enter the city, which they did by way of

London Bridge on 3 July, disabling the bridge's hoist-system so that it could not be closed behind them. *James Fiennes* was dragged from the Tower along with twenty others, all of whom were condemned to death there and then.

James appealed for a proper trial by his peers, which only served to infuriate Cade. He was, however, allowed to confess to a priest before his execution, and according to the records he confessed to involvement in the murder of the Duke of Gloucester. It was also stated by his confessor 'that of all the thynges that ever he dyde in his life, this was moost in his consciens' (which referred to his acquisition by corrupt practices of his Romney Marsh estates). The Cade mob composed a 'dyrge made by the comons of Kent in the tyme of their rysynge', which ran:

> So pore a kyng was never seene
> Nor richere lordes alle bydene;
> The communes may no more.
> The lorde Say biddeth hold hem downe,
> That worthy dastarde of renowne,
> He techithe a fals lore.

In better prose, Shakespeare quotes Cade as telling *Saye*:

Thou hast most traitorously corrupted the youth of the realm in erecting a grammar school: and whereas, before, our forefathers had no other books but the score and the tally, thou has caused printing to be used; and, contrary to the king, his crown and dignity, thou hast built a paper-mill. It will be proved to thy face that thou hast men about thee that usually talk of a noun and a verb, and such abominable words as no Christian ear can endure to hear. Thou hast appointed justices of peace, to call poor men before them about matters they were not able to answer. Moreover, thou hast put them in prison; and because they could not read, thou hast hanged them; when, indeed, only for that cause they have been most worthy to live.

Shakespeare replies for *James Fiennes* with the words:

> I sold not Maine, I lost not Normandy;
> Yet, to recover them, would lose my life.
> Justice with favour have I always done;
> Prayers and tears have moved me, gifts could never.
> When have I aught exacted at your hands,
> But to maintain the king, the realm and you? . . .
> Have I affected wealth or honour?
> Are my chests fill'd up with extorted gold?
> Is my apparel sumptuous to behold?
> Whom have I injured, that ye seek my death?
> These hands are free from guiltless blood-shedding,
> This breast from harbouring foul deceitful thoughts.
> O, let me live!

At the Guildhall trial *James* was accused of murder. The record states that he 'knowlachyd of the dethe of that notabylle and famos prynce the Duke of Glouceter. The Bury Parliament 'was maad [set up] only for to sle the noble duke of Gloucestre, whoz deth the fals duke of Suffolk . . . and ser Jamez Fynez lord *Say* . . . hadde longe tyme conspired and ymagyned.'

Cade's mob dragged *James* on foot to Cheapside where

they hacked off his head even before his confessor could forgive him the sins of his confession. His head was then impaled on a long pike and paraded in front of Cade.

At Mile End, James's son-in-law, William Cromer, the much hated Sheriff of Kent, was also decapitated, his head mounted on another spear and the mob then 'made both hedes kisse to gider'. *James*'s body was stripped, tied to a horse's tail and dragged naked, 'so that the flesh clave to the stones all the way from Chepe to Southwark'. Then the heads were put on to spikes and the bodies hanged and quartered.

The opinion of many military historians, both at the time of *Saye*'s death and in the twentieth century, has been that, between them, Suffolk and *Saye* produced the peace policy that pleased their king but finally lost England the Hundred Years War. As a royal councillor, *Saye* was seen as synonymous with and symptomatic of 'the poor leadership that was considered responsible for the military failures in France and the surrender of Maine'.

A year after *Saye*'s death, Jack Cade was hunted down and killed by Alex Iden, the successor as Sheriff of Kent to the man executed alongside Saye, William Cromer (whose widow married Iden!).

My great to the power of thirty grandfather, *Count Eustace II of Boulogne*, who commanded the army of William the Conqueror, advised William, in the midst of the Battle of Hastings, to retreat to the ships because the English appeared to be winning. William ignored him, carried on the fight and the Normans successfully invaded England. Thus began the set of events that led to the Hundred Years War, including the great Battle of Agincourt. *Eustace*'s direct descendant, *James Fiennes*, that 'dastarde of renoune' and my great to the power of eighteen grandfather, helped end that same war 384 years later.

By the early 1440s, long before Henry VI's mad spells began, English military abilities and the state of their French colonies were already in slow decline. By the early 1450s, when Henry lost his capacity to rule for long periods, that decline had become irreversible. The ruling clique's desire for peace and less tax at all costs had become paramount, the very policy espoused by Suffolk and *Saye* and implemented by *Saye* in his key months at the treasury before his execution.

Even back in the mid-1430s, before the death of Bedford and serious military setbacks in Normandy and Gascony, Henry had made clear that his views on the English monarchs ruling France were the opposite to those of his father. His deeply felt religious beliefs demanded that he try to halt the death, destruction and suffering caused by this war between Christians. Not to mention the huge financial strains involved.

When Henry's great war commander in France, *Richard Beauchamp, Earl of Warwick*, died in 1439, Henry replaced him with the inexperienced Earl of Somerset. His period at the helm soon revealed his disastrous incompetence, and in 1444 he committed suicide.

In 1445 the successful murder, organised, it was generally believed, by Suffolk and *Saye*, of Gloucester, the chief opponent to the king's peace plans, opened the way for Henry to sponsor a final peace treaty with the French and to hand back to them the province of Maine. Various half-hopeful truces were, indeed, being arranged when, in 1449, a long-time ally of the English, a Spanish mercenary knight, attacked and held the wealthy Breton town of Fougères, and this precipitated a series of successful French attacks on castles and towns all over Normandy, at which point France declared open war on the English. The English garrisons of towns hard won over the past two years often surrendered without resistance. Others, including Harfleur and Rouen, received too little support to last out for long.

In April 1450 at Formigny the French won their first major pitched battle against a British army for many years, and by August the only remaining English-held town in Normandy was Calais.

Three years later and following the hard-fought battle of Castillon, the last of Henry's southern French territories also fell. The death there of John Talbot, the greatest of all Henry's generals, signalled the unofficial end of the Hundred Years War.

If only that bastard, William the Conqueror, had listened to my cousin *Eustace*'s advice and had retreated back to his ships, none of what followed need have happened.

Postscript

The area of northern France where the Battle of Agincourt took place is still a landscape of wide fields and big skies. You can visit the battlefield on your own or there are guided tours. There's no mighty monument to the English or French who died. While researching this book I was hoping to find descendants of the French Fiennes who fought at Agincourt, but sadly all my efforts were in vain. Clearly that branch of the family suffered the fate of so many others whose ancestors lie beneath what is still a field ploughed each autumn.

Since 2004 a history festival has been held each year in the nearby village, but the organisers had to move it from October to July 'due to the inclement weather and the heavy local clay soil'. Plus ça change . . .

Appendix

The Arming Of An English Man-At-Arms, c.1415

By Tobias Capwell, Curator of
Arms and Armour, The Wallace Collection

A full armour for war was usually referred to as a 'field' armour, or sometimes a 'hosting harness', but was never called a 'suit of armour'. 'Armour' is most usually a singular noun (plural – 'armours'). 'Suit of armour' is analogous to 'suit of suit', i.e. meaningless.

There is a fair amount of very good evidence that many among the higher English nobility had their armour made by the masters of the London armourers' company (today the Worshipful Company of Armourers and Brasiers). There is good documentary evidence for the London masters supplying high-ranking nobles for the Agincourt campaign in particular. Lower quality, 'off the peg' armour was often purchased in large amounts for archers and lower-ranking men-at-arms from Italian merchants, since the English armourers were few in number and could never manufacture en masse. Instead, English craftsmen seem to have focused on the fine quality, 'bespoke' market – Savile Row vs. Marks and Spencer . . .

A full armour of the early fifteenth century was a complex

system, with many different parts which had to be put on in exactly the right way and in the correct order. The arming process was carried out as follows:

1) Undergarments: first a linen shirt and braies were put on next to the skin. Then closely tailored stockings of wool (hosen) and over them, tough leather arming shoes. The arming doublet, a closely fitted foundation garment on to which the plate armour is attached, was usually made of fustian (a fabric combining a linen warp and silk weft, or some similar combination of materials) and lined with silk or linen.

2) Mail was still an essential element of the knight's armour in *c.* 1415. This ingenious form of armour, a sort of metal fabric made of interlocking steel or iron links, was a stout but flexible form of armour and provided good protection against bladed weapons. It should never be called 'chain mail'. The word mail or maille derives from the Latin *macula*, meaning 'web' or 'net'. On an English armour of this period the mail configuration was very distinctive. Small pieces of mail were worn on the front of the ankles to cover the gap between sabaton and greave. Patches of mail, or gussets, are often worn on the backs of the knees, covering vulnerable but necessary gaps in the plate armour. A mail skirt or paunce helps protect the groin and hips, especially the juncture between the leg armour and the cuirass skirts. On the arms the English knight might wear either full mail sleeves, or a combination of voiders, protecting the underarms, and the separate gussets to protect the inner elbows. The neck was protected by a mail collar or pisan, also sometimes called a standard.

3) Plate armour – in arming order:

- Sabatons; articulated covers for the arming shoes. Sabatons do not hamper one's movement or footing. English sabatons are especially well designed to continue functioning even when clogged with mud, pebbles, etc.

- Greaves, encasing the lower legs.

- Cuisses, incorporating solid thigh plates front and back, and articulated poleyns or knee defences.

- Cuirass skirt or paunce of plate, a set of hoop-like plates forming an articulated defence for the lower torso, from the level of the bladder to the naval, in general terms. The English wear the cuirass skirt as a separate assembly – it is not attached to the cuirass.

- Cuirass, or upper body armour, composed in the period of a one-piece breastplate with attached plates for the back, which could take various forms. The most common in *c.*1415 was probably a sort of 'saloon-doors' arrangement. The sides of the breastplate, under the arms, carried hinges, to which was affixed on each side a rear plate which swung round the back to buckle on to its facing partner, usually down the middle of the back.

- Arm defences, which in this period were composed of plates for the lower arm (vambrace); elbow (couter); upper arm (rerebrace) and shoulder (spaudler or 'paltron'). All of these sections were permanently attached to each other, so that the whole arm and shoulder went on as a single element.

- Besagews, circular or ovoid plates laced or buckled on to the mail at the front of shoulder, designed to increase frontal protection without impeding mobility. English knights of this period sometimes painted their personal arms on the besagews, at a time when many English were electing not to wear a heraldic surcoat or 'coat armour', to instead show off their polished 'white armour'.

- Gauntlets, composed of a short flared cuff, solid metacarpal plate, and articulated finger and thumb assemblies. The English especially favoured gilded or copper alloy 'knoklys', or knuckle plates, sometimes raised into pointed gadlings. The original brass knuckles . . .

- Helmet, usually one of two forms. The older, tried-and-tested bascinet with mail aventail was still commonly worn throughout the reign of Henry V. This tall, pointed helmet gave excellent protection against downward blows, while the heavy, densely woven mail of the aventail, spreading down over the neck and shoulders, provided flexible and yet still quite robust protection, even against arrows and crossbow bolts. It was however vulnerable to spear thrusts, and by the early fifteenth century throat wounds were clearly becoming a major problem. In response, the great bascinet was developed, which took the same bascinet skull, and added large, solid neck plates to it, front and rear. Essentially, the mail aventail was replaced with one of the solid plates. Mail was still worn under the great bascinet, however, in the form of a long-mantled pisan.

Both helmet types could be worn with a visor, either the pointed, snouted type which has been popular since *c.*1375, or the more up-to-date rounded or globose form. Knights sometimes elected to fight without a visor, referring the increased vision, ventilation and communication over protection, but many were more cautious. One of the primary accounts specifically states that Henry V himself wore a visor at Agincourt, but of what form, we cannot know.

Sir John Cornwaille in armour of the type worn at Agincourt.

Jean, Sire d'Aumont, a French knight who fought at
Agincourt.

Acknowledgements

I am extremely grateful to Danny Smith (USA) for his prodigious and meticulous research work over many years into the genealogy of our early Fiennes/Boulogne ancestors. Also for the patience of my family Louise, Elizabeth and Alexander. Also for the hard work and diligence of Jill Firman for producing everything on time as always. Also for the ongoing support of Rupert Lancaster and his great staff at Hodder & Stoughton and that of Ed Victor and Maggie Phillips. Thanks also to Nicola Tallis (for all her careful and dedicated work into the genealogy of everybody in the Fiennes family mentioned throughout the book), Charlie Campbell and Bridget Clifford, Keeper of the Tower Armouries at the Tower of London.

Members of the Fiennes family who have been extremely kind in checking family tree details are Nat and Mariette Fiennes (Lord & Lady Saye & Sele), Martin Fiennes, Nick Fiennes, Elizabeth Randall. Thanks also to Aude de la Conté, Geoffrey Cardozo and Julia Korner.

I am indebted to Dr Tobias Capwell at the Wallace Collection in London for all his superb advice on arms and armour of the period, and for granting permission to include his article as an appendix.

Bibliography

AGINCOURT: The King, the Campaign, the Battle by Juliet Barker, published by Abacus 2006

THE PERFECT KING: The Life of Edward III, Father of the English Nation by Ian Mortimer, published by Vintage Books 2008

THE FEARS OF HENRY IV: The Life of England's Self-Made King by Ian Mortimer, published by Vintage Books 2008

1415: Henry V's Year of Glory by Ian Mortimer, published by Vintage Books 2010

HENRY V by Christopher Allmand, published by Yale University Press 1997

A BRIEF HISTORY OF THE VIKINGS: The Last Pagans or the First Modern Europeans by Jonathan Clements, published by Running Press 2008

THE LIFE AND TIMES OF EDWARD II by Caroline Bingham, published by Book Club Associates 1973

THE LIFE AND TIMES OF EDWARD III by Paul Johnson, published by Book Club Associates 1973

THE LIFE AND TIMES OF HENRY V by Peter Earle, published by Book Club Associates 1972

THE LIFE AND TIMES OF EDWARD IV by Gila Falkus, published by George Weidenfeld & Nicholson and Book Club Associates 1981

LONGBOW: A Social and Military History by Robert Hardy, published by Haynes Publishing 2012

A GREAT AND TERRIBLE KING by Marc Morris, published by Windmill Books 2009

THE FACE OF BATTLE by John Keegan, published by Pimlico 2004

EDWARD II by Mary Saaler, published by The Rubicon Press 1997

Picture Credits

Index

Acre 33, 34–5, 50
Adelof of Boulogne,
  Count 6
Agincourt, Battle of 6, 121,
  213–15, 217–34
  arrival of troops at area
    of 189–90
  England's reputation
    enhanced by 241,
    242–3
  French numbers involved
    in 201
  Henry V at 5, 190–98,
    204–5, 210–15, 218,
    221, 226–30, 234,
    237–8, 295
  Henry's army see Henry
    V's army
  map of Henry V's route
    to Agincourt 138
  map of troop positions
    before 216
  meeting of heralds
    212–13

mercenary English
  archers fighting for
  French 205
numbers killed 233
preparations for 192–6,
  210–12
treatment of French dead
  and dying 232, 233,
  237–9
Agincourt, Ysambart d'
  (Lord of Agincourt) 231
Agnes de Dammartin, later
  Agnes de Fiennes 35, 47,
  202
Aire, Jean d' 82
Aiscough, Bishop 275, 280
Albigensians 45
Albret, Charles d' 161, 174,
  180, 182–3, 186–7, 189,
  196–7, 198, 199, 200, 201,
  205, 212, 213, 218, 220,
  233–4
Alfred the Great 9
Allmand, Christopher 248–9

American Bill of Rights 40

Andres, Andrieu d' 82

Anglo-Saxons 9, 11, 12, 13, 20, 29, 39

women 13

Ango-Norman war 6

Anjou 15, 27, 89, 279

Anne of Bohemia 97, 99

Anne of Burgundy 269

Anselm of Canterbury 61

Antoine, Duke of Brabant 226

Appellants 98–100, 101

Aqueche, Gobin 77

Aquitaine 3, 27, 31, 36, 74, 89, 213

archers *see* longbows/ archers

Ardres, Lord of 196, 202, 207

Ardres, siege of 92

Armagnac–Burgundian Civil War 112–14, 121–2, 147, 206, 246–7, 249

and the French failure at Agincourt 219–20, 238

armour, English (c. 1415) 291–7

Arras, Congress of 269–70

Arundel, Richard FitzAlan, 11th Earl of 98, 99

Arundel, Thomas, Archbishop of Canterbury, and Chancellor 112, 113, 114

Auxy, Guilbert d' 186

Auxy, Isabel d' 235

Auxy, Philippe d', Lord of Dampierre 186, 207

Baibars 49

Baldwin I of Jerusalem 23

Balliol, John de 56

Barons' War, Second 45–6

Batisford, Elizabeth, later Elizabeth Fiennes 93

Baugé, Battle of 257–8

Bayeux Tapestry 10

Beauchamp, Maud, later Maud de Saye 76

Beauchamp, Richard, Earl of Warwick 120, 137, 241, 255, 259, 260, 262, 264, 265, 271, 273, 284

Beauchamp, Thomas, Earl of Warwick 76, 77, 98, 99

Beauchamp family 266

Beaufort, Henry 112, 115–16, 243–4, 257, 260, 262–3, 266–7, 269, 272–3

Beaufort, John 115–16

Beaufort, Thomas, Duke of
    Exeter 112, 115–16,
    119–20, 255, 260
Beaumont, Jean 205
Bedford, John of Lancaster,
    Duke of 257, 259, 260,
    261, 262–4, 265, 269, 270
Belgae 7
Bensell, Mr 143
Berkeley Castle 67
Bernard, Sir John 228
Bernard of Armagnac 246–7
Berwick 56
Black Death 85–7, 90, 96
Blanche de Brienne 47
Blanchetaque, Battle of
    77–8, 80
Blanchetaque ford 77–8,
    177, 180, 182–3
Bohun, Eleanor 74
Bohun, Henry de, Bishop of
    Hereford 36, 40
Bohun, Humphrey de (son
    of Bishop Henry) 36
Bohun, Humphrey (VI) de,
    3rd Earl of Hereford and
    Essex, Constable of
    England 47, 52
Bohun, Humphrey (VII)
    de, 4th Earl of Hereford
    59, 63

Bohun, Mary, later Mary
    Bohun, Queen 74
Bohun, Maud de, née
    Fiennes (daughter of
    Ingelram de Fiennes)
    47, 74
Bohun, Maud de, née
    Fiennes (daughter of
    William de Fiennes) 36
Bolingbroke, Henry *see*
    Henry IV
Bonet, Honoré 87
Boniface of Savoy 42
Bordeaux 41, 43, 54–5, 87
Born, Bertrand de 117
Boroughbridge, Battle of
    64, 66
Boucicaut, Geoffrey de 223
Boucicaut, Jean II Le
    Maingre, Marshall 174,
    182–3, 186, 189, 196–7,
    198, 199, 201, 205, 220,
    223, 226, 234, 237, 242
Bouillon, Godfrey de 1,
    22–3, 32
Boulogne 7, 12, 15, 25–6,
    80, 135
    Counts of 6, 8–9, 10,
    16, 20, 23, 27, 92, 202,
    283
Boulonnais 7–8

Bourbons 30
  John I, Duke of Bourbon
    242
Bourges, Treaty of 114
Bournonville, Aléaume de
  235
Bournonville, Alice de 231
Bournonville, Bertrand de
  196, 235
Bournonville, Gaviot de 235
Bournonville, Ingelram I de
  122
Bournonville, Ingelram II de
  207, 235
Bournonville, John de 235
Bournonville, Mahaut de
  235
Brabant, Antoine, Duke of
  226
Bradmore, John 110
Brétigny, Treaty of 89, 90
Brinton, Thomas 86
Brittany, John VI, Duke of
  200, 259, 264
Brittany 15, 84, 207
Broughton Castle 2, 100,
  191, 280
Bruce, Robert 57, 58
Brussels 1
bubonic plague 85–7, 90,
  96

Buchan, John Stewart, Earl
  of 257, 258
Bureau, Jean 277
Burgundian–Armagnac
  Civil War *see*
  Armagnac–Burgundian
  Civil War
Burgundy, Anne of 269
Burgundy, John, Duke of
  see John the Fearless,
  Duke of Burgundy
Burgundy, Philip III, the
  Good, Duke of 255, 260,
  264, 269–70
Burley, Simon 98, 99
Burnell, Robert 54

Caboche, Simon 121
Cade (page of James
  Fiennes) 208
Cade, Jack (John Mortimer)
  279–83
Caen 247–9
Caesar, Julius 7
Calais 80–84, 89, 92,
  99–100, 106, 135, 239–40,
  270, 278, 285
Cambridge, Richard of
  Conisburgh, 3rd Earl of
  135
Cameron, David 2

Camoys, Thomas, 1st Baron
209, 210
Canute, King 9
Capet, Hugh 30
Capetian dynasty 30–31, 40
Capwell, Tobias, on English
armour 291–5
Cardiff Castle 24
Carew, Lord Thomas 120
Carolingian Empire 7, 30
Castillon, Battle of 285
Caudebec, siege of 252
Channel Islands 74
Charlemagne 6
Charles V of France
90, 92
Charles VI of France 99,
105–6, 112, 114, 121–2,
127–8, 147, 200, 203, 240,
246, 255, 256
death 260, 261
Charles VII of France 261,
267, 268, 269, 271, 277–8
as dauphin 249, 254,
255, 256, 257
Charles of Anjou 49
Charles, Duke of Orléans
189, 196, 226, 234, 242
Chaucer, Geoffrey 87, 97
chevauchée 87, 88
Cheyne, John 164

chivalry 122, 163–4, 176,
203, 240, 248
Christianity
Lollardy and the Church
124–5, 152–3, 244
and William the
Conqueror 19
Chronicle of England 114
Churchill, Winston 46
Clarence, Thomas of
Lancaster, Duke of 113,
166, 170, 177, 247–8, 254,
255, 257–8
Clinton, Lady Elizabeth,
née Fiennes 277
Clinton, Lady Idonea, née
Saye 73–4, 101
Clinton, John, 3rd Lord
73–4, 100, 101
Clinton, John Fiennes, 6th
Lord 277
Clinton, Lord John
(treasurer of royal
household under
Henry V) 261
Clinton, William, 4th Lord
135, 140–41, 177, 207, 269
Cobham, Eleanor, Duchess
of Gloucester 272, 275
Cochon, Pierre 203, 205,
235

Coleman, Robert 64
Comyn, John 57, 58
Comyn, Margaret, née Fiennes 57
Constance, Council of 152
Corbie 185
Cornwaille, John, 1st Baron Fanhope 5, 121, 137, 160, 161–2, 163–4, 185, 225, 230, 231–2, 245, 250, 251, 258, 260, 262, 265, 271–2
    at Agincourt/Maisoncelles 190, 207, 210
Courtrai, Battle of 55
Crécy, Battle of 77–80
crime 119–20, 264–5
Cromer, William 283
crossbows/crossbowmen 75, 77–8, 79, 150, 172, 180, 201, 202, 205, 221
Crusades 22–3, 26, 32–3, 47, 48, 49–50

Dacre, Joan 280
Dacre family 280
Dammartin, Agnes de, later Agnes de Fiennes 35, 47, 202
Dammartin, Count of 196, 202, 207, 226

Dampierre family
    Isabel, Countess of Flanders 186
    Isabel d'Auxy 235
    Philippe d'Auxy 186, 207
Danes 18, 19
David, Prince of Wales 52
David II, King of Scotland 85
de Gaulle, Charles 7
Despenser, Hugh the Elder 63, 64, 65, 67
Despenser, Hugh the Younger 63, 64, 65, 66, 67
Domesday Book 11, 20
Dover Castle 12, 27, 38
drummers 155–6
du Guesclin, Bertrand 92
Duguesclin, Bernard 146–7
dysentery 49, 157, 169, 171, 174, 176, 177, 182, 188, 210, 213, 260

Edith, Queen 16
Edmund Crouchback 55
Edmund of Langley, Duke of York 95, 102–3
Edmund of Norwich, 2nd Duke of York 137, 188, 191, 210, 221

Edmund of Woodstock, 1st
Earl of Kent 48, 62, 72
Edward I 3, 43, 45–58, 62,
150, 151
Edward II 48, 52–3, 58,
59–61, 62–4, 65–70, 146
Edward III 3, 63, 65, 67,
68–9, 73, 74, 93, 115,
123, 145
death 93
and France 74–83, 85,
88–91, 94
and Mortimer 71–3
old age and senility 90,
93
and Perrers 90–91
Edward the Black Prince
48, 77, 79, 87–8, 91, 93
Edward the Confessor 6,
9–10, 17
Eleanor of Aquitaine 26,
28, 30, 31, 33
Eleanor of Castile 47, 49,
52, 59
Eleanor of Provence 42, 43,
59
Elizabeth of Lancaster,
Duchess of Exeter 162
Elizabeth of Rhuddlan 59
Epiphany Conspiracy 139,
162–3

Erpingham, Sir Thomas
209, 210, 214
Ethelred the Unready 9
Eton College 273
Eustace II, Count of
Boulogne and Seigneur of
Fiennes 3, 8–9, 10–12,
16, 20, 22, 283, 285
Eustace IV, Count of
Boulogne 26
Evesham, Battle of 46
Exeter, Elizabeth of
Lancaster, Duchess of
162
Exeter, John Holland, 1st
Duke of 139, 162–3
Exeter, John Holland, 2nd
Duke of *see* Holland,
John, 2nd Duke of Exeter
Exeter, Thomas Beaufort,
Duke of 112, 115–16,
119–20, 255, 260

Falkirk, Battle of 57
Faramus of Boulogne
27–8
Fastolf, Sir John 209
Fiennes, Agnes de 47
Fiennes, Baldwin de 43
Fiennes, Elizabeth, Lady
Clinton 277

Fiennes, Elizabeth, née
 Batisford 93
Fiennes, Elizabeth, née
 Holland 92, 121, 143, 162
Fiennes, Eustace 202
Fiennes, Françoise, Dame de
 235
Fiennes, Sir Giles 46, 47,
 48, 56, 64, 74
Fiennes, Ingelram
 (Enguerrand I) de 8, 28,
 33, 38, 146
Fiennes, Ingelram II de 43,
 46, 47
Fiennes, James 5, 93, 97,
 111, 120, 121, 137,
 140–41, 143, 171,
 240–41, 247, 252, 253,
 255, 262, 269, 270, 271,
 272, 273, 274–7, 279,
 283
 at Agincourt/Maisoncelles
  190, 207, 208, 209, 210,
  232
 and Cade 280–83
 imprisonment, trial and
  death 280–83
Fiennes, Jean (baker of
 Calais) 83
Fiennes, Jean du Bois de
 233

Fiennes, Joan, née Dacre
 280
Fiennes, Joan, née Saye 74,
 93, 101, 120, 276, 278
Fiennes, Joan of Kent 48,
 96, 121
Fiennes, Joanna 48
Fiennes, John, 6th Lord
 Clinton 277
Fiennes, John, Baron of
 Fiennes and Tingry
 59–61, 65, 66, 67, 71, 74,
 82, 146
Fiennes, John (cousin of
 Ingelram) 33
Fiennes, John II, Knight of
 Herstmonceux 93
Fiennes, John (soldier at
 Battle of Hastings) 28
Fiennes, Louis du Bois de
 233
Fiennes, Margaret, later
 Baroness Wake 48
Fiennes, Margaret, later
 Margaret Comyn 57
Fiennes, Margaret, later
 Margaret Mortimer 48,
 65
Fiennes, Margaret, née
 Wykeham 93, 100, 120,
 162

Fiennes, Martin 2

Fiennes, Maud (cousin of
Queen Eleanor; married
Humphrey de Bohun,
Constable of England)
47, 74

Fiennes, Maud, Lady Maud
de Monceaux 93, 101

Fiennes, Maud (married
Henry de Bohun, Bishop
of Hereford) 36

Fiennes, Michael 47, 48,
50, 54

Fiennes, Nathaniel, 21st
Baron Saye and Sele
2, 279–80

Fiennes, Oliver, Dean of
Lincoln 40

Fiennes, Sir Richard, Lord
Dacre 280

Fiennes, Robert, Captain
146–7, 172–4, 179, 186,
196, 198, 200, 201, 205,
207, 223–4, 225, 230, 233

Fiennes, Sir Robert Fiennes
of Fiennes and of Tingry,
Constable of French
Army 74, 83, 84–5, 87,
89–90, 92, 146, 234

Fiennes, Robert (son of
John Fiennes) 77

Fiennes, Robert (son of
William II Fiennes) 59,
66, 67, 71, 146–7

Fiennes, Robert (son of
William of
Herstmonceux, married
Joan de Saye) 100–101

Fiennes, Roger 5, 93, 110,
111, 121, 137, 140–41,
143, 162, 164, 170, 185,
240–41, 245, 247, 252,
255, 262, 269, 270,
271–2, 274, 277, 278

at Agincourt/Maisoncelles
190, 198, 207, 208, 210,
232

Fiennes, Thomas Dacre
280

Fiennes, Tougebrand 33

Fiennes, William I 35, 36,
37, 38

Fiennes, William II 43, 47,
56

Fiennes, William (married
Elizabeth Batisford) 93

Fiennes, William (married
Margaret Wykeham) 93,
100, 120

Fiennes, Sir William of
Herstmonceux 74, 93,
101

Fiennes, William, Sheriff of
Sussex 101, 111
Fiennes family 17, 23,
27–8, 33, 73–4, 92
in England 2, 92–3, 280
family tree vii–ix
in France 92, 196, 234
Fiennes Mountain, Mount
Fiennes 80, 238
Fiennes (village) 6, 7, 80
Castle Fiennes 80, 89–90,
91, 92
Flanders 9–10, 35, 36, 55–6
Fougères 284
France
1067 invasion of Norman
Britain 12
Armagnac–Burgundian
Civil War *see*
Armagnac–Burgundian
Civil War
Boulonnais 7–8
Bourbons *see* Bourbons
Capetian dynasty 30–31,
40
chevauchée in 87, 88
and Edward III 74–83,
85, 88–91, 93
and Edward the Black
Prince 77, 79, 87–8, 91
and Henry I 25

and Henry II 28
and Henry III 41–3
and Henry IV 105–6,
110–11, 112–14, 123
and Henry V's 1415
campaign *see* Henry
V's 1415 French
campaign
and Henry V after 1415
campaign 245, 247–57,
258–60
and Henry V before 1415
campaign 122, 123–35
and Henry VI 274–5,
278, 284–5
Hundred Years War *see*
Hundred Years War
nationalism 89
origins 30
peasant rebellions 87
Royal Council 201
and the Scots 89, 151,
257–8, 264
Valois kings of 7–8, 30,
84
Franks 7
Froissart, Jean: *Chronicles* 81
Fromyard, Friar 210

Gascony 3, 43, 51, 55, 57,
87, 106, 114

Gaucourt, Raoul de 167,
168, 170, 171, 173, 174–6,
186, 268–9
Gaulle, Charles de 7
Gaveston, Piers 60, 61,
62–3
Geoffrey le Baker 69
Geoffrey Plantagenet,
Count of Anjou 25, 26,
29, 96
Gesta Henrici Quinti
184–5, 187–8, 211, 222,
245
Gloucester, Eleanor
Cobham, Duchess of
272, 275
Gloucester, Gilbert de
Clare, 7th Earl of 46
Gloucester, Humphrey of
Lancaster, Duke of
141, 210, 222, 259, 260,
262–3, 264, 265, 266–7,
269, 270, 271, 272
imprisonment and death
275–6, 281, 282, 284
Gloucester, Margaret de
Clare, Countess of 62
Gloucester, Thomas of
Woodstock, 1st Duke of
74, 95, 98, 99–100, 101,
103

Goda of England 9
Godfrey of Bouillon 1,
22–3, 32
Godwin, Earl of Wessex 9
Godwinson, Harold *see*
Harold II, Harold
Godwin of Wessex
Golden Spurs, Battle of the
56
Gray, Thomas 70
Grey, Sir Thomas 152
Guînes 7, 12, 80, 89, 234,
238
Guy, Count of Flanders 60

Hainault, Jacqueline,
Countess of 264
Harald Hardrada of
Norway 10
Harfleur 130, 160, 164,
166, 177, 213, 285
garrison upkeep 244
siege and capture of
165–72, 174–5, 206,
242–3
Harold II, Harold Godwin
of Wessex 6, 9–10, 11,
14
Hastings 92
Battle of 3, 10, 14, 283
Henry I 21–2, 24–5, 26

Henry II 26–7, 29–31
Henry III 38, 39, 41–6, 47, 49, 50
Henry IV 74, 105, 107–12, 115, 116–17, 124
  and Cornwaille 162
  coronation speech 105
  coup and coronation 103
  death 114
  Epiphany Conspiracy against 139, 162–3
  and France 105–6, 110–11, 112–14, 123
  and Hotspur and the Percy dynasty 107–10
  and Richard II 96, 98, 99, 100, 101–3
  and the Scots 106
  Welsh campaign 107
Henry V/Prince Hal 112, 113, 114, 115–16, 117–20, 245–6
  1415 campaign *see* Henry V's 1415 French campaign
  army of *see* Henry V's army
  Battle of Agincourt *see* Agincourt, Battle of
  death 260
  and France, 1415 campaign *see* Henry V's 1415 French campaign
  and France, after 1415 campaign 245, 247–57, 258–60
  and France, before 1415 campaign 122, 123–35
  Home Guard under 153
  and Hotspur and the Percy dynasty 108–9, 110
  and Ireland 154
  Joan of Navarre accused of witchcraft by 272–3
  and the Lollards 124–5, 152–3, 244
  marriage to Katherine of Valois 213, 252–3, 254, 259, 260
  musicians under 155–6
  public relations 131–2
  and the Scots 106, 125–6, 154
  Shakespeare's portrayal 116, 168–9, 170–71, 204
  Southampton Plot against 134–5, 152, 163
  spy network 154, 161
  and surgeons 110, 156, 253

and the Welsh 110, 113,
125–6, 150, 154, 157,
246
will and beneficiaries
159, 260
Henry V's 1415 French
campaign 5, 137, 180,
235
army *see* Henry V's army
arrival in Calais 239–40
Battle of Agincourt *see*
Agincourt, Battle of
challenge to the Dauphin
175–6
and the French army
161, 164–5, 173–5, 180,
181, 182–4, 185, 186–7,
188–9, 194–204, 206–8,
217–21, 222–6, 230–31,
232–4
and French prisoners of
war 226–30, 231–2
Harfleur siege, capture
and repair 165–72,
174–5, 177, 206, 242–3
march towards Calais
181–9, 234, 237, 238
preparations 137–46,
158–60
sailing of the armada
161

and the security of his
kingdom in his absence
151–4
voyage home and loss of
ships 242
Henry V's army 140–42,
154–8, 208, 247
at Agincourt/Maisoncelles
5, 138, 190–96, 204,
207–8, 209–15, 218–32
archer treatment 204
and the armour of the
time 291–7
at Harfleur 165–72,
176–7
map of troop positions
before Agincourt 216
march towards Calais
181–9, 234, 237, 238
at Meaux 259–60
musicians 155–6
rations 178, 239
specialists 253
supplies 140, 147–9
surgeons 156, 253
Henry VI 260–61, 262, 269,
270–73, 280
and France 274–5, 278,
284–5
marriage to Margaret of
Anjou 274–5, 279

Henry the Young King 31
Herstmonceux Castle 92,
   208, 274, 280
Hever Castle 262
Higden, Ranulf 61
Holland, Elizabeth, later
   Elizabeth Fiennes 92,
   121, 143, 162
Holland, John, 1st Duke of
   Exeter 139, 162–3
Holland, John, 2nd Duke
      of Exeter 5, 121, 122,
      137, 139, 141, 160,
      161–4, 170, 171, 183,
      185, 240–41, 245–6,
      247, 251, 254, 255, 258,
      261–2, 263, 265, 269,
      270
   at Agincourt/Maisoncelles
      190, 191, 207, 210, 232
   death 276
Hollande, François 2–3
Honfleur, naval battle of
   247
Honour of Boulogne 12, 16
Hotspur, Harry (Sir Henry
   Percy) 107–9
Hubert, Alain 1
Humphrey of Lancaster *see*
   Gloucester, Humphrey of
   Lancaster, Duke of

Hundred Years War 3, 8,
   11, 14, 71, 75–84,
   87–93, 105–6, 110–11,
   112–14, 123–36, 235,
   264, 277, 280, 283–4
   1415 campaign *see* Henry
      V's 1415 French
      campaign
   Battle of Agincourt *see*
      Agincourt, Battle of
   Battle of Baugé 257–8
   Battle of Orléans 267
   Battle of Pataye 267
   Battle of Verneuil 264
   and the Black Death
      85–7, 90
   chevauchée 87, 88
   end of 285
   Richard II's attempts to
      end 97
   Scottish army fighting for
      the French 89, 151,
      257–8, 264
   siege of Meaux 259–60
   and the Treaty of Troyes
      255–6, 260–61
Hungerford, Sir Walter 211
Hus, Jan 152–3

Iden, Alex 283
Irish immigrants 265–6

Isabel of Dampierre, Countess of Flanders 186
Isabella of Flanders 60–61
Isabella of France, Queen of England (wife of Edward II) 61, 62, 65, 66–70, 72, 73, 123
Isabella of Valois, Queen of England (wife of Richard II) 99, 103

Jacqueline, Countess of Hainault 264
James I of Scotland, James Stuart 113, 151
Jean, Dauphin of France, Duke of Touraine 246
Jerusalem 22–3, 32
Jews
  killed in the Crusades 23
  in London 13, 37
Joan of Arc 267–8
Joan of England 85
Joan of Kent 48, 96, 121
Joan of Navarre 107, 240, 272–3
John, King of England 30, 31–4, 35–8, 44
John II of France 87–8, 89, 90

John I, Duke of Bourbon 242
John de Balliol 56
John of Bohemia 79–80
John the Fearless, Duke of Burgundy 112–14, 121–2, 126, 133, 199–200, 206, 226, 246–7, 249, 254–5
John of Gaunt, Duke of Lancaster 91, 93–4, 95, 96, 98, 100, 102, 124
John of Lancaster *see* Bedford, John of Lancaster, Duke of
jousting 116–17, 162
Juvenal des Ursins, Jean 194

Katherine of Valois 126, 213, 252–3, 254, 255, 259, 260, 269
Knights Templar 49
Knole Manor, Sevenoaks 274

Lancaster, Henry, 3rd Earl of 71, 72–3
Lancaster, John of Gaunt, 1st Duke of 91, 93, 95, 96, 98, 100, 102, 124

Lancaster, Thomas, 2nd
  Earl of 63–4
Lannoy, Gilbert de
  200–201, 223, 230, 233
Legge, John 97
Léon, William de 173
Leopold of Austria 33
Lewes, Battle of 46, 48
Limoges 91
Lincoln, Battle of 26, 38–9
Lionel of Antwerp, 1st
  Duke of Clarence 95,
  123
Llewelyn, Prince of Wales
  52
Lollard movement 124–5,
  152–3, 244, 266
London 280–83
  bubonic plague 85
  Jews 13, 37
  de Mandevilles attack on
    37–8
  Southwark Bridge 266
  Tower of *see* Tower of
    London
  William the Conqueror in
    16
longbows/archers 52, 53–4,
  76, 77–8, 79, 84, 90,
  109, 113, 122, 133, 141,
  145, 149–51, 164, 185,

195, 201, 202–5, 209,
  210, 214–15, 218–21,
  223, 231, 241–2, 246
see also crossbows/
  crossbowmen
Lords Appellant 98–100,
  101
Louis, Dauphin of France,
  Duke of Guyenne 121,
  122, 135, 167, 172, 173,
  174, 176–7, 178–80, 200,
  246
Louis VII of France 26,
  30–31
Louis VIII of France 36,
  38, 39
Louis IX of France 41,
  49
Louis I, Duke of Orléans
  112–13
Lusignan clan 42
Luxembourg, Jacquetta of,
  Countess Rivers 269

Magna Carta 36, 37, 40,
  41, 44
Maine 15, 89, 279, 283,
  284
Maisoncelles 5, 190–200,
  208, 211–12
Mancini, Dominic 241–2

Mandeville, Geoffrey de 34, 36, 37, 38, 40

Manny, Sir Walter 81–2, 84

Margaret of Anjou 274–5, 279

Margaret of France, Queen of England 58

Marshal, William, 1st Earl of Pembroke 38

Martock, manor house 16

Mary de Bohun 74, 105

Matilda, Empress 25, 26, 29

Matilda I, (Maud) Countess of Boulogne 8, 25–6

Meaux, siege of 259–60

Meaux Abbey Chronicle 61

Merciless Parliament 98–9

Monceaux, Lady Maud de 93, 101

Montfort, Eleanor de 52

Montfort, Simon de, 5th Earl of Leicester 45

Montfort, Simon de, 6th Earl of Leicester 43–6

Mortimer, Edmund, 2nd Baron 48, 65

Mortimer, Edmund, 3rd Earl of March 96

Mortimer, Edmund, son of 3rd Earl 107, 123

Mortimer, Edmund, 5th Earl of March 131, 134–5, 152, 170

Mortimer, Glendower 106

Mortimer, Ian 248

Mortimer, John (Jack Cade) 279–83

Mortimer, Margaret, née Fiennes 48, 65

Mortimer, Roger 48, 50, 52, 63, 65, 66–9, 70, 71–3, 134–5, 146

Mortimer family 95

Mowbray, Thomas 98, 100, 101–2

musicians 155–6

Muslims 22–3, 32, 34–5

Nazareth 50

New College, Oxford 100

Nieulay, Battle of 85

Norman Conquest 3, 10–14, 15–20

revolts 11–12, 17–18

Normandy 8, 9, 11, 14, 16, 19, 24, 27, 76, 89, 264, 267, 277, 285

Calais *see* Calais

Harfleur *see* Harfleur

and Henry V's 1415 campaign 160, 164–78

Henry V's conquest of 247–54

in the time of Philip II 32, 35, 40

Northampton, Battle of 45–6

Nottingham Castle 73

Oldcastle, Sir John 124, 125, 153, 244, 252

Ordericus Vitalis 18, 20

Oriflamme 187, 207, 214, 225

Orléans, Charles, Duke of 189, 196, 226, 234, 242

Orléans, Louis I, Duke of 112–13

Orléans, Battle of 267–8

Paris 88, 121–2, 205, 246–7, 254–5, 271

Treaty of 43

Pataye, Battle of 267–8

Paul, St 13

Peasant's Revolt

under Henry VI 279

under Richard II 97

Pelham, Sir John 164

Pelham, Sir Nicholas 143

Pepin III, the Short 6

Percy, Henry, 1st Earl of Northumberland 113

Percy, Sir Henry (Harry Hotspur) 107–9

Percy dynasty of Northumberland 107–10

Péronne 187–8

Perrers, Alice 91

Peter of Savoy 42

Philip I of France 19

Philip II of France 31, 33, 34, 35, 38, 40

Philip III of France 51

Philip IV of France, the Fair 54–6, 60–61

Philip VI of France 3, 77, 79, 81

Philip III, the Good, Duke of Burgundy 255, 260, 264, 269–70

Philippa of Hainault 76, 83, 91, 123

Philippa, 5th Countess of Ulster 95

Plantagenet dynasty 27, 74, 84

see also individual Plantagenets

Poitiers, Battle of 88

Poitou 42, 74, 89

Pole, Michael de la 98

Pole, William de la, Earl of
    Suffolk 264, 270, 271,
    272, 275–6, 279, 283
Pontoise 254, 277
Portsmouth 245, 253
Prinkle, Robert 143, 208
Provisions of Oxford 44

Ramsey, Sir James 228
Renaud I of Boulogne 35
Richard I, Lionheart 31–5
Richard II 94, 95, 96,
    97–103, 115, 131
Richard, 1st Earl of
    Cornwall 42, 44, 46, 50
Richard, Duke of York 273
Rivers, Jacquetta of
    Luxembourg, Countess
    269
Rivers, Richard Woodville,
    1st Earl 278
Robert Curthose, Duke of
    Normandy 19, 20–24
Robert I, the Bruce 57, 58
Robert III of Scotland 106
Rodin, Auguste 83
Romans 7
Rouen 173, 174, 179, 180,
    206–7, 247, 250–52, 285
Royal Council, England
    261, 264, 266, 271, 279

Royal Council, France 201
Royal Navy 132–3, 160,
    244, 245, 247, 253
Runnymede 37, 44
Rye 92

St Cloud, Battle of 113
St Denis, Michel Pintoin,
    monk of 194, 205
St Esprit 92
St George's cross emblem
    143–4, 175
Saint Pierre, Eustace de
    82
Saintes, Battle of 42
Saladin 32, 34
Salisbury, Thomas
    Montacute, 4th Earl of
    258, 259, 261, 264, 267
Salisbury, William
    Longespée, 3rd Earl
    of 38
Saracens 22–3, 32, 34–5
Savoyard family 42
Saxons *see* Anglo-Saxons
Saye, Geoffrey de, Admiral
    of the Fleet 73–4, 75, 77,
    93, 132
Saye, Geoffrey de, Baron
    (loyalist to Richard
    Lionheart) 34

Saye, Geoffrey de, Baron
(Magna Carta signatory)
40
Saye, Geoffrey de (loyalist
to Edward II) 64
Saye, Idonea, later lady
Clinton 73–4, 101
Saye, Joan, later Joan
Fiennes 74, 93, 101, 120,
276, 278
Saye, Maud, née Beauchamp
76
Saye, William de (loyalist to
Richard Lionheart) 34
Saye, William de (recipient
of land from the
Conqueror) 16
Saye, William de Saye,
Lord of Sele (knight) 46,
48, 55
Saye family 16–17, 73, 92,
93
Scrope, Henry, 3rd Baron
135
Second Barons' War 45–6
Shakespeare, William 116,
159, 168–9, 170–71, 192,
204, 270, 273, 281–2
shigella (bacterium) 169
Shrewsbury, Battle of 64,
108–10, 120, 137

Sigismund, Holy Roman
Emperor 125, 126, 127
Sluys 75
Soissons 122, 196
Somerset, John Beaufort, 1st
Duke and 3rd Earl of
271, 284
Somme, River 77, 177, 180,
182, 183, 186, 187
Southampton 132, 133,
135, 142–3, 145, 146, 147,
158–9, 247, 253
Southampton Plot 134–5,
152, 163
Stamford Bridge, Battle of
10
Stenton, Sir Frank 18
Stephen of England
(Stephen of Blois) 8,
25–6, 27, 29–30
Strecche, John 140
Suffolk, William de la Pole,
Earl of 264, 270, 271,
272, 275–6, 279, 283
surgeons 110, 156, 253
Sybil de Tingry 8, 27

Taillebourg, Battle of 42
Talbot, Sir John 154, 265,
271, 277, 285
tax-raising 243

under Edward I 54, 55, 57

under Edward III 79

under Gaunt's regency 96–7

under Henry I 24

under Henry III 42

under Henry V 131–2, 243, 244–5

under King John 36, 37

under Richard I, the Lionheart 32

under Richard II 99

under William the Conqueror 11, 13, 19–20

Thatcher, Margaret 132, 139

Thomas of Lancaster, Duke of Clarence 113, 166, 170, 177, 247–8, 254, 255, 257–8

Thomas of Woodstock, 1st Duke of Gloucester 74, 95, 98, 99–100, 101, 103

Tinchebray, Battle of 24

Tingry, Sybil Boulogne de 8

Titus Livius (Tito Livio da Forli) 194, 223

tournaments, jousting 116–17, 162

Tower of London 16, 37, 45, 52, 56, 65, 69, 73, 113, 125, 145, 150, 162, 280

trailbastons 57

Troyes, Treaty of 255–6, 260–61

Tunis 49

Umfraville, Gilbert 164

Umfraville, Simon 164

Valois kings of France 7–8

Vaurus, Bastard of 259

Vendôme, Louis I, Count of 223, 224, 225, 263

Verdun, Treaty of 7

Vere, Robert de 98, 99

Verneuil, Battle of 264

Vienne, Sir Jean de 81, 82

Wake, John, Lord 48, 56–7

Wake, Margaret, 3rd Baroness 48

Wake, Thomas 66

Wallace, William 56

Walsingham, Thomas 195

Warwick, Richard Beauchamp, Earl of *see* Beauchamp, Richard, Earl of Warwick

Warwick, Thomas
  Beauchamp, Earl of 76,
  77, 98, 99
Warwick family 98
Waurin, Jean de 109, 110
Waurin, Robert de 186, 187
Westminster Abbey 47, 49
Whittington, Dick 111
William Adelin 24–5
William the Conqueror,
  Duke of Normandy
  10–11, 12, 13–14,
  15–21, 123, 283, 285
  companions of the
  Conqueror 16–17
William II, Rufus 21, 24
William of Boulogne 36
William of Poitiers 17
William of Valence 42
William of Wykeham,
  Chancellor 91, 93, 94,
  97, 100, 134, 162
Winchester College 100
Wissant, Jacques de 82

Wissant, Pierre de 82
witchcraft, allegations of
  269, 272–3
Wycliffe, John 124, 152,
  244
Wykeham, Margaret, later
  Margaret Fiennes 93,
  100, 120, 162
Wykeham, Thomas 162,
  172, 191
Wykeham, William of
  (Chancellor) 91, 93, 94,
  97, 100, 134, 162
Wykeham, William (son of
  Thomas) 162, 171,
  190–91, 207

York, Edmund of Langley,
  Duke of 95, 102–3
York, Edmund of Norwich,
  2nd Duke of 137, 188,
  191, 210, 221
York, Richard, Duke of
  273